Wrongful Imprisonment

Elizabeth the Second,

by the Grace of God of the United Kingdom of Great Britain and Northern Ireland and of Our other Realms and Territories Queen, Head of the Commonwealth, Defender of the Faith, To all to whom these Presents shall come Greeting!

Whereas...................... at........................
on the.................... was convicted of..................
.... and was sentenced to imprisonment for.... ......

Now know ye that We in consideration of some circumstances humbly represented unto, Us, are Graciously pleased to extend Our Grace and Mercy unto the said . . . .

and to grant him Our Free Pardon in respect of the said conviction, thereby pardoning, remitting and releasing unto him all pains penalties and punishments whatsoever that from the said conviction may ensue; and We do hereby command all Justices and others whom it may concern that they take due notice hereof;

And for so doing this shall be a sufficient Warrant

Given at Our Court at St James's
the . . . . day of . . . .
19 . . . . in the . . . . year of
Our reign

By Her Majesty's Command

Wrongful Imprisonment

Mistaken Convictions and
their Consequences

Ruth Brandon and Christie Davies

Archon Books
1973

Library of Congress Cataloging in Publication Data

Brandon, Ruth.
  Wrongful imprisonment.

Bibliography: p.
  1. Judicial error—Great Britain. 2. False imprisonment—
Great Britain. I. Davies, Christie, joint author. II. Title.
III. Title: Mistaken convictions and their consequences.
KD8464.B7   345'.42'05   72-12829
ISBN 0-208-01337-7

© 1973 by George Allen & Unwin Ltd.
First published 1973 by George Allen & Unwin Ltd, London
and in the United States of America as an Archon Book by
The Shoe String Press, Inc., Hamden, Connecticut 06514
Printed in Great Britain

For our parents

Foreword

I am very glad that Ruth Brandon and Christie Davies decided to write this book and that I have been allowed to write this brief foreword. It is the kind of book which is greatly needed and which I would have liked to write if I had been able to do so.

I have for a long time believed that a true and objective appraisal of the merits and defects of the English system of criminal prosecution and trial has been bedevilled by the controversies which have raged over a few sensational cases of capital murder. Supporters of capital punishment must of necessity close their minds to the possibility of an innocent man having been hanged in error and are therefore led to maintain that we have a good system and that any serious mistakes made by the court of trial can be corrected by the Court of Appeal or by the Home Secretary. Opponents of capital punishment have been equally anxious to maintain that the system is capable of error, because for many people this has been, and still is, a powerful argument against hanging. Apart from the Timothy Evans case, the Home Office has kept its files under seal so that the legal profession and the general public have never been given the chance of making up their own minds or of knowing what to believe.

The virtue of this book is that it removes the argument about the merits of the system from this highly charged and prejudicial atmosphere by focusing attention on the numerous ordinary and often unreported cases in which the authorities have admitted that a mistake was made and the victim has been wrongfully imprisoned.

The authors have gone about their task of investigating and presenting the cases in an objective spirit and wherever I have personal knowledge of the cases cited I can confirm that the accounts given and the conclusions drawn from them are fair and accurate. What is perhaps more important, they have isolated and identified the various areas in which the system is at fault and the successive hazards which may confront an innocent man once he falls under suspicion of having committed a criminal offence.

The extent to which the various remedies they suggest would

reduce the hazards is difficult to estimate. They would undoubtedly help but I have myself come to the conclusion, after fourteen years of looking into wrong convictions and how they come about, that there are so many areas of discretion, and so many ways in which the accusatorial system can conceal or pervert the truth, that without a radical reshaping it can never be anything else but a gamble in which far too frequently the guilty will go free and the innocent end up in prison.

To those who believe that Society as a whole (that is to say every one of us) is ultimately responsible for what is done in its name by the various law enforcement agencies, the most disturbing thing about this book will surely be its revelation of the obstacles that have to be overcome by a wrongfully imprisoned man seeking to establish his innocence and regain his liberty. We have no effective Court of Appeal—no mechanism for a full judicial review, no Ministry of Justice and no Public Defender—in short we have no authority or public agency which is not, by its very nature, more concerned to uphold the sanctity of the system and its rules than to remedy a wrong for which it has been responsible.

London
1972

TOM SARGANT

Contents

Preface

We first got the idea for this book when Christie Davies was a radio producer at the BBC, and Ruth Brandon came to him with an idea for a radio documentary on the subject. This was in the spring of 1969. While compiling the programme we both became very interested in the subject, and decided that we would like to research into it at greater length and in more depth and detail. It became easier to do this when Christie Davies left the BBC and went to take up an academic post at Leeds University later in 1969. This book is the result of our joint research over the last three years. We do not regard the research as finished by any means, if only because we have had neither the time nor the money to do it as fully as we would have liked.

We may have had neither the time nor the money we needed, but we have been helped by a very large number of people whom we would now like to thank.

We wish to thank the Home Office for providing us with the list of cases contained in Appendix A. We must make it clear, however, that the Home Office did not provide us with any details of individual cases and has no responsibility for the suggestions and inferences we have made. All the information about individual cases has been drawn from other sources, from newspaper reports, from trial transcripts, from books and from interviews with the persons concerned. Where we only discovered the existence of a particular case from the Home Office list, we have obtained the written consent of the individual concerned before mentioning his name.

We have in many cases changed the names of the people involved in order to avoid causing harm and embarrassment to all concerned in the matter. However, in cases which have been extensively reported in the press or where it seemed to us that justice should be seen to have been done we have deliberately retained the real names of those involved.

We owe an enormous debt to Tom Sargant, Secretary of 'Justice', whose files of individual cases we have consulted and quoted, and whose advice has often been sought and always willingly given. We must also thank him for reading the final manuscript and for making number of invaluable suggestions and corrections; and for writing the foreword of this book.

Master Thompson, the Registrar of the Court of Appeal, has been most helpful in letting us consult the transcripts and records of individual appeal cases, and his staff have been consistently diligent and co-operative in assisting us.

Mr John E. T. Viner helped us at a critical stage in our research by sending us a veritable library of press cuttings on the subject which he had been collecting from national and local papers for many years. We are greatly indebted to him for this generous action, coming as it did from someone we had neither met nor been in contact with before. We are also grateful to L. M. Clay who sent us a number of useful cuttings. We should also like to thank our fathers, Mr Christopher Davies and Mr Maurice Brandon, for providing us with every relevant press cutting they could lay their hands on. Also, the research assistants in the Department of Social Studies in the University of Leeds, for systematically clipping the national press during the period of our research.

We should like to thank the following people for providing us with invaluable information and introductions: Marc Ancel of the *Centre Français de Droit Comparé*; Louis Blom-Cooper; Clement Drakes; Ivan Geffen; Desmond Joyce; E. Rex Makins; Gilbert Marc; Norman Marsh; C. H. Rolph; George I. Devor; W. P. W. Elwell; R. Hylton-Potts; Perimans; C. Sheward; Stephen N. Simes; N. W. Wicks.

Inspector John Newing, Michael Horowitz, Neil MacCormick and Dr John Tobias all read an early synopsis of our research and made helpful comments. Professor Brian Hogan read a later version and made invaluable suggestions. We were also helped at this stage by the Director of Public Prosecutions, by Peter Archer, QC, MP, and by David Napley.

At a time when we were under pressure to complete our references, David Davies and Elizabeth Onians gave us a great deal of assistance. David Davies and David Pettit also assisted us with the calculations involved in Appendix A.

Colin Low and Arthur Royce of Leeds University advised us on the gathering and processing of the statistics in Appendix A. They are of course not responsible for any mistakes nor are any of the people who advised us in other capacities.

We should like to thank the staff of the Brotherton Library, Leeds University; the Library of the Institute of Criminology, Cambridge; and the library of the Bradford *Telegraph and Argus*. And Miss Elizabeth Day for typing and copying large sections of the manuscript.

And finally we should like to thank all the many convicted people and their lawyers who wrote to us about their cases. We received so many that we couldn't possibly follow them all up properly, but we are nevertheless extremely grateful.

Acknowledgments

We found the following books particularly helpful and would like to thank all those authors and publishers who have given us permission to include extracts.

Bartlett, F. C.	*Remembering* (Cambridge University Press, 1932)
Bedford, Sybille	*The Faces of Justice* (Collins, 1961)
Besnard, Marie	*The Trial of Marie Besnard* (Heinemann, 1963)
Block, E. B.	*The Vindicators* (Alvin Redman, 1963)
Borchard, E.	*Convicting the Innocent* (Plenum Publishing Co., 1970)
Cobb, Belton	*Trials and Errors* (W. H. Allen, 1962)
Cornish, W.	*The Jury* (Pelican, 1971)
Devlin, Lord	*Trial by Jury* (Stevens & Sons, 1966)
Du Cann, C. G. L.	*Miscarriages of Justice* (Muller, 1960)
Eysenck, H. J.	*Crime and Personality* (Routledge, 1964)
Floriot, René	*Les Erreurs Judiciaires* (Flammarion, 1968)
Frank, Jerome and Barbara	*Not Guilty* (Gollancz, 1957)
Furneaux, R.	*Michael John Davies* (Stevens & Sons, 1962)
Hinds, Alfred	*Contempt of Court* (Bodley Head, 1966)
Hobson, J., *et al.*	*The Silence of the Accused* (Conservative Political Centre, 1966)
Justice	*Complaints against Lawyers*, a report (Charles Knight, 1970)
	Home Office Reviews of Criminal Convictions, a report (Stevens & Sons, 1968)
	2nd Memorandum on Identification, submitted to the Criminal Law Review Committee
	10th Annual Report
Kalven, H. and Zeisel, H.	*The American Jury* (Little Brown & Co., 1966)
Laurie, Peter	*Scotland Yard* (Bodley Head, 1971)
Lewis, D., and Hughman, P.	*Most Unnatural: An Inquiry into the Stafford Case* (Penguin, 1971)

17

Lustgarten, E.	*Verdict in Dispute* (Allan Wingate, 1949)
Moulton, H. Fletcher (ed.)	*The Trial of Steinie Morrison* (William Hodge, 1922)
Permiter, Geoffrey de C.	*Reasonable Doubt* (Arthur Barker, 1938)
Parris, John	*Under My Wig* (Arthur Barker, 1961)
Rolph, C. H.	*Personal Identity* (Michael Joseph, 1957)
Svartvik, Jan	*The Evans Statements: A Case for Forensic Linguistics* (Gothenburg Studies in English, 1968)
Symons, Julian	*A Reasonable Doubt* (Cresset Press, 1960)
Thompson, D. R. and Wollaston, H. W.	*Court of Appeal, Criminal Division* (Charles Knight, 1969)
Williams, Glanville	*The Proof of Guilt: A Study of the English Criminal Trial* (Stevens & Sons, 1963)
Wyndham-Brown, W. F.	*The Trial of William Herbert Wallace* (Gollancz, 1933)

The Civil Evidence Act, 1968
The Mental Health Act, 1969

Donovan Committee Report
Mars-Jones Report
Report of the Royal Commission on Capital Punishment
Report of the 'Justice' Committee on the Laws of Evidence

Chapter 1

Wrongful Imprisonment?

Wrongful imprisonment we will define as follows: the man who has been wrongfully imprisoned is the man who has been convicted of a crime he did not in fact commit and who has been sent to prison on the basis of this conviction. There are other meanings that can be given to the term 'wrongful imprisonment'[1] but the above definition seems to us to correspond to the common usage—such people are thought of as having been wrongly imprisoned. It can of course be more complicated than this. Some men are partly wrongly imprisoned in that they were implicated in a crime or were accessories to it in a minor way but not guilty of the more serious charge for which they were convicted. Even when one has succeeded in defining 'wrongful imprisonment' there is still the difficult problem of demonstrating that it exists and measuring it. How can one possibly prove that someone has been wrongfully imprisoned? For the purposes of this book, we have considered as proved those cases where a free pardon has been granted, or where the case has been specifically referred to the Court of Appeal by the Home Secretary,[2] and the conviction has subsequently been quashed. We have deliberately excluded those cases where the basis of the pardon or referral was simply a legal technicality. (In Appendix A at the end of this book there is a list of pardons and referrals kindly provided by the Home Office.)[3]

We felt justified in accepting these kinds of cases as proved. In general, the executive does not like to interfere with the decisions of the judiciary. When, therefore, the Home Secretary decides to advise a pardon or to refer a case back to the Court of Appeal, it can be assumed that he has very good reasons for doing so. In the case of pardons, the normal burden of proof is reversed—a convicted man is assumed to be guilty; he now has to *prove* his innocence.[4]

In the lists provided by the Home Office (which covered the years 1950–70), there were fifty-two pardons and eighteen referrals. The

19

figure for pardons is much smaller than the total number of pardons granted, since a much larger number are in some sense granted on technical grounds.[5]

For obvious reasons the Home Office was not willing to give us any details of the cases in the lists they sent us. Our two main sources of information were press cuttings and interviews with the people concerned, whom we located from details given in the press. Another useful source of information was the numerous books which have been written on individual miscarriages of justice. The difficulty with using the press as a source of information is that they are only interested in certain kinds of cases—the newsworthy ones. The great value of the Home Office list was that it enabled us to make sure that the cases we culled from the press were a representative. sample of the cases of officially acknowledged wrongful imprisonment.

In addition to these 'hard' cases of wrongful imprisonment, we also looked at some cases where the balance of sentence has been remitted because of doubts about the prisoner's guilt. Most remissions are granted on grounds which have nothing to do with the conviction, such as medical or compassionate grounds, or as a reward for assistance to the authorities. But there are some which stem from doubts about the original conviction.

We have occasionally accepted as instance of wrongful imprisonment a case where the conviction has been quashed on appeal, or a retrial has resulted in acquittal. We felt that such cases as we have used were similar to those which resulted in a pardon—for instance, the issue was generally one of fact rather than law. We have used them where they illustrated particular points especially well. In general, though, we have tried to avoid cases outside the 'hard' category.

Seventy cases of acknowledged wrongful imprisonment in a twenty-year period is a very small proportion of the total number of people who went to prison during that time. Indeed, it is so small that it is very hard to believe that it is anything like an adequate measure of the true number of wrongful imprisonments. It looks more like the tip of a much larger iceberg. This view was reinforced when we came to look into how the 'hard' cases came to be exonerated. In a very large proportion of the cases, the new evidence which got the case reopened only came to light as a result of some completely chance occurrence. Our inference from this is that there must be many other victims of wrongful imprisonment who have not had such luck. We therefore decided to examine, in addition to the 'hard' cases, some of the many other cases which came to our attention though unproved. We came across many of these cases in the files of 'Justice', who kindly allowed us to look through some of their records. We also had many press cuttings, and we advertised in various newspapers. Many of these cases turned out to be similar in important respects to the 'hard' cases. Patterns which emerged frequently in both groups as causes of imprisonment were: unsatisfactory identification, particularly by confrontation between the accused and the witness; confessions made by the feeble-minded and the inadequate; evidence favourable to the defence withheld by the prosecution; certain joint trials; perjury, especially in cases involving sexual or quasi-sexual offences; badly-conducted defence; criminals as witnesses. We could almost go so far as to say that for every 'hard' case we have examined, we could produce another matching case where the only difference is that the defendant has not been exonerated. This is not to say that all undetected cases of wrongful imprisonment must follow the same patterns as the proven cases. There were other definite patterns which emerged in the doubtful cases which were not to be found in the proven cases, for instance convictions following an affray amongst Asian immigrants. The very existence of these patterns seems to us significant, and might indicate that there are certain types of wrongful imprisonment that are as yet not detected at any stage.

How big is the iceberg? It is naturally impossible to say. One minimum estimate is that made by 'Justice' in its tenth annual report:

'In criminal cases, an analysis has been made of several hundred cases spread over a period of three years. This was done mainly by law students. Their evaluations have been checked, and all cases except those which could be classified as highly convincing or probably true were eliminated. These remaining cases (ninety-three in all) amounted to 15 per cent of the complaints received, but the true figure could well be higher, because it sometimes turns out that happenings which on first consideration might be regarded as impossible did in fact occur.'[6]

It must not be thought that we believed everybody who told us that they were wrongfully imprisoned. Indeed, we came to wonder why it was that so many of the truly and sometimes obviously guilty went on proclaiming their innocence for so long. Various reasons for this eventually suggested themselves. There was the group who, though guilty, were of the opinion that they had been convicted on insufficient or incorrect evidence, and it was unfair that they should have been convicted on this basis. In some cases, the prisoner felt that the prosecution's reconstruction of the crime was wrong, and since he had been there, he knew best. Such a one was the man who, when convicted on the basis of incriminating forensic evidence taken from his clothes, said: 'I wasn't wearing that suit anyway.' Others feel aggrieved, either at being caught at all, or at the circumstances of their conviction, especially if an accomplice gave evidence for the prosecution. Some, though admitting to various other crimes, feel that the one of which they stand convicted this time falls outside such moral code as they had—a burglar may not wish to be accused of pimping, or a bank robber of petty fraud. To be convicted of such an offence is an affront to their own self-respect, and will affect their standing with their friends and their family. They may go on proclaiming their innocence to keep their own and their family's morale up. Finally, there are the pettifoggers, who have a long sentence to serve and a long transcript to pick holes in, such as the man who wrote to us that he felt he had been wrongfully convicted because at his trial the prosecution had got wrong the date of the Larceny Act 1916, and the number of his admittedly stolen car.

Who were the people who did get wrongfully imprisoned? On the whole, they seemed to be a normal cross-section of the people who normally get sent to jail. Most of them have previous records of committing the kind of crime of which, this time, they were wrongly convicted.[7] Most of them did unskilled work; many were unemployed or only did casual jobs. Very few were drawn from the middle class or from the respectable working class.

The pattern of crimes which cropped up remarkably resembled the pattern of crimes for which people are sent to prison anyway (see Appendix A). The only significant differences were that a much larger proportion of them had been convicted of robbery and malicious damage than would have occurred in a random sample of the prison population. This is not surprising in view of the kind of evidence which is normally adduced for these crimes. In the case of robbery, identification made under adverse conditions is often the main evidence for the prosecution.[8] The malicious damage cases seem to involve people of low mentality who are apt to make false confessions to irrational crimes of this sort.

People have asked us why we have written this book. There are, they say, a number of books about cases of wrongful imprisonment already in print, which have fully covered the subject. Indeed, we have found these very helpful. But for our purposes they tend to be either too specific or too general. Many devote a whole book to the consideration of one case. In these books, the author sometimes gets very involved with the subject, and finds it hard to be detached about the case and to draw objective conclusions. Also, since they have only one case to draw upon, the conclusions cannot be very general. The others tend to list and describe many different miscarriages of justice, which are often too diverse for any helpful conclusions to be reached. There is, so far as we have been able to find out, no English book which deals systematically with the problem of wrongful imprisonment, with all its implications for the working of the criminal law.

Chapter 2

Identification Evidence

The position of the law in England and Wales at present is that you can be convicted on the uncorroborated evidence of identification of a single eyewitness. Depending on the circumstances, this can happen at an identification parade, by identification from a photograph, or by direct confrontation, in court or elsewhere, between the eyewitness and the accused. This is in contrast to the law in Scotland, where a single eyewitness identification must be corroborated, either by another eyewitness, or by other evidence.[1]

Since eyewitness identification is a very common form of evidence in criminal cases, it is perhaps not surprising that a large proportion of the mistakes we have come across occur in this field. Nevertheless, a greater number of mistakes seem to occur in this field even than one would expect. Of the cases we have examined of people who have subsequently been pardoned, or whose convictions have been quashed, or sentences remitted, a remarkably high proportion have involved misidentification. This impression is borne out by the second 'Justice' memorandum on identification, which states: 'The number of cases of alleged mistaken identification submitted to 'Justice' either by prisoners themselves, or by defence lawyers and MPs, has increased to a disturbing extent.'[2] Our view that eyewitness misidentification is a major cause of wrongful conviction is reinforced by numerous studies of wrongful conviction in other countries, notably America, which show it to be a major source of error there also.[3]

It has always been recognized that identification evidence can cause problems, and because of this, a standard method of handling it, in cases where the accused is unknown to the eyewitness, known as the identification parade, has been devised. This is so well known that there is no need to describe it. What are perhaps less well known are the rules set out by the Home Office for the guidance of police officers holding such parades. These rules are not mandatory, but in practice police officers usually conduct parades in accordance with them, since if not so conducted they carry less weight as evidence in court. The rules are listed in Appendix B.

Perhaps it is worth pointing out that, even if the rules are strictly observed, and the parade satisfactory in every way, all that is proved is that the person picked out looks more like the culprit than anyone else on the parade. However, there is a natural tendency on the part of the courts to regard such identification as proof that the person picked out is therefore the guilty man.

As a result the courts may make a mistake, as the following recent case shows. Ronald John Barker was convicted of burglary involving the deception of an old woman whose house he was supposed to have got into by posing as a gasman. He was identified on identity parades by three different people. He was sentenced to four years' imprisonment on this evidence, and, as he said: 'That was what the whole case hinged on.' His application to appeal against conviction was refused by the single judge; so he went on hunger-strike, which lasted 375 days, until he was granted leave to appeal. At the appeal he was granted a new trial, at which he was acquitted.

This was a case where the identification evidence was made in good faith. (It might be worth noting that the man convicted with Barker, who really did do it, was only identified by *one* person.)

A similar mistake was made in the case of the Cross brothers, who were convicted of robbery with violence in 1964. They were convicted on the identification evidence of a single witness. Subsequently, the real culprits were caught, and the three brothers were awarded a free pardon. Kenneth Cross describes the identification parade: 'Mrs . . . [the witness] went straight to me. She didn't walk up and down the parade. As soon as she walked in I knew she'd pick me out. My heart sank. It was very embarrassing. I knew two of the people on the parade.' The fact that he knew these two people was not altogether surprising, since the incident took place in a small provincial town. What was more to the point, it was also possible that the witness had met the Cross brothers before. This was a matter of contention at the trial:

Q: (Mr Cowley cross-examining): At 6.58 that night did you again attend a third identification parade?
A (eye-witness): Yes.
Q: Again, I do not know how many people there were on it.
A: There were eight.
Q: Did you manage to pick out anybody on that parade?

A: Yes, the young one on the left.

Q: That is John Cross. Had you ever seen either Kenneth or John Cross before the night of the 29th?

A: No, I had never seen any of them before. If I had seen them before, I would have told you. I had not seen them before.

Further cross-examining by Mr Hopkin disputed the point:

Q: You have told us that you have never seen any of these before.

A: I have never seen any of these before. If I had I would have told you I had, but I have not.

Q: I just want to ask you, because at least one of them recollects that you have. There may be a perfectly reasonable explanation in relation to the other two. Do you know a public house in Mansfield called the Nag's Head?

A: Yes I do. I used to go into it to have a drink in there.

Q: Have you ever seen these three young men in the Nag's Head?

A: No.

Q: They will tell the members of the jury that they have in fact seen you in there.

A: Well, I have never seen them in there.

Q: In relation to the smallest one, John, you have told us that you have never seen him before?

A: I have never seen him.

Q: Would you just cast your mind back three or four months ago, Do you know a public house just on the outskirts of Mansfield called the Oak Tree Inn?

A: No, I do not.

Q: Have you ever been to the Oak Tree Inn?

A: No, I do not know where it is; I could not tell you.

Q: It is John Cross's recollection that one evening he met you with a friend of his in Mansfield and you all went to the Oak Tree Inn?

A: No, I am sorry.

Q: The friend's name was Butch.

A: I know Butch.[4]

The reason why the counsel for the accused were so concerned to establish whether or not the witness had met the Cross brothers before was that, if she had, it would make a nonsense of holding an identification parade, which is specifically designed to deal with the situation where the eyewitness has not recognized the culprit.

In most cases, though, where an eyewitness has known the accused previously, this, far from invalidating the identification, reinforces it, since identification in these cases is based not only on observation but on recognition. But even in cases involving (supposed) recognition mistakes can occur. One such occurred in the case of Gerald Morris, who was convicted of robbery with violence in 1969, solely on evidence of identification. He was subsequently granted a free pardon. Morris was accused of attacking and robbing the man who handled the cash in a Swansea garage where Morris was known, but only slightly. The acquaintanceship was so slight that the victim wasn't even sure of his name, though he knew where he lived. The police then went to Morris's house. 'They asked for a Mr Williams. He doesn't live here, I said, I'm Mr Morris. That'll do, said the policeman.' They then took Morris to the police station, where he was confronted with the victim. Morris again: '"That's the one", the old man said.' Subsequently, someone else was convicted of the crime, and Morris was released and compensated.

Where the eyewitness knows the accused even better, there need not even be a confrontation. Thomas Hall was arrested and brought to court simply on the statement of the man who identified him—who knew him well enough to refer to him by his nickname, 'Pecky'.

Hall was tried in June 1964. In a statement subsequently made to the police, in the course of the investigation that eventually exonerated him, Hall described his arrest: 'Whilst my mother and I were sitting drinking the beer, three detectives came to the door. I don't know what time it was when they arrived. . . . Then the detectives told me that they were going to take me to the police station. . . . When we got outside the house and into the police car, one of the policemen, Detective . . . , said: "A witness seen you." I had no idea to what he was referring but I still did not ask any questions. At the Central Police Station, Detective . . . examined my hands, then he looked at my clothes, and he took possession of my trousers. I was then put into a cell and about an hour later Detective . . . took me out of my cell and he also took a chap called Whitfield out of another cell. He took us both upstairs to the charge-room and he jointly charged Whitfield and I with breaking into Tate's radio shop.'

Hall only met the eyewitness in court, where the following exchange took place:

Q: Are you able to recognize the man whose half-face you saw that night in court?
A: Yes.

Q: Where is he?
A: Just behind you, sir.
Q: Just behind me. That is the man between the two warders?
A: Yes, sir.
Q: Did you know him before or not?
A: Well, I know him well, by a nickname.[5]

Hall was convicted of shopbreaking and larceny, and sentenced to two years' imprisonment on the basis of this single identification. Leave to appeal was refused, but subsequently the Home Secretary referred the case back to the Court of Criminal Appeal, which ordered a new trial at which Hall was acquitted.

We have chosen these four cases to illustrate in different ways how mistaken identification can result in conviction, even though in each case the correct procedure was followed. The identity parades and confrontations were properly conducted, and were in each case appropriate to the kind of identification being tested.

We have no reason to suppose that these cases are unique. In all of them, the accused's innocence was established fortuitously. In the cases of the Cross brothers and Morris, the real culprits subsequently admitted the offence; and in the cases of Hall and Barker, extra alibi witnesses were later produced. It would be reasonable to infer that there have been many similar cases where the accused has not been so fortunate.

If this is true of cases where the identification procedure has been properly conducted, then clearly there will be even more errors where it has not.

The most common complaint is that the accused did not look like the other people on the identification parade. Here are some examples; all of whom were convicted, some of whom were subsequently exonerated, some not. In view of the unsatisfactory nature of the parade, there must remain a considerable element of doubt.

Ex-PC Frederick Charles Luckhurst: convicted of larceny. 'Everybody on the parade was a policeman, a serving policeman. The criticism of the parade was that it didn't consist of the correct number of people that should have been on such a parade. We were not in the least all alike, of the same age or appearance, in fact the most striking difference among us was that one was wearing a sergeant's stripes. We were told, or we have since been told, that the parade was not an official identification parade to find the criminal or to pick out the suspected person. The parade was held, in the words of the local police chief, to ascertain if one of the members of the local force was in fact involved.'[6] 'Despite considerable pressure from a number of organizations, including the Police Federation, and certain peers in the House of Lords, ex-PC Luckhurst has never been able to clear his name.

Referring to the case of John Bird and Roy Pett, convicted of attempted robbery, Lord Parker, then Lord Chief Justice, said: 'From the start we have felt a degree of uneasiness in this case.' He criticized the police for not allowing the two men time to wash and shave off two days' growth of beard before being put up for identification. 'I cannot understand how this was allowed to happen', he said. 'They were in their working clothes and to say the least, they were scruffy. In fact, they were the scruffiest and dirtiest on parade.' The two men had their convictions quashed on appeal.[7]

Gerald O'Halloran got seven years for possessing gelignite and assaulting a police officer. Mr O'Halloran is bald, and his identity parade was originally lined up in hats. But when the witness came in, the inspector made them all remove their hats.[8] O'Halloran was then the only bald man. All the others had lots of hair. (In cross-examination the eyewitness said that the man he had seen had long, well-groomed hair.)

Detective-Inspector . . . , who is a serving police officer, did not wish to be identified. He was suspected in a larceny case, and was for a while suspended from the police force, but subsequently exonerated and reinstated. 'In the afternoon there was a badly-run identity parade. The identity parade was run not by a neutral police constable but by the senior policeman involved in the case. . . . Everyone else on the parade was younger than me and dressed differently. I had the fairest hair and the lightest suit.'

Naturally enough, an innocent man will be the least punctilious about seeing that the parade is properly run. After all, he has nothing to fear. This is even true where he has had previous experience of identification parades. An interesting case is that of William Thomas Davies, who was convicted of receiving a stolen cheque and obtaining a vacuum cleaner by fraud. Later his conviction was quashed, when his case was referred back to the Court of Appeal by the Home Secretary.[9] Of his case, it was said: 'About the identity parade he [Davies] said there had been people on it with different coloured hair [he being dark-haired], and that he had been the only person in a light suit, the others all being in dark clothes. [The victim agreed that the men were not of the same colour of hair and that they were all dressed somewhat differently, but he had been sure about the identification.] The appellant said he had not objected to the parade because he had been certain he would not be picked out.'

Although it is clear in the light of experience that identification is an unreliable form of evidence, juries continue to place great faith in it. Curiously, this only works one way. Juries do not seem to place the same faith in the person who says: 'This is not the man' as in the person who says: 'This is the man'. Similarly, uncertainty or disagreement tends to be disregarded by juries. This was illustrated dramatically in the case of Patrick Crundall, who faced six charges of stealing money from elderly women. Only two of the six women who were alleged to be his victims picked out Mr Crundall at an identity parade while the others selected another man. All six, however, positively identified Mr Crundall at the committal proceedings. (Crundall was cleared when another youth admitted the offences.) Stanley Porter, who was convicted on the same sort of evidence, was sentenced to seven years for robbery with violence, and did not get off. The only evidence connecting him to the robbery was that of identification. The 'Justice' second memorandum on identification says this about the case: 'He was put on a parade with eight other men. They all had handkerchiefs over half their faces, as in the robbery. Mr Shuter was introduced to the parade first and picked out a man called Garvey who was unconnected with the offence. Garvey is 53, 5 ft 11 in. tall, and weighs 16½ stone, with dark hair greying considerably. Porter is about 5 ft 7 in.' Mrs Shuter came in and walked along the line and she went down the back of the line and picked Porter out from the rear. The police were also behind the line and so no one could see if any signal was made. Afterwards there appears to have been an argument between Mr and Mrs Shuter in which Mr Shuter said that he thought of picking out Porter but did not do so because he thought that the man in the robbery was taller.[10] The jury chose to accept Mrs Shuter's evidence.

These are cases where the uncertainty and disagreement on the part of eyewitnesses has come up in court, and the jury has at least had a chance to consider them. Often witnesses who fail to make an identification, or who identify the wrong man, are not called. Why identify anybody at all, if you are uncertain? Probably because the identity parade situation tends to make the witness feel he has to pick someone, even where he is specifically told that he need not. Where he dispels his uncertainty by picking out the suspect, this is seized upon; where he picks somebody quite other, this is disregarded.

However unsatisfactory an identity parade may be, where the witness does not know the accused, it is better than confrontation, either in the police station or in court. If you are confronted with a suspect in a police station, you assume that he has some guilty reason for being there. This applies equally to court, where anyone in the vicinity of the dock appears to be at risk. A witness asked in court at Clerkenwell recently to identify an alleged thief pointed to the usher and said: 'That's him!' The police are equally at risk, as the following report shows: 'Two policemen standing with an accused man in the dock (at Tottenham Magistrates' Court) were told by the chairman: "All three of you will be remanded in custody for one week." . . . "Only the one in the centre, sir", pleaded one of the police officers. And the remand order was graciously amended.'[11]

Usually, however, witnesses have no such difficulty in homing in on the suspect. The *Police Review* gives such a case: 'A man had been convicted of stealing a handbag by snatching it from a woman, and a nurse had given evidence of the hue and cry after the snatch but admitted she couldn't at the time identify the thief. The deputy chairman, after she had left the witness-box, recalled her and wanted to know whether she could recognise anyone in court. And can you guess to whom she pointed? Correct. When the man appealed, the Court of Appeal said it was usually most unfair to ask a witness for the first time to attempt to identify someone in court. The jury in this case had not been warned of the danger of accepting such evidence.[12]

The illusion still prevails, however, that the witness called on to make a courtroom identification is in some sense choosing from a variety of possible subjects. This assumption, of course, depends on the view that witnesses are in general ignorant of the geography of the courtroom. This is why defence lawyers may go to great lengths to prove that the witness concerned knows the layout of the courtroom and what the dock signifies. Here is an excerpt from one trial transcript:

Q: Have you ever watched trials of people on television?
A: No, I do not watch television very much.
Q: Or on the cinema screen?
A: No.
Q: Never seen any sort of representation of what a criminal court looks like?
A: No, I have not.

Q: Have you ever heard that people who are accused in criminal cases are put in a place called the dock?

A: Well, I have not really, no.

Q: Are you sure?

A: Yes, sure . . .

Q: You have never heard of people charged with serious crimes being put in a dock?

A: I have heard of them being charged with serious crimes.

Q: You know this *thing* is called a dock?

A: Yes.

Q: And while you were being asked questions by my learned friend you were staring hard at the dock, were you not?

A: I do not know that I was.

Q: And realizing, I suggest, that these two, who are the only two there in ordinary clothes, are the persons on trial?

A: No.

Q: Are you sure this did not in a sense lead you to think that you had seen them?

A: I have seen them.

This witness must have known what the dock was, since it was subsequently discovered that she had spent a lot of time there herself. She had previous convictions for soliciting for prostitution, insulting behaviour, being drunk and disorderly, attempted suicide, larceny, obtaining a cheque by false pretences, obstructing the police, and street betting and taking bets from children. She had also been a witness in court many times before.

It should be noted in fairness to the police and courts that some people in effect force the confrontation method to be used by refusing to take part in identification parades.

Clearly, a lot of people get wrongly identified, but who are they? The National Council for Civil Liberties stresses that: 'It is still possible for a man of good character to be picked out and imprisoned if he is picked out by even one witness on an identification parade.'[13] All, then, are at risk; but some are more at risk than others. The people most at risk are those known to the police: people with criminal records, people with criminal associates, and other policemen.[14]

This is most obviously so for a man with a criminal record. Such a man is often automatically picked up and put in an identification parade for every offence that takes place in his neighbourhood. Even if such a man is now going straight, on statistical grounds alone the chances of his being picked out sometime are obviously considerable and greater than for other people, since he goes on a lot more parades.

The man with criminal associates is also at risk; this, for instance, is how Ronald John Barker was picked up. He was accused of committing a robbery with a known criminal called Ross. He said: 'Ross was picked up, and the description of the man with him fitted me. The police said: "Who do we know who looks like this and knows Ross?" The police said they'd seen me with Ross in a club I frequented.' This was also the case with the Cross brothers (see pp. 25–26). A lawyer who knew the case said: 'The Cross brothers were well known in town as local toughs ... The police must have thought: Three of them involved? Who goes round in threes? The Cross brothers? Where were they at the time? In the Eclipse pub. Aha!'

We have earlier mentioned the case of ex-PC Luckhurst and another policeman who were wrongly identified, and we have several other cases in our files where policemen have been wrongly identified and accused. Clearly the police are known to the police.

And who wrongly identifies? The people who make wrong identifications are curiously like those who get wrongly identified. Criminals and their associates are more likely to be called as witnesses, and less likely to be reliable. This is especially dangerous where, as is often the case, this is not known to the jury. Such a case is that of the lady who denied all knowledge of the dock (see p. 31). A similar case is that of John Devers, convicted solely on the identification evidence of the victim of the robbery, Michael Masterson. At the trial, Masterson was put forward as a man of good character, as described by the judge: 'You saw Mr Masterson, you heard what he said. You heard what he said about his feelings in respect of what had happened. He seemed to have little or no malice against those who had perpetrated what you might think a dreadful outrage on him. He talked about a higher authority, and you may think it abundantly clear, if you come to the conclusion he was sincere, he was a man actuated by very strong Christian principles. ... The most important evidence for the case for the prosecution is that of Mr Michael Masterson. You have heard him express what you may think are high Christian principles. Principles which permit him to give expression to his desire for nothing to befall these two persons [Devers and his co-accused], but which prevented him from coming here and telling you other than what he said was the truth.' It later turned out that Masterson was an Irishman with an enormous string of convictions, who had served twelve prison sentences. When this came out, the Home Secretary referred the case back to the Court of Appeal, Criminal Division, who quashed his conviction. The Appeal Court, when quashing the conviction of Jones, his supposed accomplice, said: 'Of course, this record is wholly irreconcilable with the mannner in which he [Masterson] was guilelessly by the Commissioner presented to the jury. Cases of identification are said from time to time to be notoriously difficult. A truer way of putting it would be that they are cases which call for the most careful consideration.'[15]

Identification, then, is a risky business. Its unreliability is shown in an analysis quoted by Jerome and Barbara Frank in their survey of American cases of wrongful imprisonment: 'Perhaps erroneous identification of the accused consitutes the major cause of the known wrongful convictions . . . An analysis of the testimony of 20,000 persons who were asked to describe the physical characteristics of the man they saw commit a crime . . . revealed that on average they overestimated the height by five inches, the age by eight years, and gave the wrong hair colour in 82 per cent of the cases.'[16]

This inaccuracy is not surprising when one comes to consider the original circumstances in which the witness saw the culprit. In a very large proportion of cases it is fair to assume that the witness was disturbed, startled or frightened by what happened, which would distort his judgment. This would be particularly true where the witness was also the victim—as in many cases of rape, robbery or personal assault—and perhaps the sole identifier.[17]

In many cases where the witness is *not* directly concerned in the crime, by virtue of his distance from it, he is not in the best position to describe the people taking part. Arthur Thompson, convicted of robbery with violence and later pardoned, describes the circumstances under which he was wrongly identified: 'Well, according to the evidence, it was 3 o'clock in the morning, she was three storeys up, and there was just a small electric light bulb. And when I visited the scene of the crime two or three years later, there was three big trees that would have made it impossible for her to have seen anyone.'

The identification of the Cross brothers (see p. 25) took place under rather similar circumstances. The judge in his summing-up said of the key prosecution witness: 'You have got to consider, of course, what sort of view she had of these three men. She was in a bedroom on the third floor looking out of a window. She had, when the men were glancing up and down the road, a profile view of them, and when they were running across the road to go towards the entrance, then she had a full-face view of them. But that, of course, would only be for a very short space of time.

'You have got to consider the lighting. . . . There was one [light] almost opposite where this incident is said to have occurred, there was one light further down West Hill Drive in the direction of Clifton Place, which was some considerable distance away and would not help much with the lighting of this spot, and there was one at a shorter distance away on the other side, which also would not help much.

'You have had the advantage of seeing the photograph which was taken at night. You can see how much you can identify of that police officer; what appearance he presents in the light in which that photograph was taken. It has to be borne in mind that the lights of those two houses shown in the photograph were not in fact on at the time, though, as [the witness] says, there was a light on in the house next door to her, and, of course, you have to bear in mind the period of time during which [the witness] was able to make her observations' [three or four minutes at the most].[18]

Often, witnesses who misidentify are found to be myopic. Albert Chapman, convicted of stealing a van in Bradford and later exonerated, described the man who identified him as 'having glasses on half an inch thick', whilst Gerald Morris (see p. 27) said of his identifier: 'When he claimed to recognize me in the police station he'd just been hit on the head, he'd lost his glasses, and he was very short-sighted anyway.'

In the 'Justice' second memorandum, great stress is laid on the problems of using photographs to assist identification. 'We recognize that the showing of photographs may be necessary when there are no clues to the identity of the culprit, but it presents considerable hazards in that when the witness later goes on the parade, he inevitably has in mind the photographs he has selected and studied rather than the face he has seen at or near the scene of the crime. Whenever, therefore, there is more than one witness to identification, only one witness should be invited to study photographs to identify suspects, and the other witness be taken on the identification parade. We understand this practice is followed in some forces, particularly in Scotland.'[19]

Most police officers are aware of the dangers involved in identifications involving photographs, since this is an important part of

their basic training. Their instruction leaflet on identification says:
'It is improper for the police to assist the identification of a suspected
person already under arrest by showing photographs, including that
of the suspect, to persons who may be or are likely to be called upon
to identify him.'[20]

Nevertheless, allegations that this has happened are sometimes
made, though they aren't often substantiated. Such a case was
that of a man we shall call Harry Boyle, who was found guilty of
passing a worthless cheque, and later acquitted on a re-trial. A lawyer
who knows of the case writes: 'The description given by the complainant would undoubtedly suggest to the police that someone like
the accused, Boyle, had committed the offence. It is believed that
the shopkeeper did see a photograph before the identification parade.'
(For a dramatic description of the effects of using a photograph of
a motor car, see the description by Thompson of what happened
in his case below.) One may not that the police only had Boyle's
photograph because he had been in trouble before, and that once
again it is such people who are most at risk of being misidentified.[21]

Something that often happens in cases of misidentification is that
at each stage of the judicial process the eyewitness becomes more and
more confident that he is right in his identification. He is more
confident when identifying the culprit than when initially describing
him; more confident still at the committal proceedings; and practically unassailable at the trial. F. C. Bartlett in his classic experiments
on 'Remembering', shows that this is a general psychological phenomenon. He shows that people tend to become more confident in
their descriptions of what they have seen over time and repetition;
and secondly, that witness confidence may be an inverse guide to
accuracy.[22]

Unfortunately, the legal process reinforces this psychological
tendency. One way in which it does this is by its very repetitiousness.
Thompson (see p. 34), showed how this process worked in his
own case: 'A woman witness did identify another man quite dis-
tinctly in the assize court, but at the magistrates' court she was not
sure at all. But after being in the witness-box two or three times, she
picked the third man out without hesitation. This I think was because she'd been in the witness-box so many times that she became
word-perfect. . . .

'After they'd been in the magistrates' court for the third or fourth
time their evidence became much more detailed, and when they

came to the assize court they became word-perfect. It was impossible to break them down. The fact that they'd appeared three or four times in a magistrates' court and never been cross-examined and the prosecution had just asked them whatever questions they wanted to ask them, this made them word-perfect. . . .[23] [The three men accused of this crime were riding in a Wolseley when arrested; it was later found that the men who actually committed the crime had used a Jaguar.] Well, they identified the motor at the finish as a Wolseley. First of all, in their first evidence, at the police court, it was just a black motor. But then at the final assize court one of the witnesses definitely identified it as a Wolseley. . . . We were in a Wolseley when we was picked up, when we was stopped. She [the witness] was shown photographs of a black Wolseley. Just the one photo, she was shown, and first of all she said that it was like that photo, and finally she said that *was* the motor.'

If in the future written depositions come to replace repeated verbal descriptions of the same events, at preliminary hearings; and given that defence lawyers need not cross-examine the witness at the hearing but can reserve their questions for the trial, this sort of mistake ought to become less common.[24] Nevertheless at present this sort of reinforcement goes on happening even under apparently favourable conditions. John Lovesay and Tony Peterson were convicted of robbery (and also of murder, which conviction was later quashed). One of the main pieces of evidence against them was that of a man who claimed to have seen them in the car used in the crime. Three weeks after the crime, when this man was first interviewed by the police, he refused to attend an identity parade on the grounds that he could not be sure of recognizing the car's occupants. But three months later, in court, he identified Lovesay, who had lost a stone and a half while in solitary confinement. Even an astute lawyer is no match for human nature.

Just how universal this aspect of human nature is, can be shown by another reference to F. C. Bartlett's experiments on 'Remembering'. His subject were given a series of postcards to look at, depicting the faces of various military men. Bartlett describes his method thus: 'After all the cards had been seen, an interval of thirty minutes was allowed to pass. The subject then described the various cards in the order in which he judged them to have been presented, and answered questions about some of the details. A week, or a fortnight later, another description was given by the subject, and further questions answered. The procedure was continued after longer intervals.'

Among the cards was one of a naval captain, a three-quarter face view. Bartlett: 'A . . . subject gave the captain "a grave appearance." "He was a very serious-looking young man." The face was turned into complete profile and assigned a prominent and heavy chin. After a lapse of three weeks the seriousness appeared to have become intensified, and the captain was now referred to as "the young man in profile, to the right. He had a square face, and is very serious and determined-looking." Seriousness and decision were emphasized again and again, and a fortnight later were more striking than ever. This subject had to terminate her experiment at this stage, and so I showed her the card once more. She was amazed, and thought at first that I had substituted a new card. Her captain, she said, was very much more serious; his mouth was firmer, his chin more prominent, his face more square.'[25]

The very role that the prosecution witness is expected to play in the case, and the fact that he has to play this role in public, will reinforce his natural tendency to appear more certain than he really is.

Judges in the courts have a very specific idea of what constitutes a good witness, and the witness is left in little doubt of what this is. A 'good witness' is expected to be certain and consistent. Judges often congratulate a 'good witness' in the summing-up. At this stage, the judge makes explicit the assumptions about 'good witnessness' which are in fact present throughout the whole proceedings.

Such a witness was Miss Frayling, the prosecution's most important witness in the case of Michael John Davies. Her identification of him as the boy she had seen from the top of a bus was a mainstay of the prosecution case on which he was convicted of murder in 1953. Prosecution counsel referred to her as a witness 'upon whom the prosecution place great reliance', and in his final speech Mr Christmas Humphreys described her as: 'That marvellous witness, you may think.' 'Miss Frayling said that she was sitting on the front seat on the right-hand-side of the top of the bus, with her friend Margaret McCarthy on her right. She said that she heard a scuffle on the left side of the bus and that people on the top were standing up and looking round. She saw some seven or eight boys running along the pavement just in front of the bus, spread out slightly. She declared: "Then one of them seemed to go up to another boy and shake him. I say shake; he seemed to shake him, making a motion as if he shook his shoulders", and the boy who was shaken fell to the ground. Asked what happened to the boy who seemed to shake him, Miss Frayling said he crossed over the road.'

Later she was asked:

Q: Are you able to see him here to day?
A: Yes [indicating the prisoner].
Q: It is Davies, is it?
A: It is Davies.
Q: Have you any doubt about that?
A: No, not a single doubt.'[26]

Not unnaturally, most witnesses want to be 'good witnesses'.

The police and prosecution, too have their idea of what is a 'good witness'. He must, among other things, possess the qualities that will impress the judge, and so, consciously or unconsciously, he is pushed in that direction. To some extent, the attitude and expectations of the prosecution witness are by-products of the process of investigation and prosecution. Before he ever comes to court, he will have collaborated with the police, answered their questions, and have come to know and to feel part of the prosecution's case. Indeed, often the witness comes to feel more prosecution-minded than the police. This is what happened in the case of Bernard Beatty, who was convicted of murder, the sole evidence against him being one single eyewitness, who picked him out on an ID parade, as having driven one of the vehicles involved in a robbery resulting in the death of the victim. At the trial, Beatty's lawyer said of the ID parade: 'Then there are the discrepancies as between [the witness's] recollection of what occurred and the police sergeant's, particularly the very significant one of which the police sergeant was quite clear, namely, that the lady had said: "I am not sure, it may be one of two of them." She denied, your Lordship will remember, ever having said that.' This is one of several cases in which there has been a contrast between the certainty of the witness and the fair-mindedness of the police.[27]

Finally, the witness has his own concept of how he wishes to appear in public, both as a witness and as a person. He feels himself to be playing an important part in the trial, and doesn't want to lose this sense of his own importance, or be made to look a fool in public. For all these reasons, he has everything to lose by contradicting himself at a late stage.

All these factors can be seen at work in the separate trials of two different men for the murder of George Henry Storrs in 1909, where the same eyewitnesses were called at both trials. This case is described by Julian Symons: 'Miss Lindley admitted that Howard was the only one of the nine men at the ID parade who looked in the least like the murderer, and agreed also that she had at first thought Howard (who was 5 ft 8 in. in height) was not tall enough to be the murderer. The coroner persisted:

' "This man Howard, you say, not only resembles the man who came, but is the same man?"

' "Yes, unless he had a double about somewhere exactly like him." '

'There is a hint of doubt, perhaps, and so there seemed to be, in Mary Evans's remark that "of course Howard had no moustache". Under questioning, however, she reacted as some witnesses do, and became more positive. "Is that the only ground which makes you feel at all doubtful?" the coroner asked.

' "He is very like the man; the eyes, cheeks and forehead are the same. In fact, I feel convinced now he is the man. . . ." '

'Mrs Storrs alone among the witnesses who had seen the man was unable to identify him, and in fact picked out the wrong man at the police station. When she was giving evidence, however, she suddenly cried out that Howard had looked at her in exactly the same way as had the man in the hall [the murderer].'[28]

[Howard was in fact acquitted because of a strong alibi, and another suspect, Wilde, was subsequently tried for the same offence.]

The case against him broke down finally on the question of identification. Having been so positive and so completely mistaken before, the eyewitnesses flinched from being equally positive now. Mary Evans said that she could not swear that Wilde was the man, but she would say that he resembled him closely. Eliza Cooper said that Wilde and Howard were so much alike that one might pass for the other, but "I cannot go so far as I did at the trial and say I feel quite sure this is the man." Miss Lindley had picked out Wilde at an identification parade. But what, defence counsel asked ironically, of her certainty that Howard was the man? Miss Lindley said that she was not so sure about Howard now. . . .

'Finally Mrs Storrs was asked in the witness-box whether she could identify Wilde. She thought so, but she was not sure. Howard was in court. He stood up and looked at her, and defence counsel reminded her of her dramatic cry: "He has the same look in his eyes as there was in the eyes of the man who attacked my husband!" What did she say to that now? And what could she say, but that she had been mistaken?'[29]

Wilde was acquitted, despite strong prosecution evidence.

Many judges, of course, realize that confidence and certainty in a witness are not necessarily a sure guide to reliability. Some even err in the opposite direction. This is what happened in the case of John Devers (see p. 33). The sole identifying witness against him was rather hesitant in giving evidence, giving rise to the following remarks in the judge's summing-up: 'He [the witness] said: "I am quite satisfied [that] I am certain that these two are two of the three who attacked and robbed me." He said: "I saw these two dark boys, or coloured boys, and I wasn't able to be certain about them. Therefore, I said I wasn't certain." Does that indicate to you a man who is very reckless in the case of his identification of persons or not?'[30] Devers was convicted; his case was later referred to the Court of Appeal by the Home Secretary, where he was acquitted.

This chapter has considered at length and in detail various ways in which identification evidence can lead to a miscarriage of justice. Many others before us have concluded that this kind of evidence is unreliable. The Royal Commission which in 1904 reported on the Adolf Beck case, one of the most famous cases of wrongful imprisonment based on identification evidence, said: 'Evidence as to identity based upon personal impressions is, unless supported by other facts, an unsafe basis for the verdict of a jury.'[31] Why then do juries continue to place such faith in identification, and why are so many 'guilty' verdicts based on the flimsiest of identification evidence?

Perhaps it is because they confuse identification with recognition. As E. Lustgarten puts it: 'Recognizing someone at the time is one thing; identifying someone subsequently is quite another, especially when a substantial period has elapsed. If you say: "I saw so-and-so whom I know" the room for error is infinitesimally small. If you say: "This is a stranger whom I saw on one occasion" the room for error there is almost without limits.'[32]

Glanville Williams makes a similar point in his study, *The Proof of Guilt*: 'Common sense suggests that it is also necessary to distinguish between the witness who has merely made a brief acquaintance with the criminal and the witness who knows him well. There is all the difference between saying: "I saw the defendant whom I have known all my life", and: "I saw a man I recognized as the defendant whom I had met once before." The former statement in ninety-nine cases out of a hundred is satisfactory identification; the latter in the absence of corroborative evidence never is.'[33]

Most of us, in our everyday lives, when we meet someone, *recognize* him; it is relatively unusual to have to make an identification that does not involve a large area of recognition. Because this generally works in everyday life, we trust it; and this trust is mistakenly extended to areas of identification where it ought not to apply.

If you are asked to identify someone by the police, it is unlikely that this will involve recognition in the sense we have been using the word. In very many cases, the victim will not have 'met' his assailant before.

It isn't only juries that put too much trust in identification evidence. A lawyer who has had a lot of experience of criminal work and specifically of cases involving misidentification, wrote to us: 'We think that most solicitors and barristers accept the evidence of identification. I do not. I challenge it on each and every occasion, and by testing it by a method I have devised, case after case has been won and the evidence of identification shattered. Truly the eyewitness is a most dangerous and unreliable person.'

If this is so, then whom ought the jury to trust? Paradoxically, juries seem to place most reliance on those forms of evidence that we have found most likely to lead to error, namely identification and (as we shall explain) confessions and statements made by the accused. By contrast, juries and even, to some extent, lawyers, are chary of evidence involving expert testimony or technical expertise of any kind; yet very few errors seem to arise from this. Juries, for instance, are sometimes reluctant to accept fingerprint evidence (perhaps the technical evidence with which they are most likely to come into contact). C. G. L. Du Cann says: 'So far as the author can discover, since its inception by Sir Edward Henry in 1901, not a single miscarriage of justice has resulted from identification by fingerprint evidence. . . . The Scotland Yard bureau seems infallible—though juries do not always accept it.'[34] Lawyers have even incorporated their distrust in institutional form. When the Court of Criminal Appeal was founded by the Criminal Appeal Act of 1907, this Act provided that where any question arising on appeal involved scientific investigation or expert knowledge, either it may be referred to a special commission for inquiry and report, or else a skilled assessor may be appointed to assist the court.[35] On one level, this may simply seem a routine, sensible provision of expert assistance to the court; but looking at it another way, it also reflects a distrust of scientific and technical evidence. After all, there is no provision for a special inquiry into evidence of identification or statements and confessions.

Although these often seem quite straightforward, their proved un-reliability indicates that they may be equally in need of special investigation.[36]

The reason for this irrational state of affairs is that juries and lawyers—that is all of us—rely continually in our everyday lives on our ability to identify other people, and to trust in the statements they make to us. By contrast, because we are not so familiar with scientific and technical expertise, we are more inclined to distrust it. Also, psychologists have shown that we acquire our ability to recognize and to communicate with other people very early in life, and it is very disturbing for us to accept the fact that these basic beliefs and skills may be fallible. Scientific and technical skills are acquired much later and are much less deeply ingrained; we have a much smaller emotional investment in them. Consequently, juries are not going to discard this order of priorities simply because they are sitting in the jury-box.[37]

In view of this over-ready acceptance of doubtful identification evidence, we feel that the system ought to provide more safeguards than it does in this area.

Firstly, we feel that in general a single uncorroborated eyewitness identification ought not to be sufficient grounds for conviction—some form of corroboration should be required, as is already the case in Scotland. Of course, we need not follow the Scots model in every detail. Our own suggestions about corroboration are:

1. There are some 'weak' forms of corroboration which we feel should not be sufficient in themselves. These are (a) the use of an ID parade to buttress other evidence of identity by the same witness; (b) evidence from someone else that an ID parade did in fact take place and the suspect was picked out; (c) identification by different witnesses which refer to a different occasion and a different crime, for example a series of cheque frauds where a large number of separately defrauded merchants identify the accused.

2. The corroboration required will not necessarily be that of an independent witness, but can be other circumstantial evidence connecting the accused to the case.

3. Corroboration should not be needed (a) in a robbery, or assault case where no one was present except the criminal and his victim. (If corroboration was required in this instance, then very few criminals of this type would ever be convicted.)[38] (b) In cases where

the evidence of identification is really recognition, as where someone is robbed by a person well known to him.

Our further suggestions about identification evidence are:

1. Even where corroboration is not required, the judge should warn the jury about the dangers of convicting on the basis of uncorroborated evidence of identification. (Great care should be taken in the working and timing of such a warning, as experimental research has shown that such warnings can have an opposite effect from that intended.)[39]

2. Evidence of confrontation, whether in the dock, the police station or elsewhere, ought not to be allowed where the witness and the accused are not previously known to each other. (Such evidence should certainly not be admitted in cases where the witness has actually previously failed to pick out the accused on an ID parade—see the case of Lovesay and Peterson, p. 37).

3. If point (2) is to be viable, then ID parades must evidently become compulsory. This would both protect the innocent and also assist the police. The *Police Review* (21 February 1969) spells out the reason for this with reference to the Cannock Chase murder trial: 'However, that form of identification [in court or in the police station] cannot possibly be ruled out. In the Cannock Chase murder trial at Stafford Assizes . . . Chief Superintendent Ian Forbes said in evidence that he had made five separate attempts to put the prisoner, Raymond Morris, on an identification parade—"Even if only in favour of the accused. I knew", said Superintendent Forbes, "how important identification was going to be in this matter; the whole thing hinged on identification." When Morris was asked to go on a parade, he said: "No, no, no—nothing will make me and you can't make me." During the interview he had maintained long periods of silence, and it was during this time that he made his five refusals to be put up for identification. And in due course one of the witnesses, Mr Victor Whitehouse, was asked if he could identify Morris in court as the man he had seen on Cannock Chase at about 4 p.m. on the day of the murder. According to the *Daily Telegraph* report on 14 February, he looked at Morris for twelve seconds and then said: "Yes, I say yes." Which could be taken to be either confident and deliberate or hesitating and uneasy, according to which side you are on.'

The *Police Review*, in another issue (24 January 1969) makes suggestions for getting round this dilemma. '. . . There is absolutely no power in this country to *require* a prisoner or suspect to take part in a parade if he doesn't want to. In some of the Commonwealth countries this difficulty is surmounted by getting the suspect into a room with eight or ten other people where they walk about and are watched through a window. The suspect can't be *made* to walk about; but if he sits down defiantly while the others are walking, he draws upon himself the very attention which he presumably wants to dilute. In Western Australia the suspect walks about on the footway in a crowded street, with police in plain clothes watching from strategic doorways. He can run away, of course, but he's unlikely to get far, and his running away is the classic gesture of admission that he is the right man. (He *might* not be, but why did he run away ?)'

4. Regarding the conduct of identity parades:
(*a*) The Home Office instructions regarding the conduct of identification parades should be made mandatory. A police inspector commented on this: 'Cutting corners in identification procedure by the police is more dangerous than anywhere else. The problem is not one of devising new procedural rules, but of bringing the practice of all police forces up to that of the bulk. These recommendations are in practice in most forces already.'

(*b*) It should be an absolute rule that photographs are shown to a witness only to bring in a suspect, and that witnesses attending a parade should be given no assistance either by way of photographs or descriptions. (Recommendation of the 'Justice' 2nd memorandum on identification.)[40]

(*c*) The whole parade should be photographed with the suspect being touched by the witness, and this photograph should be available to the jury so that they can judge for themselves how fair the parade was. This is already the general practice in the Republic of South Africa.

(*d*) Some neutral official should be present whenever an ID parade is held, to ensure that it is properly conducted.[41]

5. Greater weight should be given to the evidence of those witnesses who fail to identify the accused in an identity parade, and the defence should be enabled and assisted to call them as witnesses.

6. The witness's original description of the culprit as well as his

evidence at the preliminary hearing should be taken down and made available to the defence.

7. Transcripts of the evidence of identification by each witness at earlier hearings, and even before the indictment, should be made available to the jury. The court shorthand writer should provide transcripts of the evidence for the jury as the case proceeds.[42]

Chapter 3

Confessions and Statements

After identification, we found that confessions and statements alleged to have been made by the accused were the most common cause of wrongful imprisonment. The law recognizes the problems involved in this kind of evidence. The law lays down that: 'No statement by the accused is admissible in evidence against him unless it is shown by the prosecution to have been a voluntary statement in the sense that it has not been obtained from him either by fear of prejudice or hope of advantage exercised or held out by a person in authority. In addition there are the Judges Rules (listed in Appendix C) which attempt to lay down a framework for the questioning of suspects.[1] These rules were first formulated in 1918, and revised in 1964. They don't carry the force of law, but failure to conform with them may render answers and statements liable to be excluded from evidence in subsequent criminal proceedings. But when the new rules were published in 1964, the Magistrates' Association drew attention to the uncertainty of their tone, inferring that a magistrates' court may well be justified in admitting an accused person's statement in evidence against him, even when the Judges' Rules have not been complied with; the words 'may' and 'liable to be' adding further uncertainty. Perhaps the judges do not have the courage of their convictions.

The main points in the Rules are as follows:

1. Free questioning of persons in custody is permitted so long as they have not been charged or informed that they may be prosecuted. However, the police must keep a record of the length and place of this questioning, and of those present at it.

2. 'As soon as' the investigating police officer has 'evidence which would afford reasonable grounds of suspecting that a person has

committed an offence, he shall caution that person' saying to him: 'You are not obliged to say anything unless you wish to do so, but what you say may be put into writing and given in evidence.' After a person has been charged, he must again be cautioned in a similar manner. Further questioning after this point is not allowed except where such questioning is 'necessary for the purpose of preventing or minimizing harm or loss to some other person or to the public.' Before these further questions can be asked, yet another type of caution must be administered, and the answers to these questions must be recorded in full at the time and signed by the suspect.

3. In order to ensure that the statement made by the suspect after being cautioned was genuinely voluntary, the suspect must, if he so wishes, be permitted to write it himself. If the police officer takes it down, it has to be in the exact words spoken by the suspect, and not translated into formal language. The police cannot prompt the suspect or ask questions except where these are needed to make the statement 'coherent, intelligent and relevant'. The statement must then be read by the suspect and signed by him as being made 'of my own free will'. In addition, administrative directives to the police are attached to these rules. From our point of view the most interesting of these provides safeguards for certain vulnerable groups of individuals. Foreigners who have made a statement in their own language sign that statement and not the translation of it into English which they may be unable to understand. Children should only be questioned in the presence of one of their parents or some other responsible person.

In addition to this, the Home Office circularizes police forces with further recommendations.[2]

The revised rules, like their predecessors, have aroused a great deal of controversy: some people think that they hamper the police in their investigations, others that the suspect is not sufficiently protected. It seems to us that both these statements are true, but that the people who put them forward have missed the essential points. Two main points emerge from the cases which are publicly acknowledged to have gone wrong on the basis of this kind of evidence. Firstly, whilst the rules may provide sufficient protection for the average suspect, there are a large number of people who are mentally or psychologically inadequate, and whom the rules do not sufficiently protect. Secondly, the rules and their critics seem over-concerned with the balance of powers and rights as between police and suspects, as opposed to the question of getting at the truth.

One striking fact which has emerged from the cases of people whose conviction has been quashed, or who have been pardoned, after having been convicted largely on the basis of their own confessions, or statements, is how many of them are in some sense inadequate. When the revised Judges' Rules came out in 1964, the *Police Review* commented: 'The man who does not decide to keep his mouth shut after all this is probably more of a fool than a knave.' This ties in only too well with our own findings.[3]

Our 'fools' seem to come in three categories. Firstly, the mentally retarded. Timothy John Evans, convicted of murder, hanged and later pardoned, was described to Mr Justice Brabin's inquiry as 'an illiterate youth of 25 with an IQ of 65 and a mental age of $10\frac{1}{2}$.'[4] Ron Avard, placed in Rampton at the age of 21 for attempted rape and indecent assault, was found by a doctor to have a mental age of 7. Colin Temple, convicted of attempted rape, and whose case is currently the subject of much controversy, has an IQ of 86.[5] Andrew Campbell, convicted of wilful damage and later pardoned, entered a mental deficiency institution as a result of his conviction.[6] We have come across many other cases where it is reasonable to infer, from the way the defendant has behaved, that he is of very low intelligence. Often these people are illiterate as well.

Secondly, a surprising number of youths and children are recipients of free pardons.

Thirdly, people of normal adult intelligence but who are psychologically disturbed in some way, seem prone to make false confessions to crimes with which they have no connection. Every time some particularly gruesome crime is reported in the press, police stations and hospitals are likely to receive visits and phone calls from unbalanced people claiming to be the criminal. Normally little notice is taken of such confessions, but sometimes they are believed. One such case was that of Kenneth Archibald, who 'confessed' to murdering a 26-year-old prostitute. Fortunately for him, he was acquitted at the Old Bailey—after a six-day trial and fifty-six days in gaol. He said afterwards: 'Why did I say I did such a terrible murder? I must have been mad.' A psychologist, Dr Peter Duncan Scott of the Maudsley Hospital, said at his trial that he was the type of man who could well have faked the story in a mood of depression.

Why did this case come to trial at all? Archibald says of his case: 'Thank goodness I retracted my false confession in time. I will never admit anything again, especially murder. . . . I should never have shot my mouth off in such a ridiculous way. I just kept talking, thinking up the story as I went along, and by amazing coincidence certain details fitted in with what the police knew.' Archibald had even shown the police the spot where, he said, he had strangled and undressed the girl before burning her clothes. Also, the prosecution said at the trial that a visiting-card had been found at the dead girl's address with the name 'Kenny' on it, and the phone number of a public call-box at the tennis-club where Archibald worked. (But the cards had in fact been printed by a friend of Archibald's to advertise a club that was to open at the tennis-club.) The odds against such coincidences seem large, but from time to time they are bound to happen.[7]

One might fairly comment that these are just the kinds of people who tend to be accused of crimes anyway—and usually of crimes which they have committed. There is no doubt that among criminals generally, a large proportion are either juvenile delinquents or mental and psychological inadequates. We feel, nevertheless, the proportion of such people among those who have been pardoned or exonerated after conviction seems to be even greater.

Why are these people particularly prone to get convicted in this way? Perhaps we should begin by asking why they are suspected in the first place.

The answer to this question is implied in the kinds of crimes of which, typically, the mental inadequates are accused. Here, for instance, is a list of the crimes of which the mental inadequates who came to our notice were accused: attempted rape, child murder, indecent assault, attempted rape, indecent assault, wilful damage and arson, stealing church candlesticks, indecent assault, wilful damage, indecent exposure, attempted buggery with a chicken, malicious damage. None of these involve any exercise of intelligence or foresight. For some of them, the local 'idiot' might be the obvious suspect, or even the obvious scapegoat.

Possibly, a similar inference can be drawn from a list of the crimes alleged to have been committed by the children: theft of savings stamps from a school, theft of 20p from a seven-year-old boy, theft of money from the purse of a woman they knew—in fact, petty thefts of very small amounts.

The psychologically disturbed, as we have already said, often tend to put themselves forward; and if they are picked up, perhaps quite by chance, incriminate themselves in an irrational way.

The next important question is, why are these people liable to make false confessions when they are picked up as suspects? It would be fair to say of all three groups that they are very—in some cases, abnormally—suggestible. Ron Avard, for instance, will accept and repeat almost everything anyone tells him. Here is a transcript of part of a tape-recorded interview with him and his mother:

Ron: Well, they thought I was the one, you see.

Mrs: They thought he was the one.

Ron: Yes. So what they did forced me to say it, you see, but I didn't know. I asked my mother when she come.

Mrs: And you didn't use any rude or dirty words, did you?

Ron: No. . . . Well, what they did, put me in a cell, and they took a —a photograph with me handprints to see if it was me, you see, and then after that they sent me to—what was it? Birmingham was it?

Mrs: No, Leicester for three weeks.

Ron: Leicester—jail for three weeks.

Mrs: He'd had to have been tried.

Int: What was it like in Leicester?

Ron: Well, I wasn't there long. I forget how long I was there.

Mrs: Three weeks.

Ron: Three weeks.

Mrs: And then you came back to the trial at Rampton and then you were sent to the assizes, Birmingham.

Ron: Birmingham.

Not very difficult to get a confession out of someone like that, is it?

Ron went on to describe, in part, what happened:

Ron: So what they did, forced me to say it, you see, but I didn't know. I asked my mother when she come.

Mrs: And you didn't use any rude or dirty words, did you?

Ron: No.

Mrs: But in the photostatic copy, you've never seen such dirty words and vulgar words as he's supposed to have said . . . Poor Dad was broken-hearted, and the policeman said, sign here, Mr Avard, they said to him, sign here. Of course, when you sign, that's it, isn't it?

Not difficult, but how do you do it? Dr William Sargant, consultant psychiatrist at St Thomas's Hospital, at the 5th annual scientific meeting of the British Academy of Forensic Sciences described how it's done: 'Firstly, suspects must be got into a sufficiently anxious state. Secondly, a state of artificially-induced tension must be prolonged so that normal behaviour and judgment become disturbed. This takes the form of being friendly, offering cigarettes and cups of tea, and suddenly changing to a hostile attitude. . . . The final phase is the ultra-paradoxical, when even the most secretive suspects become most anxious to tell all and make so-called "voluntary confessions".'[8] Or, as the police call it, 'hard and soft'.

Almost anybody could be worn down by this process if it goes on long enough, and is tough enough. With the kind of people we are at present discussing, it happens very easily and very quickly. E. B. Block describes just such a case: 'The medical men submitted a significant report. They agreed that Israel [the accused] was of low mentality and easily susceptible to suggestion. His confession, they concluded, came at a time when he was nervously and physically exhausted, and therefore it was of no value. In fact, it was their belief that he could be made to admit almost anything under the pressure of continuous questioning and suggestion.'[9]

It is easy to see why people with the mentality of children, and indeed children themselves, are suggestible in this way. Perhaps also certain personality types may be at risk. If we accept Professor H. J. Eysenck's theory that (a) introverts condition more easily than extroverts,[10] and (b) that most criminals are extroverts,[11] then what may happen is that methods of questioning designed to deal with the typical extrovert criminal may go badly wrong when the suspect is an easily-conditionable introvert. So in addition to children and the weak-minded, perhaps individuals who are exceptionally introverted are also at risk.

The very situation of the police interview tends to put these categories of people at a further disadvantage. A 'Justice' committee presided over by Mr F. H. Lawton, QC (now a High Court judge) made this point: 'It is still true in general that police officers have a psychological advantage and an advantage in numbers over the person they are questioning. This is particularly so where the questioning takes place at a police station.' For obvious reasons, these people feel even more inadequate and powerless under these circumstances than most people do. This will make them even more suggestible.

Is it possible to tell if a confession, or parts of it, result from too much suggestion? A Swedish linguist, Dr Jan Svartvik, of Gothenburg University, claims that it is, and uses as his example a study of the statements Timothy Evans made to the police, first in South Wales and later in London. Dr Svartvik bases his analysis on the hypothesis that each individual, when he writes or speaks, does so in regular patterns of vocabulary and syntax peculiar to the individual and characteristic throughout. Going through Evans's statements, he found a definite pattern established throughout, but sudden and significant discrepancies in the small incriminating section where Evans described the actual murders. These discrepancies fit exactly with what Evans maintained at his trial. The parts which have his regular sentence structure are the parts he agreed at his trial were true, and the parts which diverge from this are the parts Evans maintained he never said. Svartvik admits there are limitations to his method, imposed by 'the highly artificial linguistic situation which produced it [Evans's confession]: a policeman, probably of limited education, and subject to all kinds of prescriptive pressures in his written English, giving a graphic rendering of the speech of an illiterate', and 'our inadequate knowledge of how language is used in different situations.'[12] Subject to these limitations, it seems reasonable to assume that at a certain crucial point in his confession, Evans was 'programmed' to say things that were suggested to him.

Possibly a certain amount of stress applied to a normal person may get the truth out of him; but if a lot of stress is applied to inadequates like Evans, a false confession is very likely to be the result. Professor R. V. Jones of Aberdeen University, speaking at the meeting of the British Academy of Forensic Sciences mentioned earlier, put the matter even more strongly: 'It was doctrine with us in our wartime interrogations that you cannot get the truth out of a man under stress. Under stress a man tells you what he thinks you want to learn rather than the truth.'[13] Evans, like many of the people who confess in this way, was an illiterate. People like him are at a disadvantage because they cannot write out their statement themselves nor can they read it when it is written out for them.

Ironically, these people—who need a searching trial and a good defence more than most—may be the very ones to be denied a trial at all, either because they are too young or because they are judged 'unfit to plead'. This is what happened with Ron Avard. His mother described what happened at his trial: 'Well, at assizes they all went, and just said, this gentleman, he said, can't plead, he said, because, he said, he's unfit to plead, and yet they sent him to Rampton, a place like that. Well they didn't ask any questions. The barrister didn't ask, nobody would ask, but this lady got up [the mother of one of the little girls involved in the case] and tried to tell them that her little girl said it wasn't Ronny they had because they used to play all up the passageway together. They knew it wasn't him. Well at any rate she didn't—they pushed her down.' And Ron was sentenced to go to Rampton, where he stayed for four years.

The problem of a person found unfit to plead is that he is never properly tried at all in the legal sense. Yet he is detained in an institution against his will; and often an institution designed specifically for criminals, such as Broadmoor or Rampton. Although he may be psychiatrically odd or mentally retarded, unless it is conclusively shown that he is a menace to the public it does seem a little harsh that he should be detained in an institution of that kind. The mere fact of his being *accused* of some enormity does not really seem to be sufficient grounds for putting him in a criminal lunatic asylum. And if the issue is never tried and proven, how can we use his guilt as evidence that he is dangerous ? There does seem to be an odd presumption of guilt in some of these cases which is at odds with the usual attitudes and safeguards of the English legal system.[14] A person's psychological oddities may make it difficult to try him, but can we therefore presume he is either a criminal and/or insane ? In many cases where somebody has been found unfit to plead, he hasn't even been effectively tried in the medical sense of needing to be confined in an institution either in his own or in the public's interest.[15]

So far, we have dealt with people of feeble intellect, immature or disturbed, subjected to moderate pressure. Of course, the same sort of thing can happen when perfectly normal people are subjected to extreme pressure, and there are some disturbing cases of this kind. One such concerns a man whom we will call Henry Morgan. We will outline the salient points of the case in chronological order, to show how someone was cumulatively beaten down.

2 March, 11.00 p.m.: Morgan, in a strange town, stopped a woman to ask her the way. She screamed and pushed him, and they fell down a flight of steps. She was slightly injured, he badly injured. She ran away, and the incident was reported to police.

11.30 p.m.: Police turn up. Morgan still there (injured, and had no reason to run away). Taken to police station. He told police what had happened. They rang the hospital, where the girl was having a single stitch put in her head. She accused him of attempted rape. The police told him they would charge him with attempted murder, took away his spectacles (as a result of which he became disoriented) and put him in a cell. Police promised to inform Morgan's wife of his whereabouts.

3 March, late evening: Morgan's wife informed.

4 March, morning: Wife rang brother.
evening: Brother went to see him. 'Henry was sitting in the corner of the cell looking like a bloody animal.' He was still without his glasses. Police dissuaded brother from contacting a solicitor at that stage.

5 March: Police took statement from Morgan. At the time, he was ill, vomiting and passing blood from internal injury received during the fall. He was still without his spectacles and couldn't see. The police said: 'If you're good and plead guilty to wounding without intent, you can have your glasses. If not, we'll see that you get five years for attempted murder.' Morgan signed the statement, but couldn't read it because he couldn't see, as they refused to give him his spectacles. At the time, Morgan assumed that the statement he'd signed was really what he had said; but he, his family and his solicitor later agreed that he couldn't have dictated such a statement because it was 'too illiterate'.

6 March: First hearing. Legal aid solicitor arrived late, after the hearing, so there was no defence and no bail.

9 March: Second hearing. Police stressed the gravity of the assault. A different man turned up from the solicitor's office, didn't oppose the charge, gave no statement of Morgan's previous good character—bail refused.

At this point Morgan (and his family) became dissatisfied with the solicitors, and wanted to change to another firm, but the police dissuaded him, and implied that he was not allowed to.

16 March: Third hearing. Yet another man turned up from the solicitor's office. No defence statement made—solicitor didn't even address the court.

Morgan's family again tried to persuade him to change solicitors, but the police again intervened to oppose this.

18 March: Morgan's mother went to see the solicitor and asked him to see the accused, who still hadn't spoken to his solicitor

55

although it was sixteen days since he had been arrested. The solicitor now produced Morgan's statement for the first time, and it was discovered that he had admitted to sexual assault. He thought he had only admitted to a much smaller charge.

Shortly after this, Morgan was moved in custody to another police station and was there interviewed for the first time by a solicitor from another firm.

23 March: Fourth hearing. Morgan's previous good character now mentioned for the first time. Nevertheless, bail refused.

16 April: Fifth hearing. Charges of grievous bodily harm, attempted rape and theft, now added to attempted murder charge.

14 April: Commital proceedings. No denial of charge. Bail refused.

Morgan's family, under pressure from the defence lawyer, accepted that he should plead guilty. They said: 'Oh well, we'll rely on the appeal [as they assumed it was easy to appeal].'

8 May: Day of the trial.

Immediately before the trial, the barrister said: 'I'm sorry, I haven't a case to take into court. I've advised Morgan to plead guilty to save the girl the strain of appearing in court, to obtain a more lenient sentence and reduced charges.'

His brother said that at the trial there were no witnesses present— that is it was assumed that he would be persuaded to plead guilty, though in fact he only agreed to do so just before the trial.

Henry Morgan got twenty-one months after pleading guilty to wounding without intent.

This is probably rather an exceptional case, since everything appears to have been against the accused. He was frightened and injured and without his glasses after arrest and at the time when the statement was taken. He was kept apart from his family initially. He was unable to see a solicitor for a considerable period of time. Everywhere he turned, people seemed to be persuading him to plead guilty, though he didn't know what he would be charged with, and it wasn't what he thought he might have admitted to. The continuous pressure from the police, his own lawyers, and even from some members of his family, finally broke him down. If it hadn't been for this pressure, he might have been able to gain control of the situation, to repudiate his statement and to assert his innocence properly. Although he now denies that any offence ever occurred, and alleges that his statement was untrue and improperly taken, he cannot appeal against conviction since he pleaded guilty.

The only hope for people in this kind of situation is that one day they may be the recipient of a pardon. Fifty-two pardons have been granted in the last twenty years.[16] Of these, twenty-two were reported in the press including details of pleas. Fourteen of these pleaded not guilty, of which three had nevertheless made totally incriminating statements. Eight pleaded guilty. Our inference from this is therefore that a plea of guilty is by no means a proof of guilt.[17]

Why should so many people subsequently exonerated (and presumably many others who are not) plead guilty to crimes which they did not commit? The police, the courts, and the accused themselves may all feel their interests are better served by doing so.

The police point of view is very simple. Peter Laurie quotes a police officer: 'This may sound very shocking, but what's more use to society: me tied down for a couple of weeks getting him a couple of months more on his sentence, or the whole thing over in a day, a happy informant, me out catching more thieves, and perhaps a string of arrests in the future?'[18] If the accused does not plead guilty, this involves the police in much more detective work collecting evidence to make sure of conviction, and a much longer trial at which police attendance is compulsory. Two of these interests are shared by the accused: they also don't like long trials and long sentences.

C. G. L. Du Cann describes well these and other reasons why an innocent man should plead guilty: 'There are ultra-sensitive people who when accused panic exceedingly, worry desperately, and in a longing to escape what is to them an ordeal, wrongly plead guilty to some offence. . . . Some people plead guilty untruthfully for the sake of some real or fancied advantage: to save time, trouble and money, or because they think it means less publicity in the newspapers or less punishment by the court.'[19]

In many cases, of course, the person pleading guilty is a lot worse off, as Dr J. C. Sawle-Thomas has written: 'I have seen a number of cases in which a plea of guilty has been accepted and the alleged offender referred to me for psychiatric report before sentence. Quite often, if the person concerned had been advised to plead not guilty and remanded pending psychiatric report, no conviction would have been recorded. This could be a matter of extreme importance to one wishing to emigrate, or when applying for an important appointment. Not to mention the effects on the attitude of police or magistrates should he ever be so unfortunate as to fall into their hands again.'

Two further reasons cropped up when we were looking into the cases of those people who had pleaded guilty and subsequently received pardons. Two of these were juveniles who were associates of those really guilty, but who had not participated in the offences. Presumably they pleaded guilty out of a sense of schoolboy loyalty. There were also three people who had pleaded guilty to several associated offences, one of which they had not committed. They thought, presumably, that they might as well be hung for a sheep they had not committed as for a lamb they had.

Until recently, the judiciary, too, had an incentive to induce the accused to plead guilty in order to save time and public money, and were within the law in doing so. John Parris gives an example of this which shows that this practice also resulted in the guilty getting off too lightly. He describes a case at Leeds Assizes. It was Thursday; the judge wanted to get back to London on Friday evening; and the case looked like dragging on. 'Counsel was called to the judge's room on Thursday night.

' "Can you persuade your chaps to plead guilty to anything?"

' "I'd have to take instructions, but I daresay they might be guided."

' "Say three or four counts . . .", he suggested.

' "A great deal would depend on what they're likely to get."

' "Let's see," he glanced at his paper, "they got five years for it last time, didn't they?"

' "Yes—it was a bit stiff, if I may say so."

'He looked at me, and there was some unspoken bargaining.

' "I want to be in London on Saturday and all next week", he said frankly.

'I thought it wise not to tell him I knew that. He hesitated, and there was a long silence, while I kept a stony face.

' "Shall we say twelve months apiece?" me said at length.

'. . . I dashed down to the cells and found my two advertising gentlemen [his clients] and broke the news to them. They were delighted.

'I dared not, of course, tell them explicitly what had happened. I merely said that if they would plead guilty to two or three counts, the prosecution would probably accept it, and thought probably they wouldn't get more than twelve months.

' "Twelve months!" one exclaimed, "I was reckoning on seven years after the last stretch. We only made £3,000 that time."

' "Eight months for 25,000 nicker," chuckled the other gleefully....

'The next morning the judge and I picked out four counts to which the accused could plead guilty. They did so, and the jury were directed to return a verdict of "not guilty" on all the other counts. The judge had time for lunch before his train.'[20]

This practice is no longer permitted, but similar problems still persist, as an article by 'Diogenes' in *New Society*[21] shows:

'In Regina *v.* Turner . . . Lord Parker [outlawed] the practice whereby a judge indicates to counsel that he will give such and such a sentence on a plea of guilty, thereby conveying, albeit unwittingly, the impression that a conviction following a plea of not guilty will result in a severer penalty. In future a judge may give an indication of the kind of sentence that he has in mind only if he makes it clear that nothing will hang on the form of the accused's plea. . . . The Lord Chief Justice's statement will, however, not banish undesirable pressure from the courtroom. He sanctioned the practice whereby the prosecution accept a plea of guilty to a lesser offence on condition that a charge of a greater offence be abandoned. Some prosecutors, alas, may lay a serious charge without strong basis in order to procure such a plea, and some defence counsel fall for the bait.

'Lord Parker also said that defence counsel was entitled to advise a client that a plea of guilty showing "an element of remorse" might enable the court to give a lesser sentence. But either the accused, recognizing his guilt, feels remorse, or he does not. To advise him to fake his feelings in order to soften the judicial heart is to appeal to his sense, not of morality, but of expediency. Is not the truth of the matter that the court appreciates, not the remorse, but the fact that judicial time and public money have been saved? And is it possible that the accused will be unaware of this?'

However much they may go wrong, there are at least formal rules and controls over the taking of statements and confessions, and regarding their validity in court. These controls, however, cannot apply to the taking of 'verbals'—that is what the suspect said when arrested—a moment which is often a surprise for all concerned. As a result, verbal statements are a particularly unreliable form of evidence. Tom Sargant, the Secretary of 'Justice', in his memorandum sent to the Donovan Committee on Criminal Appeals said:

'Alleged verbal statements made at the time of the arrest or first approach are responsible for more wrong convictions than any other single factor.'[22] Such verbal statements are tricky because ultimately they reduce to: 'I say he said it, he says he didn't.'

Some striking examples of 'verbals' being used to convict men who were later exonerated occurred in the cases associated with Detective-Sergeant Challenor. One of the main cases was that involving Cheeseman, Ford, Fraser, Oliva and Pedrini, who were convicted of demanding money with menaces and possessing offensive weapons, but whose cases were later referred by the Home Secretary to the Court of Appeal, where the convictions were quashed. At the original trial, Challenor's aides claimed that the accused made verbal statements incriminating themselves. Cheeseman, told that he would be arrested, was alleged to have said: 'I do not wish to know anything about this, we were only kidding about doing him up.' Pedrini, asked what he used the iron bar for, was alleged to have said: 'It's my cigar holder.' On being arrested, Ford was supposed to have said: 'It's that bastard Gardiner [the alleged victim]. He has grassed on us.' After being cautioned, Ford was supposed to have added: 'It's a nice club he [the victim] has got. If he charges me, he won't have it for long.' With regard to Ford, Challenor himself gave evidence that, after being brought to West End Central Station, Ford had said: 'I am nackered anyway, this is all a take-on, Joe Oliva, myself and a few of the boys have been taking the mickey out of him. We would not have had his money, it was just frighteners.'

Even in cases where the accused has not been subsequently exonerated, verbals are very frequently a source of controversy. This is so, for example, in the case of two men whom we will call Seamus O'Toole and Sean Murphy. In this case, some classic verbals by both men considerably strengthened a rather shaky prosecution case against O'Toole (Murphy was almost certainly guilty and they had a good case against him anyway).

O'Toole: Look, guv'nor, you lot are always after me for blaggings, and I am not having the rent-collector.

1st police officer: Who said anything about a rent-collector?

O'Toole: That's the job you mean, isn't it? Anyway, I've got an alibi for all day Monday.

1st p.o.: Who said anything about Monday? . . .

2nd p.o.: The rent-collector has suffered a fractured skull.

O'Toole: I don't see how he got a fractured skull. He only took a couple on the nut. . . . A two-er (that is £200)—I didn't think it was that much. I'm wondering who's been had over here. Gospel. Murphy's propped the job—he's not nicked—supposed to be a two-er ? Nothing like it.

Murphy: We know about that, because you've nicked Seamus O'Toole. Was he identified ? Look, guv, let's get it over with. You know what happened. . . . Me and Seamus spanked a rent-man.
2nd p.o.: You have admitted your part in the robbery. Do you want to make a written statement ?
Murphy: Never make no statements. I told him and I tell you, me and O'Toole clocked the geezer. John never got out of the motor. Came to three score apiece and the rest in excess.

Even where the verbals are genuine, they may be twisted out of context, or put in such a way either accidentally or deliberately so as to impute guilt that isn't there. In the case of John Smith, convicted of assault with intent to rob and other charges, this is what happened. He was convicted with Frederick Robinson, who was caught on the spot, and George Roy Bell, who was also concerned in the offence. A 'Justice' memorandum on the case comments on the verbal statements made by Smith to the police to the effect that he knew both Bell and Robinson. 'The police in the depositions stated that Smith said to them when questioned: "No, not me, I know Bell, but not Fred." And after the identification parade, when asked if he knew Bell: "Yes, I know Bell, but I don't know Fred." Smith makes the following observations about his evidence.

1. The 'Bell' to whom he was referring turned out to be a different man.

2. The police twisted his statement as regards Robinson to make it seem that he knew him because he referred to him as 'Fred'. He says that he told the police that he knew *of* Robinson, who was a well known character in the underworld, but that he did not *know* him. He admits that he called him 'Fred', but explained that it was because the police were all referring to him as 'Fred' and, in his own words, 'I joined in the spirit of the thing and called him Fred not once, but several times.'

Verbals are known to be so unreliable that many police-officers do not submit them in court, knowing they are unlikely to be believed

—and indeed, they can often rebound against the police. A police-officer commented to us: 'Verbals are a police tradition known to many villains who play along with it deliberately in order to be able subsequently to cast doubt upon police evidence. When they are arrested, villains will deliberately make outrageous verbal admissions of guilt, such as "It's a fair cop", knowing that a conscientious police-officer will note this down, will report it to the court, and will not be believed.'

The great dilemma with regard to making any suggestions about the use, or restrictions upon the use, of statements and confessions of all kinds, is that on the one hand they are apt to be unreliable, and on the other hand, they are an absolutely necessary form of evidence. Dr William Sargant has estimated that 'without confessions, convictions which the police obtain might be reduced by more than 70 per cent.'[23] It is not surprising that, as Mr Justice Barry of the Supreme Court of Victoria, Australia, put it at the United Nations seminar on the role of the police in the protection of human rights, May 1963: 'Confession is the most attractive way of solving crimes. Getting one should be recognized as a genuine temptation.'[24]

We feel that the two central principles in this area of justice are, or should be, (a) to get at the truth of what actually occurred, rather than enshrining the ancient rights of one side or the other, and (b) that this should be subject to only one condition, namely, that the suspect should not be subjected to duress or intimidation. The latter condition does not in any way contradict the former, since statements or confessions obtained under duress tend to contain what the prisoner thinks the authorities want to hear rather than the truth.

We recognize that these principles are hardly new, but we do think that some of the safeguards set up in order to put them into practice under different historical conditions are no longer relevant. Some of the currently controversial issues, such as the timing and nature of the caution, or the accused's right to remain silent, seem to us to fall into this category. Both the caution and the accused's right to silence obstruct the police and do not protect the innocent; we feel that the time has come for them to be abolished—and to be replaced by more relevant safeguards.

Many people think that only radical changes in the legal framework will obtain the three vital objectives: (a) to give the police greater and more effective powers of investigation; (b) to give suspected or accused persons better protection, and to eliminate any abuses which may occur under the present system; (c) to eliminate many of the time-wasting, and often inconclusive arguments about confessions and statements which now take place during criminal trials. However, we feel that there are certain simple patching-up jobs which could improve the present system.

1. The law and the rules regarding statements by their very nature cater for the average person—the man in the Wormwood Scrubs omnibus. It cannot cater for people who are very far from that average. Thus there are some intelligent criminals who will always find a loop-hole and get off; but our investigations have been more concerned with those at the other end of the scale. These are the mental and psychological inadequates whose sad cases we have discussed. In the extreme case where a person is found unfit to plead after being accused of the crime solely on the basis of his confession, this should not obviate the need for an examination of the case. In all such cases, there should perhaps be a public re-examination of the confession before a judge or a magistrate, and all other relevant evidence should be called. But there are classes of people who, while not unfit to plead in the legal sense, are clearly insufficiently protected. The people we primarily have in mind are those of very low intelligence, the psychologically unstable, and children. For statements from these people to be admissible, they should be taken before an independent third party, and the proof that a person belongs to one of these categories should provide a valid and sufficient defence against any incriminating statement not made under these circumstances. Obviously, the police would have to exercise their discretion in regard to deciding whether someone belongs to one of these categories. But they already exercise this kind of discretion, though at a rather different level, in implementing their powers in respect of the allegedly mentally disordered under the Mental Health Act of 1959. Anyway, if the police knew that the defence was able to object to a confession or statement on these grounds, they would be inclined to be careful.

The fact that a person found unfit to plead will be sent to a mental institution and not to a gaol is no argument for not giving him any sort of trial. It is not always fairer or kinder to treat and attempt to cure rather than to try and punish. We must beware of the notion that we may confine and treat people compulsorily without giving them the same benefit of the doubt as those we seek to try and possibly punish. A similar criticism may be made of procedures involving juveniles. Things that are done to people for their own good, or to protect the public from some possible outrage, are seldom much less unpleasant than judicial punishments, and should not be imposed in a more arbitrary way than is involved in the more usual criminal trials.

It will, of course, be difficult to get a recommendation of this kind put into practice because lawyers always object to laws or rules which are not universal in their application, but which only apply to particular classes of person.

2. In order more easily to establish that statements and confessions made to the police were properly obtained and recorded, it seems sensible that they should be tape-recorded as well as written. This is obviously particularly important in the case of illiterates or people with poor eyesight. A tape would give a more accurate rendering of a statement than having it written down in longhand, especially where a person other than the accused does the writing. The tape should be sealed in to the tape-recorder so that it cannot be edited.

The pocket tape-recorder appears to be the only method of recording verbals satisfactorily, and is certainly more reliable than reconstructing from notebooks. We recognize that this creates certain problems. You cannot cross-examine a tape-recorder. Also there is the problem of the man who when arrested shouts deliberately and inaccurately into the tape-recorder: 'Aargh, you're twisting my arm' or 'Stop hitting me with that club'.

3. The problem with respect to guilty pleas has again been well-described by C. G. L. Du Cann: 'Once a plea of guilty is spoken by one fit to plead, and who understands what he is doing, courts are more than reluctant to go behind that plea. . . . You cannot in the criminal law's view, be both [guilty and not guilty] or neither, or partly one, or partly the other, and if you say nothing you are mute either "of malice" [that is intentionally] or "by the visitation of God" [genuinely unable to speak] or . . . unfit to plead [through mental incapacity].'[25] These simple categories are not sufficient, and the courts *should* be more ready to look behind the plea.

The above suggestions are all concerned with the system as it stands at present. But diverse groups of people, including the 'Justice' committee on evidence, prefer the idea of a shift to 'a new procedure of controlled compulsory interrogation before a magistrate'. These proposals differ in detail, but the basic principles seem to us to be these: (*a*) that all interrogations should be carried out before such a magistrate, or with his permission. The record of these interrogations would be admissible as evidence at a trial; (*b*) no other statements, oral or written, would be so admissible, except for tape-recorded 'verbals'; (*c*) people suspected by the police should be brought before a magistrate and required to answer certain questions. If they refuse to do so, this should be regarded as *prima facie* evidence of guilt, which they should have to dispute at their trial. We shall discuss these rather more radical proposals in greater detail in our concluding chapter.

Chapter 4

Trial Proceedings

Criminal trials and rules of evidence are complex and multi-faceted. Any discussion of them necessarily has to deal with a large number of disparate facts. For this reason, this chapter will be set out under a series of sub-headings: The Suspect's Progress; Discovery and Disclosure of Evidence; Inadmissible Evidence; Joint Trials; Unsatisfactory Defence; Judge, Juries and Appeals.

THE SUSPECT'S PROGRESS

Regardless of whether someone did or did not commit a crime, once he has become a suspect, the behaviour of the police, the workings of the court and the reactions of the accused himself may all tend to focus attention on aspects pointing to his guilt.

The process of investigation is by its very nature a process of narrowing down the field of suspects. Eventually, all efforts are concentrated on the most likely of these, and other possibilities are neglected. The purpose of the investigation ceases to be that of finding the culprit, and becomes that of proving that the chief suspect did it.[1] In view of police time and resources, this is inevitable and understandable. However, given that this is so, it is unfortunate that in most cases the decision to prosecute lies entirely with the police. In almost every other country in Europe, this decision is taken by a separate body; even in Scotland, it is not the police, but the procurators fiscal who make this crucial decision, after a rigorous and independent scrutiny of the police case.[2]

In England, certain classes of crime and of offenders are dealt with in this way by the Director of Public Prosecutions (DPP). One such category is that of policemen accused of crime. The police are well aware of the advantages of this system when they come to be on the receiving end. As the *Police Review* said in discussing the Luckhurst case: 'One of the points raised by the Police Federation in its comments on the case of ex-PC F. C. Luckhurst is that the complaint was not referred to the Director of Public Prosecutions.

If the requirements of Section 49 (3) of the Police Act, 1964, had been followed, the federation maintained, then a report of the investigation into the complaint would have been sent to the DPP and it would have been for the Director, and not for the Police, to decide whether or not criminal proceedings should be brought. What apparently happened was that the complaint was not dealt with as a complaint against the Police, but as a crime complaint. The Police Act procedure therefore was not followed. No authoritative ruling has been given as to whether or not this view was right. However, the press reports of the case of Inspector J. Warwicker and three other members of the Metropolitan Police, into which an inquiry is being sought, show that the City of London Police support the Federation's view. Like ex-PC Luckhurst, Inspector Warwicker was picked out by a single witness at an identification parade. Unlike ex-PC Luckhurst, he was not then charged with a crime. He was suspended from duty and the papers were then sent by the City of London Police to the DPP for consideration. On the Director's advice, no proceedings were brought against Inspector Warwicker. A Metropolitan Police spokesman confirmed that no disciplinary proceedings were contemplated, and that the allegation which had been made was "completely unfounded". Things might have gone very differently for ex-PC Luckhurst if the allegations against him and the evidence in support of them had been submitted to the expert scrutiny of the DPP.'[3]

This point of view was shared by the Hugman brothers, who along with Inspector Warwicker were accused of robbery. Ben Hugman said: 'If John Warwicker hadn't been involved, it might all have been different. But him being there meant that the case escalated, there was press interest, and it went up to the House of Commons and the DPP. Otherwise it would have been just a small larceny case. The whole case collapsed when it got to the DPP because for the first time it was assessed in cold blood and our alibis were considered.' Because the DPP is not tied up in the investigating process in the way the police are, he is able to be more detached in this way. This does *not* necessarily mean that he is less prosecution-minded, or less likely to prosecute. This will depend on the personality and outlook of the incumbent, whereas the objectivity we are talking about is a function of the office.

Even where the suspect is innocent, he may behave in such a way as to accentuate the tendency of the police and the courts to focus on a single suspect. Jerome and Barbara Frank discuss this process: 'To help prove a defendant's guilt, frequently the prosecution introduces evidence that he "acted guilty". Showing that he fled soon after the commission of the crime, the government argues that "the wicked flee when no man pursueth, but the righteous are bold as a lion." Or the prosecution may prove that the accused concealed or destroyed a weapon like that used to commit the crime, or invented a false alibi or false clues, or that, when arrested, he stammered or was confused or told lies. The courts say such conduct tends to show "consciousness of guilt". Without doubt, such proof which seems damning, often induces juries to convict. Yet not only the guilty show signs of apparent guilt. . . . An innocent man, when placed by circumstancess in a condition of suspicion and danger, may resort to deception, in the hope of avoiding arrest and conviction. He may be stunned under the mere imputation of guilt. . . .' The Franks quote the English case of Graham, who was tried for the murder of his niece: 'Graham, at his trial, attempted to deceive the jury by presenting another girl as his niece. The prosecution's exposure of this deception led to Graham's conviction. He was hanged. Some seven years later his niece turned up, alive.'[4]

This natural tendency towards focusing attention on evidence incriminating the accused also occurs throughout the trial. This may be particularly true in cases where most of the evidence is circumstantial. A good example of this occurred in the trial of Gerald Wentzel in America.[5] At the Appeal Court, his appeal was rejected, the Appeal Court judges being divided. One of the dissenting judges who wished to set aside the conviction commented: 'The trial judge should have given binding instructions for acquittal . . . If the evidence in this case does not prove the defendant innocent beyond a reasonable doubt, it certainly preponderates in his favour. Wentzel found himself enmeshed in a set of circumstances which raised a suspicion of his guilt, but each of these circumstances is consistent with his innocence. There is no rule at law or at logic that several suspicious circumstances, each one of which is consistent with the innocence of the accused, becomes proof of guilt when considered together. Four or five times nothing is still nothing.' The appeal, however, was turned down (though Wentzel was later pardoned). One of the majority of judges who turned it down commented: 'While none of the facts presented would be conclusive of his guilt when individually considered, yet there is no doubt in our minds that the evidence presented when considered collectively required that the case be submitted to the jury.'

Even if the trial judge does his utmost to present circumstantial evidence fairly, an innocent man can be convicted because the jury, too, tends to exaggerate the degree to which evidence points in a particular direction. This is what happened in the case of William Herbert Wallace, convicted of murdering his wife in 1931. He was convicted in spite of a summing-up favourable to an acquittal. Subsequently, the Court of Criminal Appeal set aside the verdict of the jury under Section 4 of the Criminal Appeal Act, 1907, on the ground that 'it cannot be supported having regard to the evidence'.[6] In this case the jury chose to ignore the careful warning of the judge on the danger of convicting on circumstantial evidence alone. At the trial, Judge Wright said in his summing-up: 'Circumstantial evidence may vary in value almost infinitely. Some is as good and conclusive as the evidence of actual witnesses. In other cases the only circumstantial evidence which anyone can present still leaves loopholes and doubts. . . . The real test of the value of circumstantial evidence is this: Does it exclude other theories or possibilities? If you cannot put the evidence against the accused beyond a probability; if it is a probability which is not inconsistent with there being other, reasonable possibilities; then it is impossible for a jury to say: "We are satisfied beyond a reasonable doubt that the charge is made out".'[7]

Some lawyers argue that circumstantial evidence, by very reason of its diversity, is less likely to result in this incorrect focusing of the evidence on a suspect. Chief Justice Shaw said in one case: 'The advantages [of circumstantial evidence] are that, as the evidence commonly comes from several witnesses and different sources, a chain of circumstances is less likely to be falsely prepared and arranged, and falsehood and perjury are more likely to be detected and fail of their purpose.'[8] This may well be true of false evidence. But in most of the English cases we have studied, this is not the main problem. Each piece of evidence may be true enough. It is rather a question of what interpretation the court and the jury choose to put upon the whole.

Once people have committed themselves to a particular line in this way they are (as we have already shown for the witnesses in identification cases) often reluctant to climb down and admit they have been mistaken. This is true of the police and the courts; we shall later be showing how it affects the workings of the Court of Appeal. In the case of the police it may result in a refusal to reopen a case where a suspect has already been committed, even if new evidence comes to light. Such was the case of a man who was arrested for and convicted of a robbery of which he was later acquitted at a re-trial. He said: 'They must have had some reason to pick on me. I think they made a genuine mistake when they said they saw me in the club —I can't think of anything else. . . . They did see the man who really did it. He was questioned by the police before my second trial. They didn't admit that at the trial because it would have done their case in. They didn't want to make fools of themselves.' Once again, as with the witnesses, if you make a fool of yourself in court, you make a very public fool of yourself.

DISCOVERY AND DISCLOSURE OF EVIDENCE

The main duty of the prosecution in this country is not to get a conviction at all costs, but to make sure that justice is done. It follows from this that if the prosecution has a piece of evidence which favours the defence, it ought not to suppress it but to hand it over to the defence. When this rule is not followed, and the facts subsequently become known, the judge is likely to be highly critical of the prosecution. Thus Mr Justice Salmon at Leeds Assizes in 1963, in the case of a man accused of arson and manslaughter, said: 'Scientific evidence should be presented with a view to helping the administration of justice and not with a view to assisting the prosecution. I hope that the practice of not mentioning a negative finding is not common and will never happen again. . . . I am astonished that anyone in the office of the DPP should have thought it right to put Griffin [the accused] on trial on these charges. On the deposition there is not a particle of evidence on which a jury can convict.' He also commented on the deposition of a scientist from the Home Office forensic science laboratory regarding clothes which Griffin was said to have been wearing at the time: 'I assume from the fact that he says nothing about them that there was no trace of petrol found on these clothes. In my view it is monstrous that when scientific tests reveal a negative fact which is strongly in favour of the defence, the negative fact should not plainly be said in evidence. I think it is inexcusable that it was not said here that this clothing had no trace of petrol.' In this case, the prosecution offered no evidence, and the jury were directed to acquit. But some people are less fortunate.

Such a one was William Thomas Davies, who was convicted of receiving a cheque-book and of fraudulently obtaining a vacuum-cleaner by means of a forged cheque. His case was subsequently referred to the Court of Appeal, Criminal Division, by the Home

Secretary, and the conviction was quashed. The centre of contro-versy was a report by the Home Office forensic science laboratory, which was in the hands of the prosecution, but of whose contents the defence were ignorant. The report said: 'I have examined the documents submitted and compared the handwriting in question on the four Leigh Trustee Savings Bank cheques with specimen handwriting attributed to William Thomas Davies. . . . There are features of the handwriting in question that cannot be matched in the specimens and consequently I cannot connect Davies with the handwriting on the cheques. Indeed, although I cannot be sure, my indications are that he did not write out the cheques.'[9]

The judges at the Appeal Court said: 'It seems to this Court that leaving aside all questions of the identification and alibi, that it is utterly impossible to say that if the contents of this report had been before the jury as it ought to have been, or if the sergeant had truly disclosed the effect of the report, that in all the circumstances the jury would have convicted . . . appeal allowed, and conviction quashed.'

It is still not clear what really happened regarding this report. The note of referral to the Court of Appeal (Criminal Division) said: 'Before the committal proceedings the police consulted a hand-writing expert at a Home Office forensic science laboratory about the handwriting on the cheque concerned [among others], but, having received his report, they decided not to call the handwriting expert as a witness for the prosecution.

'It has been represented to the Secretary of State that the jury might have reached a different verdict if the handwriting expert had been available to give evidence on behalf of the defence at the trial, and that although the defence solicitors were aware that an expert opinion had been obtained, they were misled by the police evidence at the committal proceedings as to the nature of the report. The solicitors say that before the commencement of the trial they did get in touch with the forensic science laboratory with a view to calling the witness, but as he was away on holiday they decided not to pursue the matter; and that had they then known the nature of this report they would have asked for an adjournment to allow him to be called. The police, on the other hand, have stated in a report to the Secretary of State, that the original report was handed to a repre-sentative of the firm of solicitors before the committal proceedings, and that having read the report he returned it to them without comment. . . .'[10]

The defence solicitors comment: 'It was at the committal proceedings on 12 July 1966 we became aware that samples of Davies's handwriting and the cheques had been submitted to the forensic science laboratory at Cardiff, when this was disclosed in the evidence of [a detective-sergeant]. At the end of his examination-in-chief, he [the police officer] said: "There is no evidence we can offer in relation to handwriting experts at the forensic science laboratory in relation to the samples of handwriting and the cheques." He was then cross-examined and said, *inter alia*: "The cheques have been to the handwriting expert. He says he cannot give evidence about the handwriting on the cheques and samples." . . . [The defence] requested from the prosecution a copy of the handwriting expert's report, but this was not provided, and we were left with the impression that the expert was not in a position to say whether or not the handwriting on the cheques was that of Davies.

'At conference with counsel and accused immediately before the commencement of the trial, it was agreed, having regard to our information at that time, that although the expert's evidence would probably take the matter no further, he should be called to give whatever evidence he could. We immediately telephoned the laboratory at Cardiff and found he was then on holiday, and his whereabouts were not known, and in view of this and the fact we were calling four witnesses to prove an alibi for our client, the trial was allowed to go on.

'Had we known the expert had found the cheques were not in the handwriting of Davies we would not have allowed the trial to go on without the expert's evidence.'

What is clear is that after his conviction, Davies obtained a copy of the handwriting report from the Chief Constable, and forwarded it to the registrar with his application for leave to appeal. The application went before a single judge, who refused it. Only much later, and by the intervention of the Home Secretary, was the case resolved in Davies's favour. (Davies's case was referred back to the Court of Appeal after 'Justice' took it up with the Home Secretary when the single judge had turned it down. The Court of Appeal quashed the conviction on the same evidence, *including the handwriting report*, which had been before the single judge.)

Not only expert evidence, but also the existence of witnesses who might be helpful to the defence, can be concealed from them. In the case of Dennis Stafford and Michael Luvaglio, convicted of murder in 1967 and still (1972) in jail, David Lewis and Peter Hughman, allege in their book that this occurred: 'The last prosecution witness to see the car was Reuben Controy, a livestock transporter who drove past at about 12.50 a.m. travelling towards Easington Lane. Approaching the car from the front he had noticed that the windscreen wipers were working and that the sidelights were on, but he didn't see any sign of damage. There is then a four and a half hour blank in the prosecution evidence before miners Leak and Marshall arrive on the scene. But this is not to say by any means that no witnesses could be found; indeed, the police had interviewed many, *though not all were made known to the defence.* The first, and one of the most important, was Mr Mauro Ferri, a confectioner of Easington Colliery. The defence first learnt of his existence shortly before their application for leave to appeal was heard, although he had been known to the police from early in their investigation. His statement is short but very much to the point: "About 12.10 a.m. on Thursday 5 January 1967 I was driving my Ford Corsair, registration number CWC 956, from Easington Lane in the direction of Easington Colliery. At this time I passed through South Hetton. I travelled under the railway bridge which crosses the road in the village. There was no motor vehicle stationary, and no one near the bridge at that time. There was quite a bit of traffic on the road, but I saw nothing unusual."

'Yet it was fundamental to the very tight prosecution time schedule that the Mark X was in position by 12.07/8 at the very latest. Here was a witness who was vital to the defence. Surely it was in the interests of justice that the jury should have had an opportunity of hearing him.'[11] (authors' italics)

Not only expert evidence or the existence of witnesses but also the statements of witnesses who do appear in court can be withheld in this way. Glanville Williams comments on this problem: 'Since the witnesses for the prosecution are generally interviewed first by the police there is an obvious risk that the manner in which the evidence is taken will influence its content. The police are naturally on the look-out for all elements that may help them to fix responsibility. Hence there is a tendency for the statement as so taken to omit matters favourable to the defence. The matters so omitted will quite possibly be forgotten. Leading questions may be asked and suggestions made so that by the time of the trial the damage may have been done—the false memory may already, perhaps in good faith, have been implanted in the witness's mind.'[12]

To alleviate this problem he urges that the defence should have access to such evidence: '. . . there should be virtually a verbatim report of the interview [of witnesses by the police]. Best of all the interview should be tape-recorded. It is a necessary corollary of these proposals that the record of the interview should be available to the defence. At present the police refuse to allow the defence to have copies of the statements taken from witnesses. The refusal appears to be quite wrong because it means that the defence is hampered in its effort to find out how the witness has changed his story in the course of time. It is true that the defence will have copies of the witness's depositions taken at the preliminary inquiry but these may not be so informative as the story first told to the police. . . . There should be the same rules for the defence as for the prosecution: the interview by the defendant's solicitor of his witness should be tape-recorded and the prosecution should have the right to demand a copy of the record.'[13]

The situation is complicated when the prosecution withholds evidence which could convict the accused on a minor charge, but which might result in his getting off on a major charge, and the accused connives at this because he hopes to get off on both. This is what may have happened in the famous case of Steinie Morrison, convicted of murder in 1911 and sentenced to death, but reprieved probably because the Home Secretary had doubts about his guilt. Julian Symons discusses this case. After Morrison had been convicted of murder, the defence lawyer discovered that Morrison had made a lot of money by forgery but had suppressed this fact at the trial. He asked the Home Office to investigate, and as a result of their findings Morrison was reprieved and his sentence commuted to penal servitude for life. 'With the remains of a successful forgery for £200 still in his pocket, why should Morrison murder Beron for a problematical £20 or £30. But there is more that must be said. Morrison's identity as the forger was known to the police and to Muir [the prosecutor]. A clerk from the Bank of England was in court expecting to be called to identify the banknotes. He was not called because this evidence was useless to the prosecution. But why was it not made known to the defence as it should have been? It must have helped them very materially on the murder charge.'[14]

Even where the prosecution do produce evidence in court which is helpful to the defence, they often do so in such a way as to minimize it possible use. This came up in yet another cause célèbre, the trial of Mrs Thompson for murdering her husband, at which she was convicted and later hung. E. Lustgarten describes this aspect of the trial: 'There had been an exhumation of Percy Thompson's body with the express object of examining for poison. Bernard Spilsbury conducted the post-mortem. . . . He found precisely nothing. There was no trace or sign of any poison. There was no trace or sign of any glass. There was no indication that either one or the other had ever been administered. . . . The Crown produced this tremendous piece of evidence in a shabby, grudging, discreditable way. They tried to make it seem that the post-mortem was nugatory by stressing that all traces might have disappeared. But the exhumation wasn't made without hope of finding something; the most famous of pathologists had said that there was nothing; and the Crown would have done better to have faced up to the fact and not tried to look as though they expected nothing anyway.'[15]

The present situation, then, seems to be that the moral duty of the prosecution is to disclose to the defence any evidence, statements or witnesses which tend to show the accused is innocent. On this subject Archbold says: 'Where a witness whom the prosecution calls or tenders gives evidence in the box on a material issue, and the prosecution have in their possession an earlier statement from that witness substantially conflicting with that evidence, the prosecution should at any rate inform the defence of that fact . . . Neither case should be regarded as an authority for the proposition that there is any general duty on the part of the prosecution with regard to statements to the police by witnesses or potential witnesses beyond what is above stated.'[16]

Lord Goddard, in a decision of the Court of Criminal Appeal, set out the position for cases where the prosecution has taken statements from witnesses whom they do not wish to call to give evidence: 'It is said that it was the duty of the prosecution to have supplied the defence with the statement which Campbell had admittedly made to the prosecution. In the opinion of the Court, there is no such duty, nor has there ever been. . . . The duty of the prosecution is to make available [that is give the name and address] to the defence a witness whom the prosecution know can, if he is called, give material evidence.'[17]

This does not seem to be sufficient. It would seem to be more satisfactory if the prosecution was required in law to provide the defence with any statements, witnesses or evidence which might be helpful to the defence.

There is one major drawback to this proposal, which is well expressed in the report of the 'Justice' committee on the laws of evidence concerning 'the availability of prosecution evidence to the defence'. They say: 'The committee recognize that the work of the police in the war against crime must not be hampered. The prosecution might be greatly burdened if copies of every statement taken in connection with an alleged offence had to be supplied. The police cannot be expected to disclose everything to the underworld. Statements might relate to other offences concerning third parties. The names of informers could not be disclosed. The public policy provision of our legislative proposals is designed to meet this type of objection. People might become reluctant to make statements to the police if they knew that there would be no confidence observed and that the statements would be given to the defence.'[18]

The relevant policy proposal by 'Justice' says: 'The prosecution shall be entitled, notwithstanding the relevancy of any statement, to refuse to supply copies or to permit inspection of the statement or parts of it, on the ground that it would be contrary to public policy so to do. In such a case, however, the objection shall be notified to the defence in writing. If the defence does not accept the validity of such objections, the court or judge shall rule thereon. In deciding upon the validity of such objections, the court or judge shall not be bound to disclose the contents of such statements to the defence.'[19]

These proposed changes would be in line with the policy which is already extending the grounds for 'discovery' of evidence in both civil and criminal proceedings; and in criminal proceedings for both prosecution and defence. 'Discovery' is the process whereby either side before the trial can require the other side to disclose the evidence it has and which it may introduce at the trial. This enables either side to know beforehand the evidence which it may have to answer, so that it can obtain evidence to answer it.[20]

This has always been true of the bulk of prosecution evidence. Before the trial there has to be a preliminary hearing at which the prosecution discloses the evidence it intends to use at the trial. It might be better at this stage if it also disclosed any evidence it did not intend to use, and which might be helpful to the defence. In the past, the defence has been able to reserve the whole of its case; but increasingly, advance notice has had to be given of certain special defences. The main instance in England is that the defence must disclose in advance any alibis it intends to use in order that the police can check them.[21] This can be as much help to the defence as to the police in cases where the accused is innocent; and conversely, where the police fail to check the alibi, this can be a source of wrongful imprisonment. This is the reaction of one man accused of robbery and subsequently exonerated: 'I wanted to prosecute the police for not checking on my alibi, for not going to see the doctor on the day that they came for me. The crime was committed on the Wednesday when I was in bed and never got out of it, and I never got out of bed that day. In fact the Friday night they came for me I'd only been out of bed two hours. They never checked on my alibi. They took [the prosecution witness's] evidence as proof. . . . Who could have corroborated my alibi? I'll tell you who. The neighbours next door above me, the neighbours below me, and the people across the street who kept—periodically with me being in bed sick and my wife downstairs sick—neighbours kept coming in to see if they could give us a little bit of a hand or do a little job or did she want a cup of tea or did I want anything, or to help her doing a bit of cleaning up.'

If a man is innocent, there are advantages on both sides in the disclosure of an alibi. Perhaps, as under Scots law, other special defences should also be revealed before the trial. Some of these defences are: insanity at the time of the crime, an allegation that the offence was committed by some other named person; the offence being committed in self-defence.[22]

INADMISSIBLE EVIDENCE

There are certain kinds of evidence which are not admissible in court, although they may be relevant. Sybille Bedford quotes a magistrate on a piece of evidence which the defence said was not admissible, and the prosecution alleged was the essence of their case: 'Oh, frequently the most relevant evidence is not admissible.'[23] In the cases we have come across, the main problems arise from two categories of inadmissible evidence: hearsay, and the accused's previous record or bad character.

Evidence is hearsay when a witness states a fact to be true, not because he himself saw or experienced it, but because somebody told him it was true. The 13th Report of the Law Reform Committee points out that three reasons are usually advanced for the hearsay rules:

(*a*) The unreliability of statements, whether written or oral, made by persons not under oath nor subject to cross-examination;
(*b*) the desirability of the 'best evidence' being produced of any fact sought to be proved;

(c) the danger that the relaxation of the rule would lead to a proliferation of evidence directed to establishing a particular fact.[24]

In general, then, it is fair to say that the hearsay rule protects the accused from the danger of being convicted on certain kinds of unreliable evidence.[25] But there are cases where its exclusion means that a piece of evidence vital to the defence cannot be used. This is what appears to have happened in the controversial case of William Curbishley and William Stupple, currently serving sentences for robbing a bank. One of the authors attended the appeal, at which one of the important points of defence evidence was that when Stupple was first confronted with Curbishley in the corridor of the court, Curbishley said to the warder regarding his alleged accomplice Stupple: 'Who is that man? Is it a policeman?' The warder could not be found for the appeal, so we have only Curbishley's word that this occurred. The Court of Appeal was very reluctant to admit this kind of evidence, and said: 'Certainly our admission of such evidence is not to be used as a precedent.' They said they were unfavourably impressed by the evidence. The fact that this evidence was admitted at all was probably only due to the extraordinary circumstances of the appeal, and the judge's distaste for this form of evidence may well have been one of the factors which contributed to the conviction being upheld. Stupple has never been exonerated, although many people have considerable doubt about the case. During a civil action against Stupple under the Police Property Act, Mr Justice Paull commented on Stupple's earlier criminal conviction in this case: 'I should like to stress the fact that I have been troubled by this case as it is contrary to what I myself would have found as a juryman.'[26]

The hearsay rule is not quite as straightforward as it might appear from the above example. There are a large number of exceptions—some of them involving rather hairsplitting distinctions. This can create a lot of confusion where one person is being tried. There are even more difficulties in a joint trial where the various accused may have different and conflicting interests as to which evidence they want admitted.

One such exception to the rule which is admissible as hearsay is the declaration of a dying man as to the cause of his death. Of this Professor Cornish says: 'If another person is charged with his murder or manslaughter then the declaration may be given in evidence by someone to whom it was made. The justification for the exception is said to be that a man is more likely to speak the truth when faced with the immediate prospect of death—a view which is certainly more pious hope than proven fact. Because of this, the exception is only applied if the dead man is shown to have had 'a settled, hopeless expectation of death' at the time of making the declaration, and some cases show curiously different attitudes among judges as to just when this is so. In one case the dead man's head was almost severed, but there was no proof that he believed himself to be dying. The evidence could accordingly not be given. In other cases death did not follow for some days after the statement, but nevertheless the statement was allowed to be given in evidence.'[27]

A good example of the complications involved in applying the hearsay rule and exceptions to it such as a dying declaration is the case of Castin and Leathlan Townsend. The Townsends are West Indians. They are half-brothers; Castin is tall and dark, and known as 'J.B.'; Leathlan is shorter, has lighter skin and ginger hair and is known as 'Boozy' or 'Budsy'. The brothers were jointly charged with the murder of another Jamaican; Leathlan was convicted of it and is now in prison. Castin was acquitted, but convicted of the lesser crime of attempted grievous bodily harm. A crucial issue at the trial was the admissibility of hearsay evidence, including a dying declaration. The hearsay that was admitted pointed towards Leathlan as the murderer. The dying declaration, which was excluded, would have incriminated Castin and possibly assisted Leathlan. Some time after the trial, Castin confessed to the murder, but has refused to sign his confession. There is some corroboration for Castin's confession, and the details given in it as to what actually happened.

The hearsay evidence that was admitted and that told against Leathlan is described by Tom Sargant of 'Justice': 'Some disquieting and highly prejudicial hearsay evidence against Leathlan was given by Detective-Sergeant Babb and other police officers and admitted at the trial. According to their statements McKensie [a witness] on arriving at the police station said: "He [Leathlan] has also stabbed my friend Norris Edwards. He is in hospital now." McKensie himself did not depose to this in his own evidence in the magistrates' court, and according to the accounts he gave of his movements in chasing the two brothers he could not have known that Edwards had been taken to hospital unless another guest in the chase had told him [when it would have been double hearsay]. Leathlan denies that he [McKensie] mentioned Edwards at all. Detective-Sergeant Babb was nevertheless allowed to give evidence of this at the trial, the judge telling the jury that this wasn't evidence but only an accusation that was being made! This evidence makes the exclusion of the hearsay evidence against Castin even more open to criticism.'

The hearsay evidence that was excluded consisted of five declarations made to different people by the dying man when he was in hospital. These statements were:

1. From Norbert Edwards, brother of the victim. 'Later I went to King's College Hospital. This was about 6 in the morning. I saw my brother Norris there; I asked him what happened and he said that he felt a pain in his stomach. Then I asked him: Who cut you? and he said: "It is the tall slim dark one." '

2. From Kenneth Edwards, also a brother of the victim: 'We went in to see him and Norbert bent over Norris and said to him, "How are you feeling?" Norris said to Norbert: "The cut is paining me, it's not the light-skinned one who cut me, but the dark one." The nurse then came and we had to leave.'

3. From Hazel Davidson, a nurse at King's College Hospital: 'The policemen then asked Edwards about the knife. I did not hear the reply. I gathered from the disjoined replies that Edwards gave that a fight had started at a party; he had not got his injuries in the house but in the street. The police officer asked him who had caused his injury and he said: "the tall man, you know, brown suit." '

4. From Detective-Sergeant Clarence Babb: 'I saw him in the X-ray room. . . . I said "Who stabbed you?" He said something like: "Jesus, the pain, the pain!" I said: "Who stabbed you?" He said: "Budsy, or Boosy. He cut me, the dark man was there as well." I said: "What does he look like?" He said: "He is tall, dark." '

5. PC Roger Hill: 'I went to the X-ray room with D.S. Babb . . . D.S. Babb said to him: "Who stabbed you?" He said something which sounded like "Buzzy or Boosey—he cut me. The tall man was there as well." D.S. said: "What does he look like?" Edwards said: "He is a tall dark man." Edwards started to complain about pain and we left him.'

These statements, which clearly had a great deal of relevance to the trial, were excluded. They were excluded for various reasons.

(a) There was considerable doubt as to whether the victim had known he was about to die when he spoke to the witnesses, and therefore as to whether the statements were 'dying declarations' in the legal sense of the term.

(b) Castin and Leathlan Townsend were tried jointly; and, given the nature of the case, any statement incriminating one of them exonerates the other. There were therefore two very different interests in the courtroom, and so two very different views as to whether they wanted the hearsay to be admitted as evidence. On balance the statements favour Leathlan and point to Castin as being guilty.

(c) Quite naturally, the defence lawyers wished to include those statements which favoured their client and exclude the rest. The judge would not allow this, and ruled that either all the hearsay was to be admitted or none of it.

This is not as rare a situation as might be supposed: it does crop up from time to time in murder cases. We have come across at least two others, including one remarkably similar to this.

Professor Cornish makes an interesting point about the fallacious psychology involved in making a special case out of dying declarations: 'Related experiments have demonstrated that statements made by a person in a highly excited or disturbed emotional state—because, for example, he has just been attacked or involved in an accident—are particularly likely to contain inaccuracies. The legal doctrine which allowed hearsay evidence to be given of the dying declaration of the victim in a homicide case runs counter to this finding. It is based on the unwarranted assumption that a person will speak the truth *in extremis* and ignores the fact that the person's powers of perception may have been seriously dulled by the circumstances.'[28] (This ties in with observations we have already made about identification evidence.)

Clearly, the rules regarding hearsay evidence, and the exceptions to these rules, are so complicated and ambiguous that they create a great deal of confusion in the courts and give rise to too many arbitrary *ad hoc* decisions. It might be better if hearsay evidence were to be admitted subject to the discretion of the judge, and all the complicated rules were done away with. This is what has recently happened in civil cases under the Civil Evidence Act, 1968.[29] Under this Act, such evidence is now admissible in civil proceedings, double hearsay, with exceptions, alone being excluded. The justification usually given for differentiating between civil and criminal courts with respect to hearsay evidence is that juries are supposed to be incapable of discriminating between good and bad evidence in this area. This seems a surprising attitude, since in everyday life the jurors, like everyone else, have to depend on hearsay evidence of all kinds, and to discriminate between the trustworthy and the unreliable. As Lord Chancellor Maugham put it: 'If the press of the entire world reported the death of the Queen everybody could safely accept it—except the courts of law on that evidence.'[30]

It also seems odd in this context that the jury whose powers of judgment and discrimination are so trusted with regard to identification and statements—perhaps too much so—shall be deemed to have lost these said powers when it comes to weighing up hearsay evidence. Paradoxically, the jury's reliance on their common sense and everyday experience, the very things which lead them into error in matters of identification and confessions, seem to us here to be a proper basis for assessing the evidence.

Another category of inadmissible evidence is the past record, if any, of the accused. This cannot be mentioned in court by the prosecution; the defendant cannot be cross-examined on it. There are exceptions to this rule. If the defence attacks the character of a prosecution witness, then the prosecution can in turn attack the character of the accused. Previous convictions are admissible to prove guilty knowledge or to show system in cases where the accused has perpetrated similar crimes before. The prosecution can bring up the accused's previous record to rebut the defence that he committed the offence by accident or mistake.[31]

This rule is rightly regarded as an important safeguard for the defendant with a record. The reason usually given for the rule is the prejudical effect on the mind of the jury on learning that the defendant does have a record. Once the accused has been labelled as a criminal, they jury tends to regard him as the sort of person who will have committed the crime of which he is accused. Under the influence of this prejudice, the jury are likely to misinterpret the prisoner's actions, as Mr Justice Darling put it in this summing-up to the jury in the Steinie Morrison trial: '. . . no one is more conscious than I am of the danger that such knowledge as you now have [about Morrison's previous convictions] should warp the judgment not only of you, but of myself. It is almost impossible to put as good a construction upon the most innocent thing a man may have done as it was when you believed him to be an unconvicted man.'[32] This is really only a lawyer's belief, and experimental work may show it to be false; but looking at those American States where this rule does not apply, or where it is applied laxly, the abandonment of the rule does seem to be a key cause of wrongful conviction. For instance, in Borchard's study, disclosure of criminal record to the court often played a major part in securing a wrongful conviction.[33]

This rule is taken seriously enough in England for a man found guilty to win his appeal and have his conviction quashed solely on the grounds that the rule was infringed. Such was the case of James Prentice Brandon who was convicted of passing bad cheques from a stolen cheque-book which he had received, and passing forged banknotes. He was refused leave to appeal by a single judge and by the full court. He had a previous record with two offences of dishonesty for which he had been put on probation and served a jail sentence, and had done seven years for sodomy with a boy of 14. It was later discovered that the jury knew of his past record, and the Home Office investigated the case. As a result, it was decided to refer the case back to the Court of Appeal and, with his letter of reference, the Home Secretary sent copies of statements made by six members of the trial jury. The Appeal Court commented: 'A newly appointed prison officer at Winchester Prison, where he [Brandon] had begun to serve his sentence, had a conversation with the appellant in which according to the appellant he was told that this officer had in fact been a member of the jury that had tried him, and he conveyed, so the appellant said, that there had been some irregularity in regard to the jury in that case.

'As a result of that, extensive inquiries have been made . . . it seems likely that from something the jury bailiff said, the jury—or some of them—understood that this man had previous convictions, as indeed he had. Moreover, that was at a time when they had been in retirement considering their verdict for a substantial period of time: after which they returned and gave a verdict of guilty.' What seems to have happened is that the jury bailiff, when escorting members of the jury out to the lavatory, told the foreman that Brandon had previous convictions and that there were other charges he wanted taken into consideration. The foreman then informed the other jurors of this. If the jury had not known of Brandon's record, they might have failed to agree and he would have got a new trial. The jury were undoubtedly uncertain about this case, for at an earlier stage in their deliberations they had called in the clerk of the court to help them because they could not all agree whether or not Brandon knew that the notes he possessed and uttered were forged. The clerk said it was up to them and left.

There are other, less direct ways in which it may emerge that the accused does in fact have a record. He will not be able to bring up in evidence the better sides of his character. If the prosecution puts indirect questions to him which might betray his record, he may refuse to answer, or appear shifty or evasive. In cases like this, the jury may convict not so much on the prosecution evidence as on the fact that the accused did give evasive or false replies, designed to conceal his record, on matters not really relevant to the charge.

There are also various indirect ways (fortuitous or deliberate) in which the jury may come to know that the accused has a criminal record. Here are some of these ways. Professor Cornish says: 'The jurors whom I interviewed were almost unanimous in thinking that knowledge of previous convictions would have been an important factor in increasing their certainty of the accused's guilt. Several recalled the relief they felt when, having convicted without knowing that the accused had a record, they then heard it read out before sentence. It appeared that juries do sometimes speculate about whether an accused has previous convictions. Some jurors informed their fellows that an accused had not given evidence because he had attacked the evidence of the police and was therefore afraid that his record would be put to him in cross-examination. They might thus have managed to sway doubters into convicting. One told of a jury which came to recognize the appearance of the police form stating previous convictions, and took account of its very existence if they saw it in the hands of the prosecution.'[34]

When Gerald Morris was convicted of robbery, he alleged that the prosecution brought up his previous convictions in a round-about way in court before the jury. The prosecution quoted him as saying: 'If I'm found guilty of this, I'll get eight years.' The implication was clearly that he had a previous record, since a first offender would not get a stretch of this magnitude.

In another case the detective-constable who made the arrest gave evidence that he identified the accused after asking to see the palms of his hands—thus telling the jury that he had a criminal record and had been fingerprinted before.

A more direct instance of a record being revealed occurred in a case where the judge inadvertently said that the accused had been 'in bother' before. He immediately withdrew it, but did not tell the jury to disregard it. The shorthand writer omitted this remark from the trial transcript.

The jury nevertheless usually does not know about the defendant's record. In this case, it is obviously important for the defence to keep the jury ignorant of it. This creates two distinct dilemmas for the defence. Firstly, it must consider very carefully before attacking the character of a prosecution witness, since, as has been explained, this will lay the character of the defendant open to attack, and his record may be produced in evidence. Secondly, the defence must be very careful about the character of its own witnesses. If a defence witness has a criminal record, then this may be brought out in cross-examination by the prosecution, with the risk that the jury may think the defendant guilty by association. Even if he is in other respects the best witness available to the defence, this may undo all the good he is otherwise able to do.

A good example of the first dilemma occurs in the case of Devers and Jones discussed earlier. Devers and Jones were convicted of robbing a Mr Masterson on the sole evidence of the victim. Masterson was presented at the trial as a witness of good character. Even the judge said of him: 'The most important evidence for the case of the prosecution is that of Mr Michael Masterson. You have heard him express what you may think are high Christian principles, principles which permit him to give expression to his desire for nothing to befall these two persons, but which prevented him from coming here and telling you other than what he said was the truth.' Masterson in fact had an enormous string of convictions, and had served twelve prison sentences, but could not be cross-examined on this. As the Appeal Court commented: 'Jones himself has a record which might have emerged if the defence had attacked Masterson in the light of his record, and the Crown had sought leave to cross-examine Jones accordingly on his [own] record.' Jones and Devers were anyway convicted: it seems likely they would have been convicted whichever course the defence had taken.

This dilemma for the defence is not limited to cases where the prosecution witness has a criminal record. It can prevent the defence alleging malpractice on the part of any prosecution witness—including the police—even if this is its only defence. This is what happened in one of the cases connected with Detective-Sergeant Challenor. In the case of Pedrini, Ford, Cheeseman and Oliva, Pedrini and Cheeseman put forward the defence at their trial for possession of offensive weapons, that the weapons had been planted on them. Oliva was unable to put forward this defence. As he had previous convictions he could not risk running the defence that the police had planted the bottle in his car.

The temptation to attack a prosecution witness is nevertheless very great, since if you can prove he has a bad character, the defence is less likely to believe him. This temptation proved disastrous for the defence in the Steinie Morrison case. Many of the witnesses in this case were somewhat shady characters. It was clearly a great temptation to the defence counsel, Abinger, to attack the character of Joseph Mintz, a prosecution witness:

Abinger: Did you ever try to hang yourself in this restaurant?
Mintz: That has nothing to do with the case.
Abinger: But is it true?
Mintz: It is true, but it has nothing to do with the case. . . .
Abinger: And did you afterwards go to Colney Hatch asylum?
Mintz: Yes, I have been there. . . .
Mr Justice Darling: I suppose you realize, Mr Abinger, that suicide is a felony, and that you are asking this man whether he attempted a felony.
Abinger: If your lordship thinks I should not pursue this . . .?
Mr Justice Darling: I am not saying you should not pursue it, Mr Abinger. I did not quite know whether you knew what it might lead to.[35]

Abinger retorted, according to Julian Symons, 'that he had not been accusing Mintz of an attempt to commit a felony. Far from it, he said. That had not been his attitude at all. He had merely been pointing out that a man who had attempted suicide and had been an asylum inmate was not a reliable witness. Darling interrupted him:

Mr Justice Darling: I hope you will excuse me; it was not a question of what was your object. The question I had in mind was what Mr Muir would claim to do, because of your questions, no matter with what object you put them. It was perfectly obvious to me that he would claim upon that to cross-examine the defendant, if he went into the witness-box, to cross-examine him as to his character.
Abinger: In this country, it is no offence to commit suicide if the Almighty afflicts you with madness—no offence at all. If a sane person wickedly attempts to destroy his own life it is an offence,

but this man was insane. Gentlemen, the rod has been held over me until it is insupportable. I was threatened then by my lord—
Mr Justice Darling: I wish you would not use that word. 'Threatened' is not the word. You say, I was 'threatened' then.
Abinger: If your lordship wishes me to withdraw the word 'threatened' I will withdraw it.
Mr Justice Darling: It is not a question of my wishing you to withdraw it. I pointed that out to you absolutely, to save you from what I thought might be the consequences of your own cross-examination—with no other motive.'[36]

The judge here conveyed to defence counsel in a skilful and subtle way, the dangers of attacking the character of a prosecution witness. The jury, unless it was very sophisticated, would be unlikely to infer from this that the judge knew that Morrison had previous convictions. Nevertheless, later in the case the defence did attack the character of another prosecution witness, Mrs Deitch, whom they accused of keeping a whorehouse. As a result, the prosecution were able to reveal that Morrison had previous convictions for burglary and other offences of dishonesty. This, as our previous quotation from Mr Justice Darling shows, probably had a great effect on the jury.

The second difficulty is with the calling of defence witnesses of doubtful character: if you call them, you may be discredited, and if you don't call them, you may lack a vital witness. In the case of Robert Snowdon and Kenneth McKenna, convicted with two others of conspiracy to cause grievous bodily harm, and causing grievous bodily harm, the second course was decided upon. The situation was this: four men, including Snowdon and McKenna, were accused of deliberately trying to run a man down in their car, and later stabbing him. All four were convicted, and an appeal was refused. After they had all served their prison sentences, the two other men in the case, together with a third man, Peter Lamb, who was not tried for the offence, wrote to the Home Secretary telling him that they had committed the crime and that Snowdon and McKenna had nothing to do with it. The Home Secretary directed that the case be referred to the Court of Criminal Appeal, but the appeal was dismissed.

Although Lamb was clearly a key witness, and offered himself to appear for either side, he was never called, though he was in court throughout the trial. He was not called because he had a bad character with many previous convictions for both violence and dishonesty. The defence feared that if he had been called, the prosecution might have suggested collusion between this witness and the defendants.

Defence lawyers are justified in their fears that the bad character of a witness will seriously harm the defence if it is brought out in cross-examination. This is shown in the case of the Cross brothers (see p. 25) — convicted of robbery, later pardoned. This is what happened in court to their main alibi witness, Mr J. G. Wandless:

Wandless: Ken definitely was with me all night. If I left Ken, or if he left me, it was to go to the bar. Then I only had to turn my head to see if he was there. If I went to the bar, he only had to turn his head to see if I was there. It is not a very big room at the Eclipse.

Pros. lawyer: Are you sure you left home and started the evening with Kenneth?

A: Yes, I definitely was with Kenneth.

Q: If he says that he met you part way through in a public house, that would be quite wrong?

A: I would say it is.

Q: The truth of this matter is that you do not mind what you say, do you?

A: I said exactly what I can remember.

Q: And you would support any man in an alibi against a police officer, would you not?

A: I would not.

Q: How many times have you been before the courts yourself for criminal offences?

A: Since just about the time I was old enough to be charged, in 1942 or 1944 when I was a juvenile.

Mr Justice Havers: Since 1942 or 1944, you have been convicted, have you?

A: When I came out of the army, I got my first prison sentence.

Q: How many times have you been convicted?

A: I cannot exactly say, but it is more than it should ever be.

Q: I know. But you can help us a bit more than that. Is it half a dozen?

A: I cannot honestly say how many times.

Q: Is it half a dozen?

A: Probably more than half a dozen. I have been up many times since I was a juvenile.

Q: At any time since you were 21 ?

A: Yes. I had a punch-up and I was in court the day before my twenty-first birthday. I was on disembarkation leave, just finishing it, and I have been pulling pretty steady-on these last eight or nine years, except for a lapse at Nottingham goose fair a year before.

Pros. lawyer: Except for a lapse, you say ?

A: Yes.

Q: Let us see how many times that has happened since you were a juvenile. Stonehaven Summary Court . . .

A: I was in the army then; I was not a juvenile.

Mr Justice Havers: What year is this ?

A: 1952.

Pros. lawyer: Housebreaking and larceny, two charges; housebreaking with intent. 1953, unlawful wounding, Moorhill Magistrate's Court, fined £20 ?

A: That was a fight at one of the dances.

Q: 1953, Newcastle Quarter Sessions, shopbreaking and larceny, two cases considered, three years' corrective training. Is that right ?

A: Yes.

Q: 1955, Wolverhampton Magistrate's Court, larceny of motor car, no insurance, no licence, six months' and three months' imprisonment concurrent. Is that right ?

A: Yes.

Q: In November 1956 at Notts Assizes for unlawful sexual intercourse: eighteen months' imprisonment: is that right ?

A: Two eighteen months concurrent.

Q: Nottingham City Magistrate's Court in 1963, at the end of last year, for larceny of cash, you were fined £25 ?

A: That is quite correct.

Q: Did you really see these brothers at all that night ?[37]

As Kenneth Cross ruefully commented after he had been pardoned: 'Our barrister thought he was our star witness. But as soon as he got into the dock, the barrister prosecuting got up and brought all his prison record out, and the judge said: 'This is an unreliable witness.' Our solicitor picked him out because he was so intelligent. We had no idea—Pete and John knew he'd been in trouble, but not to that extent. I felt sorry for him.'

Kenneth Cross felt particularly annoyed at this attack on Johnny Wandless's character, because he felt the main prosecution witness was also of doubtful character. He said: 'She was the sort of woman who would hang round the Black Boy, very loose morals. She was right scruffy, right rough. But when we went to court, she was all dressed up. She got done by the police shortly after, and she'd been had up before and been in a mental home. But the barrister said we couldn't use this because it would put my own character in the issue [Kenneth Cross had served a previous prison sentence, though his brothers had not]. . . . I felt it was unfair that Johnny Wandless's character came out but not this woman's.'

It is difficult to see how the position could be made more satisfactory in most cases. The rule that if the defence attacks a prosecution witness, the defendant's character becomes an issue, seems a fair one. But perhaps this 'knock for knock' rule could be extended. If the prosecution attacks the character of a defence witness, the defence in its turn should be allowed to attack the character of a prosecution witness with impunity.

JOINT TRIALS

Despite the fact that joint trials have many disadvantages, the joint trial of apparent confederates is a normal procedure in the courts.[38] There are various reasons for this. There is an obvious saving of public and judicial time and money. To many lawyers, it seems only fit and proper that the law should take its course in this way. This attitude is well illustrated in the case of William Henry Barber, convicted of fraud in 1844 and later pardoned. At that time the defendant was not allowed to give evidence, and Barber was put at an enormous disadvantage by being jointly tried with the real culprit, Fletcher. Belton Cobb says: 'Barber had then only one chance of a successful defence. The rule forbidding the accused to give evidence only applied to the accused in the case on hand—it did not matter that a required witness was under arrest and would be in the dock in another case. Therefore, if Barber could be tried separately from the other prisoners, he would be able to call Fletcher as a witness.

'When that application came before the judge, however, the ruling was that it could only be granted with the consent of the prosecution. On the ground that a separate trial would not be "in the interests of justice" the Attorney-General refused.' That was 130 years ago, and the rules of evidence have changed radically since then, but judges are still reluctant to grant separate trials.

One of the dangers of the joint trial when the innocent and the guilty are arbitrarily lumped together as 'the accused', is that the guilty may drag the innocent down with them. This is what happened in the case of Ronald Barker, discussed earlier (convicted of robbery, acquitted at a re-trial). He was jointly tried with James Ross, who really was guilty of the offence, but who also pleaded not guilty. Barker says of his experience: 'I knew Ross was guilty, and I knew I'd stand a much better chance at a separate trial. For one thing, under the legal aid system we'd only get one barrister between us. I thought of skipping bail to get a separate trial, but the police suspected I might do this, so they arrested me while I was still out on bail. I didn't want to lose the bond, anyway. At the trial, Ross's alibi crumbled into lies, and I had to go down with him. Ross wanted to change his plea to guilty during the trial and ask for leniency, but the barrister persuaded him not to. If he had changed his plea, I'd have got a new trial, and I might have been able to call Ross as evidence for the defence.'

This process was carried a stage further in the case of Thomas Hall (convicted of shopbreaking, conviction later quashed). The man charged with him was Harold Whitfield, who was caught red-handed running away from the shop with the stolen goods on him. In view of this, it may seem surprising that Whitfield also decided to plead not guilty at the preliminary hearing, but in a statement made later he said: 'In the chargeroom we were jointly charged with breaking and entering Tate's shop and stealing cameras. I was very surprised when they charged Hall with me for breaking into the shop. When we were coming up the stairs from the cells I was going to ask him what he was in for. He was not the man who broke into Tate's with me.

'I was pleading not guilty to the offence with which I was charged, and I decided to make this plea because I saw that the police were making a blunder in charging Hall and I thought that if they could make that mistake, there was a chance for me. . . . I did not mention to anyone in the station that Hall was not the man concerned in the offence. I was not asked. . . . When we were going back down to the cells, Hall asked me what it was all about, and I told him that I had no idea, as I had just been pulled in off the street myself. I had to say that because there were policemen around and I was pleading not guilty.'

Before the trial at quarter-sessions, Whitfield changed his plea to guilty because of the strong forensic evidence against him.

Initially, Whitfield had hoped that Hall's innocence would drag him out of trouble. What probably happened was that his guilt dragged Hall down. By pleading guilty in a joint trial, he implicated Hall. Because Whitfield only told the barrister that he was changing his plea immediately before the trial—as he put it, 'before I got in the dock'—the barrister had no chance to change his strategy. Whitfield said: 'Hall also saw the barrister before he went into the dock but only for about five minutes.' It is certainly curious that Whitfield did not give any evidence during the trial.

Another of the great dangers of joint trial is that the jury may get muddled. Professor Cornish puts it clearly: ' . . . the strangeness of the surroundings and the intricacies of procedure may well impair a juror's concentration; then he is confronted with an indictment consisting of a string of charges, and a row of individuals in the dock, each one of whom has to be associated with the charges against him and the counsel who is defending him. A number of jurors whom I interviewed spoke of the confusion which they experience during the early stages of a trial of this nature. One of them sat on a jury which in desperation asked for a diagram showing the position of each defendant in the dock and of his counsel. . . . Yet it is clear that cases still occur in which confusions arise, and remain undispelled when the time comes for the jury to return its verdict. There have been recent cases in which the Court of Criminal Appeal has considered that the jury must have been unable to appreciate that evidence concerning some of the defendants did not affect one of the others. Of one convicted defendant, the court said: "We think that he is really a typical example of a man who was sunk beneath a mass of evidence about frauds of various kinds, with the great majority of which he had no connection, either direct or indirect, and in which he took no part whatever, and in which his name was never even mentioned."[39] Mr Justice Finnemore was here referring to Wenlock, one of the men accused with George Dawson of conspiracy to cheat and defraud. Wenlock had all his convictions quashed; although Dawson's conviction for conspiracy was quashed, his other convictions were upheld.[40]

A case that is possibly of this kind is that of Joginder Singh, convicted in 1960 along with three other men on a charge of murdering another Indian. Almost every single person concerned with the case was called Singh. Presumably they were all Sikhs and therefore wore turbans and beards. The case in itself was confusing because it was the result of an affray in which a large number of people took part. The prosecution lawyer, Mr J. Hobson, QC, carefully warned the jury of the problems involved: 'Members of the jury, this case is not very easy to follow because, as you will hear, there are large numbers of witnesses who have the same name. The deceased was called Sawan Singh, one of the accused is Swarn Singh, and one of the witnesses is called Sawarn Singh, spelled S A W A R N. So it is somewhat difficult to distinguish personalities, and there are a number of cases where people bear the same names.' Mr Justice Diplock also stressed the problems and confusions involved in his summing-up: 'There are five prisoners in the dock there. You have got, as I am sure you realize, to consider the case against each of them. You must not lump them all together and say: "Well, they must have done it." You have to consider the case against each of them. . . . Of course, it is in the nature of this charge against them, that they combine together, and that is why you are trying them all together here; but do remember and think of them separately in coming to your conclusion about them.'

Inevitably, it is alleged that muddle did occur in this case in spite of all these warnings. We have come across a number of cases of this kind, in which several Indians have been involved in a fight, the situation is unclear, the names are identical or very similar, and they all look alike to English people. It seems likely that in more than one of these cases a mistake may have been made. At any rate, those involved in these cases are still protesting about the verdict.

But verdicts, however mistaken, that are reached at the end of a very muddling case, are the most difficult to reverse, because no one can ever know for certain what really happened. The other big class of cases of which this seems to be true are complicated fraud cases. It is rare for anyone involved in a case of either type to get a pardon or to have a conviction quashed. (We have therefore come to the conclusion that the person most at risk of remaining wrongfully imprisoned in our society is an Indian accountant!)

Not only juries but judges are at risk of getting confused in joint trials. A 'Justice' memorandum on the case of James William Pearce, convicted with two other men of breaking and entering a factory office and placing gelignite in the building with intent to damage a safe, says: 'The summing-up was on the whole extremely fair. The deputy chairman specifically told the jury at the outset that they had to consider the case of each man separately. He asked the jury to ignore the fact that the men had been on a visit to Dartmoor; or that they had come out of their way, or that they had set out with very vague arrangements. But in two respects it appears, perhaps without intent, to have been unfair to Pearce.

1. The deputy chairman said: "If you are satisfied that the three men set out on what we will call a joint enterprise, that is to say, all acting for a common purpose, you do not need to worry yourselves at all about who forced open the window, which one pushed the gel-ignite into the lock and, for that matter, which one stayed outside to keep guard." By introducing for the first time, the suggestion of one man keeping guard, he must have set aside any doubts the jury may have had about the absence of scientific evidence against Pearce.

2. The deputy chairman's résumé of the scientific evidence takes up five pages of the transcript. He insists that this is the most important evidence. He mentions Pearce only once, to cite the sacking fibres, and without mentioning that prosecution witnesses had said they could not be identified. The total effect of this résumé, however, is to include Pearce in its indictment, and at the end of it, he completely fails to point out to the jury as an essential part of Pearce's defence, that the scientific evidence against him was not only negligible in comparison with that against the others, but, in its negative aspect, was in Pearce's favour.'

A further difficulty in joint trials is that the defendants may have conflicting interests. Evidence which clearly favours one accused may tell against another: is it to be called, and how much weight is it to be given? This is a particularly difficult point when the evidence in question is of doubtful admissibility. Earlier in this chapter we discussed the case of Castin and Leathlan Townsend. The dying declarations involved were helpful to one defendant and directly incriminated the other. So there was a direct conflict of interest between the two defendants as to whether they wanted this evidence to be admitted. It was not an issue on which they could present a united front to the prosecution.

The conflict is not always of this simple winner-loser nature. Thinking once again of the rather special case of admissibility of evidence, there are bound to be cases where evidence is available which would be admissible for one of the defendants if he were being tried by himself, but not for the others, if they were being tried by themselves. The usual practice in joint trials is to admit such evidence, but the judge tells the jury to ignore it in deciding whether the other accused are guilty. This makes nonsense of the exclusion rules, since the purpose of these rules is to exclude evidence which the jury is thought incapable of assessing. It appears that they are now thought capable not merely of assessing it, but of putting it out of their minds when the occasion demands.

Another common circumstance in joint trials, and which can lead to a conflict of interest between the defendants, is where one of the defendants has a criminal record, and the others do not. Those of the accused who do not have a record may well wish to cross-examine prosecution witnesses as to their character; but if they should do so, they may be putting their co-defendant at risk of having his record revealed to the court. This seems to have inhibited the Cross brothers' lawyer from ruthlessly cross-examining the chief prosecution witness. (Possibly this is only a problem where the co-defendants are all represented by the same lawyer. If they had different lawyers, the rule might work to the benefit of the accused with a record. The lawyer for the defendant who had a clean record would be able to cross-examine prosecution witnesses as to their character without putting any of the defence at risk.)

More generally it has been alleged that the defence of particular defendants has been hampered by the fact that all the defendants were represented by the same lawyer, because it is difficult for him to devise a defence strategy which is the best possible one for all of them.

We have shown that the guilty may drag the innocent down with them. What perhaps needs explaining is that the innocent often acquiesce in this. They may well know the real circumstances of the case, but for various reasons they are not prepared to disclose them. The main reasons seem to be fear of reprisals and 'honour among thieves'. Take the case of James Pearce (see p. 93): once again, we quote from the 'Justice' memorandum. 'Pearce was in a dilemma throughout the whole of these proceedings. He was aware that Biggs and Brown were going to make the attempt on the egg-packing station, and that they had done so. Whether he contracted out of the attempt at the last minute, cannot be established. He says that he never wanted to join in, and that the meeting with the girl gave him something to do while he waited for them. When it came to the trial, Pearce was unwilling, partly through loyalty, partly through fear of reprisals from Biggs and Brown, who were described by their solicitors as ruthless men, to give them away. He was confident that there was no evidence against him of actual participation in the affair, and dismayed when he was convicted, not only of the breaking and entering but also of placing the gelignite. Had he had a defence counsel to bring out the absence of evidence, or a separate trial after the other two had been convicted, the result might well have been different.

'Biggs and Brown have throughout (or at any rate since their appeal failed) insisted that he went off with the girl, and have since written letters to Pearce's wife saying that he was not involved in the crime.'

Pearce himself did not want the girl with whom he was supposed to have spent the time during which the crime was committed, to be traced because he didn't want his wife to know about her.

It is not surprising that during the trial and until any appeal has been lost, those among the accused at a joint trial who are guilty are unwilling to state that some of their co-accused had no part in the crime—since this would be tantamount to admitting that they themselves did take part in it. Once a final decision has been made on their case, then they have no more to lose by trying to clear anyone who may have been falsely imprisoned with them. But at this stage, the Court of Appeal and the police are not disposed to believe them—after all, they may simply be making up a story to get one of them off, who was in fact rightly convicted.

But it may be that there is a certain rough justice about their attitude. As a police inspector put it to us: 'If A and B are jointly charged, and both plead not guilty, this suggests that B knows of A's guilt, but is prepared to remain quiet on the chance that they will both get off. He is in a sense an accomplice of A in such circumstances. In the event of his being convicted, he has only himself to blame. If he had told the police at the outset, the court would have correctly placed the blame with A alone. In a sense, justice has been served.'

This may in some cases be true, but there are others where the rough justice is very rough indeed.

Such a one appears to be that of John Henry Taylor. We quote from the 'Justice' memorandum on the case: 'Taylor was convicted in September 1962 at London Sessions together with six other men, of breaking out of an office after stealing a safe, and of being an accessory after the fact, in that he assisted those who had stolen it. At the committal proceedings Taylor had been actually charged with the stealing and breaking out, but at his trial, where he was undefended, it was agreed that he had not taken part in the stealing, and he was charged with being an accessory before the fact. He was found guilty of this, whereby he became a principle in the offence, was deemed by the trial judge to have been the ringleader of the gang, and sentenced to five years' imprisonment. He had never been to prison before and had a clean record, apart from having been put on probation while in the army for misappropriating some blankets. The case against Taylor, and his friend Byrne, rested almost entirely on the fact that the police entered Byrne's flat in the middle of the night and there found the safe and five men who had stolen it, and that Taylor was sleeping in the flat at the time. . . .

'Taylor's defence was that he had called to see his friend Byrne, had been drinking together with a neighbour, and Byrne had invited him to stay the might. Unfortunately, Taylor agreed to give misleading evidence in order to protect his friend [he admitted this to 'Justice' rather later in the investigation]. His evidence was that he had been roused by a knock on the door, had opened it, to find a man who said he was a friend of Byrne's who wanted to stay the night, had let him in and gone back to bed; and that this man subsequently let in the rest of the gang with the safe. Taylor's later account, confirmed by Byrne, was that Byrne had opened the door, Taylor had looked out of his room and asked what was happening, and that Byrne had said it was Charlie McCance with a safe, and had himself let them in and locked them in the living-room. There may have been some prior arrangement between Byrne and McCance, but it appears fairly certain that Taylor had no part in it, although he was justifiably chargeable with being an accessory after the fact. . . .

'Byrne's counsel attributes the conviction of Byrne and Taylor as principals to the fact that all the men gave differing and ridiculous excuses for going in the flat that night and that Byrne and Taylor's stories, being in part untrue, were equally disbelieved. This is one of the hazards of a joint trial.'[41]

UNSATISFACTORY DEFENCE

Unsatisfactory defence is very commonly alleged by convicted persons. Many of these complaints are without substance, and are made by people who would feel they had a grievance whatever had happened. Nevertheless, it must frequently happen that a mistake is made by the defence solicitor, barrister, or some other party; and occasionally one of these parties is guilty of downright negligence.

An example of this is the case of the man we have called Henry Morgan (see above, p. 54) whose solicitor seems to have made

D

insufficient effort to conduct his defence. He did not even bother to see his client until Morgan had been in prison on remand for nearly three weeks. Important defence witnesses were not called, no real effort was made to get him bail, and the solicitor took an active part in the illicit pressures put upon him to plead guilty.

A defence can be thoroughly unsatisfactory without neligence on the part of the lawyers or their agents. Everyone is liable to make mistakes from time to time. This is what appears to have happened in the case of Thomas Hall. Here the mistake appears to have lain not with the barrister or solicitor, but with an inquiry agent. Hall was convicted of shopbreaking; his first appeal was refused, but his conviction was later quashed on referral to the Court of Appeal by the Home Secretary.

Hall's conviction was eventually quashed on the evidence of several crucial alibi witnesses. These witnesses were not called at his trial, because the inquiry agent failed to locate them in time. The alibi as described by Hall was this: 'When I got to my mother's, she was the only one at home. Shortly after I got there, my mother asked me to go round to the off beer licence in Brookside Crescent for two bottles of brown ale. I went round to the off beer licence and I got two bottles of brown ale, and then I decided to go into Mrs Duncan's shop next to the off beer licence to buy a bag of coal for my mother.' Mr Duncan said of this visit in a later statement: 'It was either the next day or the day after that my wife told me that Mr Hall had been locked up by the police for breaking into a shop near the market in the town about 9 o'clock on the night he had been for the coal. My wife also said to me that he must have had a helicopter to get to town and break into a shop by 9 p.m.'

Why were these vital witnesses not produced at Hall's trial? The inquiry agent's statement reads: 'On about 1 June 1964 I received instructions from [the solicitors] to make inquiries to trace a Mrs Donkin at her shop at Rye Hill, Newcastle. This inquiry was in connection with the trial of Thomas Hall of Rye Hill, Newcastle, who was charged with committing an offence of shopbreaking. . . . Hall was apparently alleging that on the night in question he went to Mrs Donkin's shop and bought a bag of coal about 8.40 p.m. on that particular night. I was asked to contact Mrs Donkin to find out if she had any recollection of the incident and to obtain a statement from her.

'On receipt of the letter I made inquiries in the Rye Hill area, but could not find a Donkin's shop. I then made inquiries in the

North Fenham area and I found a "Duncan's shop" near to Hall's mother's house. My object in being in the area was to see Hall's mother to see if she could assist me, and it was whilst on my way to her home that I found Duncan's shop. . . . There were two assistants in the shop, and they told me that Mrs Duncan was out but that she was visiting a ladies' hairdresser. . . . I told the assistants that it was very urgent that I see Mrs Duncan, and that is why they told me where I could find her. I am not certain of the date I made these inquiries, but I know that Hall's trial was in its closing stages when I called at the shop, that is why I had to see Mrs Duncan that morning and could not afford to wait until later on in the day.'

In a later addendum to his statement, the inquiry agent said: 'After [my assistant] and I returned to my office about 12.30 p.m. on the day in question, I now recall telephoning the solicitors for whom I was acting and informing them that I had traced Mrs Duncan but had been unable to see her due to the fact that she was at the hairdresser's. I received a reply to the effect that the trial was in its concluding stages, or in effect concluded, and that it was too late to introduce Mrs Duncan's evidence, which at that stage was unknown.'

Hall describes what happened in court: 'Just before the start of my trial whilst I was standing in the dock a man came up and said "Are you Mr Hall?" I replied "Yes". He then said: "[the inquiry agent] has been to Rye Hill but he can't find that woman witness anywhere." I couldn't understand this because when I told the solicitor about my visit to Duncan's shop he took a statement from me and wrote down Mrs Duncan's name and address.'

Most of the complaints that we have come across seem to point to solicitors as having been responsible for errors in the defence, but the 'Justice' report *Complaints against Lawyers* comments: 'Barristers have comparatively little personal contact with their clients, and those contacts are mainly concerned with advocacy and courtwork. When the outcome of court proceedings is unsatisfactory to the client, it is difficult for an investigating body to ascertain whether the barrister was in any way at fault. Solicitors' contact with their clients is far more personal, and consequently a more fruitful source of complaint; moreover, they are often blamed for what may be a mistake or error of judgment on the part of the barrister.'[42]

In the Chicago Jury Project, judges and jurors were asked their opinion of the abilities of counsel in different cases. The jurors were asked why they reached a particular verdict; in all cases, the judge was asked whether he would have come to the same verdict. An attempt was then made to match up disagreements between judges and jurors and the abilities of counsel on either side.

Judges' opinion of abilities of counsel
  No difference: 76 per cent.
  Prosecution superior: 13 per cent.
  Defence superior: 11 per cent.

Where judge and jury disagreed as to what the verdict should have been, difference in ability between counsel on one side was given as *one* reason for disagreement in 9 per cent of the cases.

Where judge but not jury wanted to convict, the effect of the defence counsel being superior to prosecution counsel accounted for 3·4 per cent of the disagreements.

Where the judge wanted to acquit but not the jury, effect of prosecution counsel being superior to the defence accounted for 2·5 per cent of disagreements.[43]

One inference to be drawn from this is that the jury are more liable to be influenced by a good counsel than the judge, who has more experience of these things.

The figure of 2·5 per cent of cases where the defendant's case appears to be sabotaged by a bad advocate is anyway remarkably small, especially in view of the very poor quality of the worst lawyers in America. The gap between good and bad lawyers is much greater there than in this country, so one would expect the equivalent figures here to be correspondingly smaller.

What these figures refer to is of course largely the quality of presentation of the case. A more important cause of the defence going wrong is likely to be the kind of mistakes and misjudgments which go on behind the scenes and are not apparent to the jury.

It is difficult to assess the objective effects of legal aid in this field. But what does seem clear to us is that in some of the cases we have come across where lawyers were retained on legal aid, the defendants lacked confidence in them and felt that they might have done better as paying clients. Henry Morgan, for instance, felt that his solicitors expended little effort on their legal aid clients. He felt their attitude was indicated by the fact that they failed at a series of hearings to get bail for him, whereas they did get bail for another (paying) client accused of a much more serious offence. Even ex-PC Luckhurst, who felt that the lawyers who defended him had been good ones, said: 'I think if I'd been in a position to have instructed a better defence I may have fared better.'[44]

One man who did benefit from paying for a good defence was Philip Berry. He was accused of burglary, and there was strong forensic and other evidence against him. Nevertheless, with the assistance of a very able defence lawyer, he was acquitted by a majority verdict at his second trial, the jury having been unable to agree at his first trial. He said: 'I tried various friends and connections to get a solicitor who could handle this kind of thing, and I finally got one who in turn asked me whether I would like a low price, medium price or high price counsel. And I said a high price, because I wasn't prepared to economize in such a terrifying situation. And so I said I would go for a leading silk, and this is what I got. . . . I think that the reputation of the man defending me had something to do with the way the case went. . . . As it stands, it's cost me £650 out of my pocket. Had I been poorer, there is no question about it, I would almost certainly have been convicted.'

One of the concrete points about the working of the legal aid system that emerged from talking to Berry and Luckhurst, was the greater continuity possible if you pay for your lawyer. Berry had two trials; his counsel, having been through the first, knew what points to stress at the second. In Luckhurst's case, the counsel and solicitor acting for him at his trial (on legal aid) ceased to act for him directly after it; a new set of lawyers had to be instructed for the appeal.

However, it is not necessarily an advantage to have enough money not to need legal aid. The man who is in the worst possible position is the one who has just too much money to be granted legal aid, but not enough to afford a really good lawyer. But even if he can afford one, he may not know who is a good criminal lawyer and who isn't. Most people when caught up in this kind of situation would most likely go to their family solicitor, who is very unlikely to specialize in criminal work. For most solicitors their bread and butter work lies in other fields. Criminal cases are only a small part of the job and hence a single solicitor or a small partnership will acquire little expertise in this field. This will be especially true in smaller towns where solicitors do not get much criminal work anyway. The person most likely to know who is a good criminal solicitor is of course an experienced and successful criminal.

If you feel you have been inadequately defended at your trial and have been convicted, there is very little you can do about it. An inadequate defence is almost certainly not grounds for appeal, whether the failure lies with your lawyers or with your expert witnesses. Arthur James Lomas, convicted of murdering his wife in 1967 and sentenced to life imprisonment, was fortunate to have his appeal allowed, and a verdict of manslaughter substituted with a sentence of five years. The appeal was allowed because of disagreement over the evidence from the pathologists. But at the Appeal Court Lord Justice Fenton Atkinson said regarding the relevant section (23) of the Criminal Appeal Act: 'Although the section in its terms appears wide enough to embrace fresh evidence of scientific or medical opinion, it seems to this court that only in most exceptional circumstances would it be possible to say that there was any reasonable explanation for not producing such evidence at the trial. . . . It is said with force by Mr Inskip [prosecuting] that if the defence are content to go into trial with a somewhat inexperienced pathologist A without asking for an adjournment to secure the assistance of a more experienced pathologist B they should not be allowed in this court to have a second chance.' Mr Inskip asked rhetorically if this application were allowed, where is it to stop?. . . . 'We regard this as an exceptional case, depending on its own special facts, and not as a decision giving any encouragement to similar applications in the future.'[45]

Even if you feel aggreived about your defence, it is seldom profitable to sue your solicitor. Henry Scudder sued the firm of solicitors who represented him at his trial at the Old Bailey. Scudder, on parole, and conducting his own defence, contended that his solicitors were negligent in failing to call two key alibi witnesses, a bus conductor and a chimney-sweep. He was awarded only nominal damages of £2. Judge Melford Stevenson commented in the High Court: 'There was in relation to the failure to call the bus conductor a breach of duty—although I think a technical one in this case. Scudder wholly failed to satisfy me that if these two witnesses had been called, it was probable he would have been acquitted.' Scudder was ordered to pay costs but it is unlikely that any effort was made to recover them. (Scudder had claimed damages for shame and humiliation, loss of liberty and gross inconvenience he had suffered, and also for financial loss while he was in jail.)[46]

It is very rare for someone who feels his defence has been inadequate to win an appeal on those grounds or successfully to sue any of the people who represented him. He is thus unlikely to get satisfaction or compensation for his grievance. Perhaps the best solution would be if the Appeal Court were to relax its attitude slightly, but this seems unlikely to happen, except perhaps in cases where gross negligence is proved.

In practice, gross negligence is relatively rare. What more often happens is that the defence is inadequate or unsatisfactory in some respect. This may be genuine and large enough to have contributed towards a wrongful imprisonment, and yet not culpable enough to warrant sanctions against the lawyers concerned. Should a defendant turn round and wish to sue his lawyer or lay a complaint against him, it is now up to him to prove negligence on the lawyer's part; the burden of proof must naturally lie with the accuser.

The lawyer, seeing his professional reputation at stake, will obviously fight such a charge as hard as he possibly can.

What is needed is an institution which will mediate between lawyer and complainant, and whose main purpose is not to allocate blame, but simply to see that in some manner the grievance is redressed. The trouble with investigating bodies whose main purpose is to impose penalties, and high ones at that, is threefold. Firstly, because the penalties are high—in this case, possibly the loss of a lawyer's livelihood—the standard of proof has to be high, and therefore it is very difficult to prove a grievance. Secondly, because the professional man naturally wishes to evade such a penalty, he will do all he can not to admit responsibility. He may, possibly with the connivance of his colleagues, cover it all up. Thirdly, a lawyer who is constantly afraid that his client may sue him or take other punitive action against him if his case goes wrong, may become over-cautious and unwilling to take risks that would probably benefit his client. It is for this reason that a barrister is not liable to be sued for negligence in his conduct of a defence.

What is needed is an institution geared not to passing judgment, but rather to asking the question: 'What can be done for the aggrieved client?'[47] Such a body could admit the client's claims without this necessarily involving sanctions against the offending lawyer. In this case, lawyers might be far more ready to admit something had gone wrong. Either this body could provide compensation out of a central fund, or perhaps a certificate from it that a real error had occurred in the conduct of the complainant's defence would enable the case to be reconsidered by the Court of Appeal.

JUDGES, JURIES AND APPEALS

The justifying qualities generally applied to the jury by lawyers and

public alike are that it is disinterested, representative and independent of the State. Admirable though these qualities are, they
are not necessarily what we are concerned with in this book. They
may protect a man from being wrongfully imprisoned for political
reasons; but they do not protect him from being mistakenly
imprisoned. The jury's traditional virtues are no guarantee that it
will efficiently reach accurate decisions as to a person's guilt or
ignorance. Yet these are the qualities mistakenly ascribed to it by
people (and groups) who strongly believe in its political and social
virtues, such as Lord Goddard and the National Council for Civil
Liberties. For this and other reasons it is very hard to get jury
decisions overturned by the Court of Appeal. The decision of a
randomly-selected jury is regarded as preferable to that of people
who might be thought in a better position to judge. A good example
of the latter attitude was given by Lord Goddard and the Court of
Criminal Appeal in 1950. In 1950, the Court of Criminal Appeal
declared that the jury might convict even despite unanimous medical
evidence that the accused was insane, because they were supposed
to look at the evidence in the case as a whole. Lord Goddard said:
'It is for the jury and not for medical men of whatever eminence to
determine the issue. Unless and until Parliament ordains that this
question is to be determined by a panel of medical men, it is to a
jury, after proper direction by a judge, that by the law of this country
the decision is to be entrusted.'[48] One wonders whether the late
Lord Goddard would have preferred to have been operated on by
surgeons or by a jury. The attitudes and decisions of the Court of
Appeal, then and now, show that this distrust of experts *vis-a-vis*
juries is extended even to include themselves. We shall be discussing
their reluctance to overturn jury verdicts more fully below. His own
unfortunate experience, stemming as it does from this reluctance on
the part of the Court of Appeal, has caused ex-PC Luckhurst to
delinate the strengths and weaknesses of the jury system very clearly:
'I now know that mistakes can be made, and if a mistake is made it's
the hardest thing in the world to unmake that mistake—it just cannot
be done. It was said in the House of Lords that the representative
at the Home Office said that even the Home Secretary or any other
person has no power at all to vary the verdicts of a jury. It's the law
of this land that the jury is an independent body who makes a
decision and that decision remains final forever. And when that jury
has made, in my case I know, and possibly in other cases, a wrong
verdict or wrong decision, then the whole system, to me, is not so

good as I thought it was.' This is an especially interesting opinion coming from an ex-policeman.

There are, however, various types of evidence that the jury is apparently not thought fit to consider. We have already discussed the instance of hearsay evidence, which the jury is explicitly forbidden to consider. But there are other types of evidence which lawyers are reluctant to let juries consider unaided. Among these are certain types of expert and circumstantial evidence. For instance, in the case of William Thomas Davies (convicted of cheque fraud, conviction later quashed after the Home Secretary referred the case back to the Court of Appeal), the expert evidence in question was that needed to match handwriting. In the absence of a handwriting expert the two dud cheques and specimens of Davies's handwriting were given to the jury for assessment. One of the reasons for the conviction being quashed was that it was contrary to previous court rulings to invite a jury to constitute themselves experts on handwriting analysis in this way, which might allow them to 'draw possible unfounded conclusions'.

Similar doubts have been expressed about letting the jury assess circumstantial evidence. These have been well expressed by an American judge, Chief Justice Shaw: 'The disadvantages [of circumstantial evidence] are that a jury not only has to weigh the evidence of facts, but to draw just conclusions from them; in doing which they may be led by prejudice or partiality, or by want of due deliberation and sobriety of judgment to make hasty and false deductions; a source of error not existing in the consideration of positive evidence."[49]

The judges and Parliament both appear to distrust the jury's powers of comprehension and decision-making in complex cases, since the right to trial by jury in civil actions has been consistently and considerably curtailed over time. Where the judge may still opt for trial with or without a jury, he usually dispenses with it.

The use of a randomly-selected jury in civil cases, then, has already been considerably cut down. Mr Justice Lawton has recently expressed similar doubts about the quality of the randomly-selected jury in complicated criminal cases, particularly involving commercial or financial matters. He recommends in these cases trial by a judge and a team of competent lay assessors.[50]

Most cases of mistaken imprisonment seem to us to occur because of mistaken identification or flawed statements or confessions, both of which are types of evidence considered fit for a jury alone to assess, rather than the forms of evidence discussed above. We are forced to come to one of two conclusions.

Either these are the most difficult forms of evidence for a jury to assess, in which case it is these types of evidence that a jury should be precluded from considering unaided (rather than those now placed in this category). Or a jury is incapable of assessing even these, the easiest forms of evidence, and the only ones really left for them to assess. If this is so, then the jury is the main cause of wrongful imprisonment.

Juries only try a very small proportion of all offences charged—only 3 to 4 per cent of all persons tried for all offences are tried on indictment. Most people are tried summarily before magistrates, even those on trial for indictable offences.[51] But just over half of the cases over the last twenty years where a pardon has been granted, or the Home Secretary has referred the case back to the Court of Criminal Appeal and the conviction has been quashed, were originally tried by juries. It would seem on the face of it that juries make a disproportionate number of mistakes. However, this assessment could be badly wrong for a number of reasons.

Firstly, a man who feels there is an element of doubt in his case is likely to plead not guilty and choose to be tried before a jury. Juries are thus faced with a disproportionate number of difficult and doubtful cases.

Secondly, we have only examined cases of wrongful imprisonment, not the wider category of wrongful conviction. A large proportion of people convicted at a magistrates' court are fined or put on probation rather than put in prison, whereas those convicted before a jury are very likely to go to jail.

Thirdly, where a person is sent to prison from a magistrates' court, it is likely to be for a much shorter time than someone sentenced by a judge after a jury trial. These people are therefore less likely to protest about their conviction, and the authorities are less likely to investigate it.

However, the kind of mistake that juries are usually credited with making is wrongful acquittal rather than wrongful imprisonment. Forty per cent of all persons pleading not guilty before a jury are currently acquitted. By contrast, Lord Parker, then Lord Chief Justice, estimated that only 10 per cent of those so tried actually deserved to be acquitted.[52] The police find it particularly galling that so many villains whom they have caught and prosecuted should finally be acquitted (very often wrongly) by naive and inexperienced juries. 'The jury', said one officer to us, 'is an important variable in the imperfectness of our legal system.' We think we know what he means.

It would seem that juries cannot be trusted in either direction. What could be done to improve the situation?

Possibly the whole concept of jury trial should be radically considered. We shall have some suggestions of this kind to make later in the chapter. Meanwhile, there are two broad innovations which could easily be grafted on to the present system. They are, firstly, that juries should be given agreed transcripts of all evidence; and secondly, that the qualifications for jury service should be more rational and more stringent, and that greater use should be made of special juries where appropriate.

The case of Augustine John Fletcher indicates that not only do juries need transcripts of the evidence, they sometimes actively ask for them. Fletcher was found guilty of attempted robbery, largely on rather shaky identification evidence. His defence was an alibi supported by his father, sister, some neighbours and a Salvation Army bandleader who had called to make a collection about the time the offence took place. He said that Fletcher had answered the door to him. The jury were out for two hours altogether. After half an hour, they asked for a transcript of the bandleader's evidence. The judge refused this, but read them his notes of it.

Firstly, this request does not seem to us unreasonable, and we feel it should have been complied with. The general point has been well put by C. G. L. DuCann: 'The points of both fact and law raised by both prosecution and defence could be tabulated in written form and their summaries made available in typescript to judge and jury. These would be very like the written pleadings in a civil action, and would be equally useful.

'Similarly, the summing-up of the judge could be summarised in a different transcript. This would contain, briefly expressed, the points of fact made on behalf of prosecution and defence as well as those which were common points to both, together with a statement of the law to be applied when considering those facts. . . . The written word is not subject to the treacheries of either understanding or memory. . . . It can be read, re-read, and studied at leisure. . . . [The present system] is productive of opportunities for mishearing, misapprehending or misremembering by one, more or all of the jury.'[53]

Secondly, we feel that an educational qualification is now more relevant to jury service than a property one. As more trials involve technical and scientific evidence, an ability to understand this without being overawed by it, becomes important. Also, the educated person is less rigid and dogmatic in his thinking, and more likely to be emancipated from 'basic beliefs'. He is more likely to be sceptical of his own and other people's everyday experience as applied to such evidence as identification and statements.

Special juries are rarely summoned at present, and we feel that they could be more often used. A special jury in a sense takes selection a stage further than we have been discussing. It will contain people who are not only educated and intelligent, but who have some special knowledge relevant to the case in point. Thus, in fraud cases—the kind of case where, as we have already pointed out, mistakes are most likely to be made and least likely to be cleared up— a jury of accountants and related professionals would be most competent to deal with the case.[54]

It seems to us that the special jury provides the only real alternative to a jury dominated by the judge. Professor Cornish, as a result of interviewing a large number of jurors, comments that jurors at any rate *feel* that they have been considerably influenced by the judge's summing-up. In particular, the judge seems to have a great influence on the verdict in cases which are finely balanced.[55] Glanville Williams writes: '. . . too obvious an attempt to overbear the jury in the summing-up may lead to rebellion or else to reversal on appeal. But an experienced judge can so marshal the facts and indicate the probabilities that, while professing to leave everything to the jury, he has in truth made their verdict himself. A tendentious summing-up becomes all the more persuasive when it is not dogmatic and purports to leave an unfettered choice to the jury. The judge, moreover, speaks with all the prestige of his position and with the appearance of impartiality deriving from the fact that he has hitherto played no prominent part in the trial. To the jury he is, in Stephen's striking phrase, "the voice of Justice itself". I was told by a recorder who was a strong supporter of the jury system, that when first appointed he used to sum-up to the jury with absolute impartiality, and the result was that the jury, being left to do its own thinking, acquitted most of the defendants. To avoid these failures of justice the recorder changed his method and summed-up in the direction he thought proper. The result was the expected number of convictions.'[56]

It is difficult to demonstrate to what extent judges influence jury verdicts. It is equally difficult to see why people are so shocked at the thought that they might do so. Presumably they fear that if the judge does exercise such influence, then the jury is revealed as redundant. There are some advantages in the judge playing a role of this sort, and perhaps it should be institutionalised. One way would be for the judge to retire with the jury while they consider their verdict, as already happens in some Continental countries.

An advantage of the judge playing a recognisedly more positive role would be that it would be easier to establish an appeal from a jury verdict. This would be true for various reasons. Firstly, there would be much less tendency to deify the jury once they had ceased to be a separate and sacred entity embodying the common man alone, sitting in judgment on his peers. Secondly, the judge could be held accountable for the verdict in a more open, direct and fair way that at present. As things stand, the jury sitting alone cannot be held accountable for its verdict. Its members are anonymous; there are too many of them; and they only play this role for a short time anyway. By its very nature, this is the only way in which a jury could ever be expected to function. By contrast, the judge holds a permanent appointment, and is a well known and accountable figure. If the judge did retire with the jury, written reasons could be given as to how the verdict was arrived at, and this could be used as a rational basis for an appeal.

We can understand that it is precisely because judges naturally wish to avoid this difficult responsibility that they regard the jury system as beyond criticism and alteration. They would appear to shelter behind the jury, yet, paradoxically, when a particular verdict is criticized, either by the Court of Appeal or more generally, the criticism is directed at the judge in his summing-up. In a sense, summings-up are made the scapegoats for bad verdicts.

Let us now return from our suggestions for greater judicial influence over the jury, to the question of the influence the judge exerts at present.

We shall discuss two aspects of the 'control' exercised by the judge over the jury. One of these is the judge's duty to warn the jury about specific problems involved in weighing-up particular kinds of evidence. These warnings are sometimes mandatory, and are a direct and legitimate exercise of the judge's influence. Secondly, there is the inevitable effect of the tone of the judge's summing-up on the jury. We speak of the judge as 'summing-up for a conviction' or 'summing-up for an acquittal'. The judge is liable to censure in the Appeal Court if he omits a mandatory warning or overdoes it when summing-up for a conviction. Paradoxically, the specific and sometimes compulsory warning may rebound and have the opposite effect to that which was intended. As Jerome and Barbara Frank put it: 'Most lawyers and judges think that the accused will be better off if the judge does not give the jury such a warning, for that sort of warning tends to rub in the very fact the jury is cautioned to disregard.'[57] In the American Wentzel case (see p. 68), the Franks discuss a slightly different instance of such warnings rebounding. In this case the jury was shown photographs of the corpse of a murdered woman. 'The judge warned the jury that: "However horrible a crime may have taken place as shown by these pictures, it does not indicate the guilt of this defendant. You will have no prejudice against anyone because of these photographs or anything like that. It may be they are to some extent shocking. They are only put into evidence for such aid as they may be to you, in determining the issue put to you for determination." The judge thus unintentionally fixed the horror of the photographs in the jury's mind.'[58]

The manifest function of the judge's summing-up is to instruct the jury. The latent function is to provide something which is essential but which is prohibited in an overt form—that is some sort of version of how the jury arrived at their verdict. The Appeal Court is chary of questioning or going behind jury verdicts. Nevertheless, they must do so from time to time. The judge's summing-up gives them a means of doing this without appearing to do so.[59] These latent aspects of the summing-up are shown in a case quoted by Lord Devlin: 'In the case in 1938[60] to which I referred, the judge was dissatisfied with a verdict of guilty because he felt he had made an error in his summing-up. So he refused to accept the verdict and ordered that the accused should be tried again. No doubt he thought that he was doing the fair thing by the accused, but in fact he was depriving him of the opportunity of having the conviction quashed on appeal.'[61]

In a sense, if someone is going to be wrongfully imprisoned, it is better from his point of view if the summing-up at his trial is biased against him. If he has been wrongly convicted and the summing-up was biased, then he will have good grounds on which to base his appeal, and the Court of Appeal will have a lever with which to overturn a jury verdict. A police inspector commented wryly: 'Any sign of bias towards the prosecution in the summing-up can lead to appeal and almost certain acquittal.' This can of course be as true for the guilty as for the innocent. A sophisticated villain who is being tried for a crime which he has committed may prefer (paradoxically, on the face of it) to be tried before a really prosecution-minded judge because he reckons that in his eagerness to secure a conviction, the judge may overdo it in his summing-up. The case is then more likely to go to appeal, and possibly the conviction will be quashed on grounds of misdirection.

Less fortunate is the innocent man wrongfully convicted despite a fair summing-up. This is what appears to have happened in the case of William Herbert Wallace. Wallace was convicted of murdering his wife, but his conviction was quashed by the Appeal Court. Belton Cobb describes the situation: 'As a rule an appeal against conviction is based on a claim of misdirection of the jury by the judge. Obviously no such claim could be made in this case where the summing-up had been all in the prisoner's favour, but had been totally ignored by the jury.

'There is, however, a clause in the Act which provides that the Appeal Court shall allow an appeal and set aside the conviction if they consider the jury's verdict one that cannot be supported having regard to the evidence—provided they feel, that a *substantial* miscarriage of justice has occurred (our italics).

'It is rare for that clause to be invoked in a case of murder, rarer still for such an appeal to succeed; indeed, there was not a single instance between 1907, when the Act came into force, [Criminal Appeal Act], and 1931 when an appeal on the ground that the verdict had been 'against the weight of the evidence' was made on behalf of Wallace.'[62]

Whereas the Court of Appeal will almost as a matter of routine quash a conviction for reasons related to the judge's summing-up, there has to be a *substantial* miscarriage of justice before it will overturn a perverse jury verdict arrived at against the grain both of the evidence and the summing-up. It is perhaps not surprising that the clause is 'rarely invoked' and that defence lawyers prefer to look for niggling errors in the summing-up.[63]

The whole process by which the Court of Appeal latches on to aspects of the judge's summing-up when considering a case of patently wrong conviction, rather than going back to the facts upon which the jury based its decision, is illustrated by Lord Chief Justice Parker's judgment delivered in the Court of Criminal Appeal on the case of Bridgeman, Francis, Brown and Pink. These were among those convicted on the evidence of Detective-Sergeant Challenor shortly before the scandal broke. The four had been convicted of carrying offensive weapons. 'The short facts were that these four appellants and Brown's wife entered the Establishment Club in Greek Street, Soho, on 25 May, introduced by the appellant Pink, who was a member. The prosecution's case was that, as a result of their behaviour, the police were sent for, and when they arrived the four men were taken, not without a struggle, out of the club, and it was said that they were searched, and that these weapons were found upon them. The defence was that they were not carrying these weapons at all, but that the weapons were planted upon them by the police officers. It is only right to say that that was not a defence just raised at the trial, it was something which they had said all along.

'These appellants have raised a number of matters in criticism of the summing-up of the learned commissioner. This court finds it unnecessary to deal with any save one of the complaints, and that concerns a passage of some length which appears on pages 19 and 20 of the summing-up. The learned Commissioner is dealing with this defence of the weapons being planted, and he points out quite rightly the coincidence, if it be that, that here there were not just one police officer but a number of police officers, something like eight involved, and accordingly the suggestion of planting involved all these eight officers. No objection can be taken to pointing that out to the jury, but the learned Commissioner then goes on in this way: "Fashions alter in defences. You are only concerned with this case. This type of defence, as has been rightly said, has become fairly common, and, indeed, since the days when every citizen like the accused can be granted and are granted legal aid, they have the great advantage of coming here, perhaps with solicitor and learned counsel supporting him, and maybe it is a great temptation for men like that to instruct counsel to make appear as respectable and plausible as possible something which otherwise, left to themselves, they would know to be quite hopeless. When learned counsel, with all the skill and oratory which they possess, put the matter, it is different. Whether that is the situation or not is perhaps only speculation. One can only judge by one's experience of these matters, and it has become as fashionable as it is now when prisoners—indeed, you read about it constantly and it is common knowledge— have made a statement confessing, getting it off their chest, and when they are brought to trial they deny they ever said anything of the kind, that the statement was never read over to them, that they did not know what it was; what is in the statement has been put down by the police. That is exactly the same thing here, with this variation: the suggestion is that these implements have been planted; not only that, but a much more extreme method of horticulture was used than the mere planting of all these implements; the words and expressions I have mentioned, they have all been planted too; the things they said, so far as they implicate them at all, they also, according to them, have been inserted by the police. Well, you cannot go much further than that. You cannot sink much lower. If the police descend to one level, it is only another short step below, for the descent downwards is easy enough, climbing up is not so easy.'

'This Court has said over and over again that there is nothing wrong in a judge in his summing-up expressing, maybe in forcible language, his views of the facts of the case, provided always that he makes it clear that the ultimate decision is for the jury and the jury alone. But there may be occasions, and this Court has come to the conclusion with regret that this is one, that even with a warning, the speech here of the learned Commissioner went so far as to make it appear patent to anyone that these men, albeit they were guilty [no one knows], were not having a fair trial. In this passage, not only is the learned Commissioner telling the jury perfectly plainly that this defence, which is the only defence and the only issue in the case, was quite ridiculous and absurd, but he was invoking references to his own experience on the Bench, and he was suggesting that with legal aid a defence such as this could be dressed up in an attractive form. It was with those two passages in mind that the jury then went away for the week-end, the summing-up being formally completed on the Monday morning.

'This Court with regret feels that it would be quite wrong to allow these convictions to stand, and accordingly they are all quashed. In the case of Brown and Pink, leave to appeal accordingly will be given, this will be treated as the hearing of the appeal, and the appeals, like those in the reference from the Home Secretary, will be allowed.'[64]

This is probably an instance of the Court of Appeal quashing a conviction for one reason while having another reason in mind. Various points arise in connection with this. Firstly, the appellants were lucky that the Commissioner's summing-up gave the Appeal Court something to latch on to. Secondly, it seems improbable that the appellants would have had their conviction quashed if there had not by this time (December 1963) been considerable doubts about the probity of Detective-Sergeant Challenor's investigations. This supposition is reinforced by the circumstances of the appeal. For Bridgeman and Francis, this was a reinstatement of an appeal earlier abandoned. When it came up again early in December, the Lord Chief Justice was at first unwilling to allow Bridgeman and Francis to appeal, on the grounds of a vague allegation of misconduct by the police. He indicated, however, that he might be prepared to give the appeal further consideration if it were referred to the Court by the Home Secretary. This seems to have two implications: firstly, that if the decision about whether the complaint had substance were in effect taken out of his hands by the Home Secretary, he would be prepared to consider it. If this happened, the judges could use the mere fact of the case having been referred to them by the Home Secretary as an indication that the complaint did have substance. Secondly, it would give them some concrete reason for searching out some suitable passage in the Commissioner's summing-up with which to overturn the jury's verdict, a procedure they were otherwise unwilling to undertake.

Before we go any further in discussing appeals procedure, it might be a good idea to consider the chance of getting an appeal heard at all, and if heard, of it resulting in a quashed conviction or a new trial. In 1969, 8,613 people applied for leave to appeal. Of these, only 608 were appealing against conviction alone, and a further 1,280 against both conviction and sentence. (The bulk of appeals were against sentence alone.) Of these 8,613 attempts, 4,579 were abandoned, and a further 3,174 were refused leave to appeal. Only 860 were granted leave to appeal. In other words, less than half these applications ever got to the stage of being considered, and only one-tenth of those who had originally wished to appeal eventually had their case heard in the Court of Appeal. Of the 860 who did reach the Appeal Court, it would appear that 281 were in one way or another appealing against conviction (out of the 1,888 who originally wanted to appeal against conviction). If you are appealing against conviction, then, the chance of your reaching the Court of Appeal are about one in seven.[65]

It is at this stage that the real sifting out occurs. If you actually get through to the Appeal Court, the chances of your conviction being quashed appear to be quite high. Of the 281 cases heard, 117 had their conviction quashed; 4 new trials were ordered; and 5 had their original conviction quashed and another substituted.

A study of wrongful imprisonment must therefore pay close

attention to the reasons why appeals fail to reach the stage of being heard by the Court.

There are two aspects of this. Why are so many appeals abandoned? And why is leave to appeal so often refused?

One important factor is the lack of proper facilities and legal advice to the prisoner when he is seeking leave to appeal.[66] At this stage, after conviction, there are not the same opportunities for legal aid and advice as there are at the original trial and again at the Appeal Court. We have earlier drawn attention to the frequent lack of continuity of legal representation between trial and Appeal Court for the person on legal aid. The break occurs at this point. A person unrepresented at this stage needs a certain amount of ability, determination and legal knowledge. An illustration of the kind of thing he may have to deal with can be drawn from the case of Ronald Barker (for details, see p. 25): 'After two or three days, I said: "I want to petition." The jailer said: "Nonsense." I said: "Are you refusing me my rights?" He said: "No, you seem to know all about it—you find out." So I got a form. Then I said: "I want to write to my MP." And he said: "No, you can't do both at once, write to your MP and put in a petition." But he denied saying this later.'

The prison authorities are not normally so unhelpful. In the case of James William Pearce (see p. 93) the Governor of Exeter Prison not only provided Pearce with facilities to make a second application to the Court of Criminal Appeal, after his first application had been refused, but went to considerable trouble, as did the Registrar of the Court of Appeal, to assist him in the difficulties he experienced when one of the crucial documents got lost.

This is by no means an unusual case. It is prison staff, and also the staff of the registrar's office, who provide much of the assistance needed by prisoners in framing their appeal applications. For them to bear the brunt of this is unfair both to them and to the prisoners. 'Justice' has put this very well in two of its reports. Its report on *Home Office Reviews of Criminal Convictions* notes: 'Individual prison and welfare officers have given their assistance in the preparation of petitions and have sometimes involved themselves in considerable effort, for example in obtaining papers and information from the former legal adviser of the prisoner. Although this assistance is gratefully appreciated by the prisoner concerned, its practical utility is limited. Prison and welfare officers have neither the time nor the resources nor the professional training to provide fully adequate advice and assistance.[67] The tenth annual report further comments:

'All those who have dealings with the registrar and his staff have nothing but praise for the helpfulness and efficiency with which, under great pressure of work, they prepare cases and assist appellants, whether legally aided or not. Their task would be very much easier if prisoners were better informed about appeal procedures and had adequate legal advice.'[68] One obvious way to improve the situation would be to extend the legal aid and advice scheme so that solicitors could be paid to visit and advise prisoners while they were framing their appeal petitions.

Another reason why many prisoners abandon appeals is the fear that if their application is refused their sentence will be deemed to run from the date when it was refused—that is they will lose all the time they spent as an appellant. Up until the Criminal Appeal Act, 1966, there was an automatic 42-day penalty for all unsuccessful applications to appeal. The Act abolished this, but the other penalty can still be applied at the discretion of the Court. This still deters some people from applying. See, for example, the case of William Thomas Davies (see p. 70). Davies applied for leave to appeal to the single judge, who dismissed the application but said: 'I have not directed any loss of time because the applicant was not unreasonable in seeking the decision of the single judge.' This masterly piece of ambiguity both encourages the prisoner to go further and discourages him from doing so. What really discouraged Davies, however, was the warning printed on the notice of rejection by the single judge that an applicant who goes on to take his application to the full Court may lose *all* the time spent as an appellant.

We have already discussed the Appeal Court's preference for basing its decisions on points of law rather than questions of fact. This applies also at the earlier stage of the appeal procedure, when an application for leave to appeal is being heard by the single judge or the full Court. In William Thomas Davies's case, the single judge said: 'This was a straight issue of fact for the jury, who took only twenty-four minutes to convict on one count of false pretences, and acquit on the other. Summing-up was completely fair and correct in law. . . . He no doubt feels—but cannot complain in law— that the prosecution was strengthened by the decision not to put in evidence the handwriting report.' It was because of this same handwriting report (see p. 71) that his case was later referred back to the Court of Appeal by the Home Secretary, and the conviction quashed. In other words, this case consisted of a straight issue of fact for the jury which they got wrong. But as the trial

116

was fairly conducted in law, Davies had nothing to complain of—in law.

Normally, the Appeal Court appears to use legal niceties to avoid the need to reconsider questions of fact. At times, however, it almost seems to use such points in order to prevent such facts from being presented to the Court at all. Patrick Moylan was convicted of robbery largely on the basis of a doubtful identification, together with two other men who also pleaded not guilty at the trial, but subsequently admitted their part in the affair. Later another man, Bernard Williams, confessed that he was the third man involved, and not Moylan. He gave a detailed and accurate statement of what had occurred, which was corroborated by the two other robbers. At Moylan's appeal, Williams refused to give evidence after being told by the judge that he need not do so. This destroyed the whole basis of Moylan's appeal. Professor J. C. Smith commented on this case: 'There was no point in warning Williams that he need not give any evidence that would incriminate him. Williams had already confessed to the crime editor of the *Daily Mirror*. He had made a full signed statement to the police, and had sworn an affidavit that was before the Court. . . . He could therefore have been put in the witness-box and questioned without incriminating himself further than he had done already. The Court's action and its failure even to ask the Home Office to have further inquiries made was an abdication of its judicial responsibility.'[69]

Appeals on questions of fact are generally granted only if some new evidence is produced which could not be produced at the original trial. The rule as to what constitutes new evidence is stringent. It is not enough to call evidence that was not presented at the trial: it has to be shown that it *could* not have been presented at the trial. This is why Thomas Hall's application for leave to appeal was refused by the three judges (though later the case was referred to the Court of Appeal by the Home Secretary, and the conviction quashed). One of the judges said on behalf of the three: 'Hall seeks leave to appeal against his conviction and asks for leave to call additional evidence in the form of two witnesses whom he says were not available at the trial. He also puts forward other grounds; suffice it to say in relation to that that, as indeed he himself admitted when he stated it at the trial after his conviction, he had a perfectly fair trial. The two witnesses whom he asks leave to call by way of additional evidence are the applicant and co-defendant Whitfield and also a man by the name of Maughan. Maughan is, significantly enough, a prisoner at Durham prison, where the applicant Hall was also taken, and it would appear that what he now seeks to prove by the evidence of these two witnesses is that he was not the person who was accompanying Whitfield on this occasion when the smash and grab raid took place, but that he was in fact accompanied by Maughan and that Maughan is the other man engaged in the crime.

'There was ample and convicing evidence of the identification of the applicant Hall as having been the man accompanying Whitfield. So far as this application for further evidence is concerned, first of all Whitfield was a witness who was available to the applicant Hall at the trial. Moreover, Whitfield, if there had been anything in this story that Maughan was the other man who was engaged, would have known that Maughan was the other man who was engaged, and consequently at the trial it could have been ascertained from Whitfield if in fact Maughan was the man who was accompanying him, or, what is much more important, it could have been ascertained from Whitfield, and Whitfield could have been called to say that Hall was not the man who was with him on that occasion. In those circumstances there was in fact nothing to have prevented Whitfield having been called to say that Maughan was the man and, he having identified Maughan, Maughan could also have been called as a witness. In those circumstances, the Court sees no ground why his application for leave to call additional evidence should be acceded to, and more particularly it is perfectly clear from the facts that were established, and from the evidence that was given, that the evidence of the additional witness Maughan it is now sought to call would be utterly lacking in conviction and could not carry any weight. Accordingly, this application is also refused.'[70] This difficulty in showing that new evidence really is new was clearly perceived by ex-PC Luckhurst: 'The final appeal was unsuccessful I think mainly because the Lord Chief Justice excluded the evidence which we had been told to get. We had been told to secure new evidence when I was given leave to appeal and then when the actual appeal came up we were denied the opportunity of providing or of giving this evidence in the Court.'

The Court of Appeal's unwillingness to reconsider evidence presented at the trial, and its stringency in assessing what constitutes new evidence, stem from its basic reluctance to re-enact the role of the jury. The Court of Criminal Appeal said, in rejecting Steinie Morrison's appeal: 'Bearing in mind that we are not entitled to put ourselves in the position of the jury, we can only come to the conclusion that the appeal must be dismissed.' But where new evidence is presented to the Court and is recognized as such, this is precisely what the Court has to do. The Court sees itself as considering how the jury would have assessed this evidence had it been placed alongside the other evidence presented at the trial. It is perhaps unfortunate that they will not use this same concept of an ideal typical jury to reconsider cases where there is no new evidence but where the trial evidence has probably been misunderstood.[71] Despite appearances, this is not what they do when they return a decision that a verdict was unsafe and unsatisfactory. What they are doing in this case is to apply powers which, as we have shown, they are extremely reluctant to use because this involves totally overturning a jury verdict.[72] There needs to have been a 'substantial' miscarriage of justice.

It is always a difficult business for the Court to imagine itself in the jury's position in considering this new evidence. This is particularly so where the new evidence is that the defendants allege that the police fabricated evidence against them. It is difficult enough for the jury to consider this sort of evidence; it is even more difficult for the Court of Appeal, at one remove, to consider how the jury would have acted. This difficulty is illustrated by two cases of this sort, which led to different decisions by the Court. In the case of Lovesay and Peterson (see p. 37) Lord Justice Widgery said: 'There were three possibilities arising out of this evidence. The first was that the evidence of the police was wholly reliable, that these pieces of paper had been found in the pockets of these two men on arrest. I pause to examine the likelihood or not of that being true. . . . The second possibility . . . was that there had been some muddle or mistake in the police station. . . . Clearly, it is a very unlikely explanation. . . . The third possibility was that these pieces of paper had been dishonestly planted by the police in and among the possessions of the accused. . . . We are impressed by the improbabilities of each of the first two alternatives, but when we come to ask ourselves: What would have happened if a plant had been run in the court below by the defence, we are up against a considerable difficulty, in that we do not know what the police evidence would have been. We do not know what the evidence would be from them, and what impression it may have made. This case has not been easy on that point, but in the end we cannot say that the verdict was unsafe or unsatisfactory on behalf of these matters, and therefore we are not disposed to grant leave of appeal on that point.'

Trevarthen and Cunliffe were convicted of burglary. Their application for leave to appeal was refused by the single judge, but their case was later referred to the Court of Appeal by the Home Secretary, and their convictions quashed. Trevarthen and Cunliffe were picked up by the police while loitering suspiciously in a road where a burglary was later found to have taken place. In the burgled house, a button from Cunliffe's cardigan was found; a jemmy and a torch were found near where the loiterers had been stopped; and a crowbar was found in their car. They were unable to give an explanation as to why they had been loitering in the lane earlier. In their defence, they claimed that the button had been planted by the police. No forensic evidence connected the instruments with the burglary.

In the course of an extensive, independent police inquiry, the Hendon forensic laboratory proved that the implements could not have been used in the crime and that the button had been cut off Cunliffe's cardigan, not pulled or frayed.

At the Court of Appeal, the appellants admitted that they had indeed been loitering with intent—but intent to steal a car, not to burgle a house. The Court of Appeal stressed that planting by the police had not been proven, and declared that: 'The question before this Court is whether the jury, having heard this evidence together with the other evidence at the trial, would nevertheless necessarily have come to the same conclusion which they did, namely that these men had been proved guilty.

'This Court has come to the conclusion that, looked at in that way, which is the only way in which this Court is entitled to look at it, it cannot be said here that if the jury had heard Dr Barclay's evidence in regard to the instruments and particularly the threads on the cardigan together with the appellant's present account of their presence in the lane, that the jury must have come to the same conclusion.'

There are several interesting differences between the two cases and the ways in which they were handled. In this case, the Court felt itself able to simulate jury reactions, whereas in the earlier case they did not. In some senses, this is a surprisingly radical move, since they were not in this case considering a 'planting' defence which had not been heard by a jury, but were reconsidering a revitalized defence which had already been turned down by a jury. But they were not being asked to consider a straight allegation of planting. Rather they were being asked to consider a situation from which an allegation of planting had emerged, and how the new evidence affected this situation.

Although in some respects these two cases are different, they do have some points in common. The fact that Lovesay and Peterson were not allowed to appeal on this issue does not preclude the fact that there is a large element of doubt in their case. The happier outcome of the Trevarthen/Cunliffe case seems to be due to the sensible way in which the Court and the police responded to the allegations made. The Court took the best possible course of action in finding the allegations of planting not proven, and yet quashing the conviction because of the element of doubt involved. This reinforces the point we made earlier that when an allegation of this kind is made, it is best dealt with if the emphasis is laid on restitution rather than retribution.

If the condition of Trevarthen and Cunliffe's getting off had been that they must demonstrate that the police had been guilty of misconduct, then this would have been to lay an almost impossible burden of proof upon them. The proof of intention is always very difficult, and perhaps the best thing is to lay the question of intention to one side—as the Court did in this case, where the most important thing was not whether planting had occurred, but whether there was sufficient doubt as to whether the men had committed the burglary.

The Court of Appeal recognized the radical nature of its usurpation of the jury's function in this case, and took pains to spell out the special circumstances which had led it to do this. In the Trevarthen and Cunliffe case the Court commented: 'It is quite clearly a matter for the jury to decide on this evidence, and in the ordinary way this would be just the sort of case in which the Court would order a new trial under the powers conferred by Section 7, Subsection 1 of the Criminal Appeal Act, 1968. That says that "where the Court of Appeal allow an appeal against conviction and do so only by reason of evidence received or available to be received by them under Section 23 of this Act, and it appears to the Court that the interests of justice so require, they may order the appellant to be re-tried."

'It is quite clear here that the interests of justice do not demand re-trial if only for the reason that these matters took place in December of last year, now a year ago, and when the only appellant who has been sentenced to a custodial sentence has had a sentence of twelve months' imprisonment and will clearly have served it by the time any re-trial took place. That is quite apart from the fact that there has already been not only the trial but a very extensive police inquiry.'

The Court took a similar line in the case of Pedrini and others (one of the cases concerning Detective-Sergeant Challenor), which came before them in July 1964. By this time the facts about Challenor had come out into the open, and perhaps they felt freer to take direct action: 'What of course this Court is concerned in these proceedings to decide is what effect that fresh evidence, if it could have been before the jury, might have had on their verdict. That it is fresh evidence this Court is prepared to accept; that it is relevant evidence there is no doubt; that it is credible evidence in the sense that it is capable of belief and of carrying some weight, is also clear. No one would suggest that the medical evidence (about Challenor's insanity) does not carry weight. Mr Buzzard for the prosecution has very fairly said that he does not require the doormen [new defence witnesses] to be called and cross-examined here, he is prepared to say their evidence, if it went before a jury, was capable of belief and might carry some weight.

'The Court has come to the clear conclusion in those circumstances that it is quite impossible to say that that evidence might not have put the jury in reasonable doubt. They say that with the full recognition that there were other witnesses, other than Sergeant Challenor, who gave evidence. There was of course the complainant, Gardiner, who as I have already said, was a man of bad character. There were also a number of police officers, of which P C Wells and P C Legge were two, who gave evidence in support of Gardiner. The Court would like to make it quite clear that they, as a Court, are in no way finding that those police constables' evidence was not honest and might not be fully believed, but at the same time it seems to this Court that with the additional further evidence before them, the jury might not have been able to attach the same weight to those police constables' evidence as they did at the trial itself. They may well have thought that, having regard to the fact that the commanding officer, as it were the officer in charge, might be tainted in the way suggested.'

These last are cases where the Court has used its discretion wisely. It is hard to see quite what difficulties would arise if it did this more often.

In this section we have repeatedly drawn attention to the restrictive nature of the rules concerning appeals on questions of fact, and the

Court of Appeal's narrow interpretation of these rules. But in fairness, it appears much broader in both its rules and its interpretation of them, than similar courts in other countries. American lawyers, writing about our Court of Appeal, lay particular stress on its liberality in regard to points of fact. Delmar Karlen writes: 'Appellate review of criminal cases in the United States is more frequent, but less broad in scope than in England. In the United States, one appeal is allowed as of right from virtually every criminal trial. . . . In England, very few cases can be appealed even once as a matter of right. Ordinarily, the Court of Criminal Appeal. . . grants leave] in not much more than 10 per cent of the cases in which application was made. . . . On the other hand, when review is allowed in England, its scope is broad. The Court of Criminal Appeal is empowered to review determinations of fact as well as determinations of law'.[73]

Edwin M. Borchard sees the latitude and liberality exercised by out Court of Criminal Appeal in this respect as an important reason why there is less wrongful imprisonment in Britain. He regards the English system as a model that the Americans should imitate. 'There should be a review by an appellate court on the facts as well as on the law in cases of felony, or at least in capital cases, as there is in New York and New Jersey and in England and Scotland. Appeals for errors of law only often defeat the interests of justice, not only in granting new trials on technicalities where no substantial injustice can be shown, but in refusing to set aside an unjust verdict merely because technical compliance with formal rules is established. The Court of Criminal Appeal in England and Scotland, fittingly enough, came into being through the egregious errors and negligence manifested in the Beck and Slater cases. In nearly all our States, the appellate courts can reverse a conviction only for errors of law. They are bound by the jury's finding of fact, however wrong they may consider the conclusion.'[74]

There are very real differences, now as when Borchard was writing, between the English and American systems. But Borchard is perhaps too much influenced by the spirit in which the English Court of Criminal Appeal was set up, rather than the way in which it has since functioned. The Court of Appeal was indeed set up following the uproar over the Beck case. Ironically, Beck's wrongful imprisonment was largely due to misidentification—a mistake of fact. This is perhaps the kind of case that the Court is most reluctant to deal with. However, this reluctance was built into it right from the start. Beck's case was merely the triggering factor which led to the implementation of an idea which had been in circulation for some time already. The Report of the Council of Judges in 1894 had earlier suggested that there should be a permanent Court of Criminal Appeal. It arose as much from conventional legal thinking as from the upset caused by a specific miscarriage of justice. The debate in Parliament on the setting up of the Act in 1907 showed that the legislature was also basically reluctant to allow appeals on points of fact. Thompson and Wollaston describe the debate: 'In the debates in Parliament during the passage of the Act of 1907, there was no controversy over the proposal that the appellant should have an absolute right to appeal against conviction on a point of law. Whether he should have a right to appeal against conviction on a point of fact was hotly debated. A major objection to the proposal was that it would interfere with the finding of the jury, and therefore infringed the sanctity [*sic*] of trial by jury. A suggestion that the Court be given power to order a new trial was strongly resisted, and the suggestion was dropped. The logic of this, which was duly followed, was the abolition of the pre-existing power to order a new trial.'[75]

When the Court of Criminal Appeal was first set up, the rules governing appeals on questions of fact were strict, and the Court interpreted them strictly. Over the last fifteen or twenty years, however, the statutes have been reformed and the Court's interpretation of them relaxed. Thompson and Wollaston show how this tendency has operated in the case of appeals where the original verdict has been set aside as 'unsafe or unsatisfactory': 'Section 4 (1) of the Criminal Appeal Act, 1907, gave the Court of Criminal Appeal power, on an appeal against conviction, to allow the appeal if it thought that the verdict of the jury should be set aside on the ground that "it is unreasonable or cannot be supported having regard to the evidence." From the outset, the Court acted upon the view that its function was circumscribed in appeals which raised issues of fact. Thus in the first case which came before the Court, Lord Alverstone, LCJ said: "It must be understood that we are not here to re-try the case where there was evidence proper to be left to the jury upon which they could come to the conclusion at which they have arrived. The appellant must bring himself within the words of Section 4 (1). Here there was evidence on both sides, and it is impossible to say that the verdict is one at which the jury could not properly have arrived." The Court continued to act upon this general principle;

thus in R. *v.* McGrath (1949) . . . Lord Goddard, LCJ, said: "where there is evidence on which a jury can act, and there has been a proper direction to the jury, this Court cannot substitute itself for the jury and re-try the case. That is not our function. If we took any other attitude, it would strike at the very root of trial by jury."[76]

The Donovan Committee pointed out: 'The view that the Court cannot re-try cases is clearly correct. What has been questioned in this context, however, is whether the Court is, or should be, debarred from interfering with the jury's verdict because there was some evidence to support it, and because it cannot therefore be described as unreasonable. Purely as a matter of construction of the language of Section 4(1) we cannot say that the interpretation adopted by the Court is open to serious doubt. If there was credible evidence both ways, and the jury accepted the evidence pointing towards guilt, it is difficult to say that the verdict was 'unreasonable' or could not "be supported having regard to the evidence" or that "there was a miscarriage of justice". If there be some defect in the situation which requires to be remedied, the defect lies in the statutory language rather than in its judicial interpretation.'[77] Thompson and Wollaston comment: 'The Donovan Committee believed that there was a defect which they illustrated by convictions based on mistaken identity. . . . The Donovan Committee considered that the law should be amended and recommended that the test should be whether under all the circumstances of the case the verdict of the jury was unsafe or unsatisfactory. This criterion had been suggested during the debates in Parliament on the Criminal Appeal Act, 1907, but had been opposed by the government on the ground that the words were too loose and obscure. The Donovan Committee pointed out that in spite of this rejection of the words 'unsafe or unsatisfactory' the Court sometimes acted as though this test was a proper test to apply to a jury's verdict; and as though the Court was entitled to quash a verdict which it considered to be unsafe or unsatisfactory in spite of there being some evidence to support it. . . . As the Donovan Committee pointed out, this evaluation of the evidence by the Court with the result that the Court found it inadequate is not easily reconcilable with the view that the weight to be attached to evidence is a matter for the jury who alone see and hear the witnesses.'[78] This recommendation has now been given effect in the Criminal Appeal Acts of 1966 and 1968.

Similar liberalisation has occurred with regard to the admission of new evidence,[79] the granting of retrials[80] and the condition under which the Home Secretary can refer a case to the Court.[81]

'Justice', in its tenth annual report, comments on such reforms: 'These reforms are gratifying, but we are not yet satisfied that the Court is making full use of its powers under the new Act, particularly in its interpretation of "unsafe or unsatisfactory" and the calling of new evidence.'[82]

We entirely agree with 'Justice' on this point. We feel too that there ought to be a greater shift towards latitude in the attitudes of the Court of Appeal—that is further steps in the direction in which they already seem to be moving.

Chapter 5

Witnesses, Credible and Incredible

This chapter is about why some witnesses are believed and others are not, when they are giving evidence about crimes they have directly experienced. From the point of view of a study of wrongful imprisonment, the two obvious categories are those where prosecution witnesses do not tell the truth, but are believed; and where defence witnesses tell the truth but for one reason and another are not believed.

Who are these witnesses, and in what kinds of cases are they involved? The two categories we have cited are very different. The prosecution witnesses who fail to tell the truth are often psychologically disturbed, and/or have been involved in a real or imaginary crime of an unpleasant and disturbing nature.

The defence witnesses' problems are much more straightforward. They are mainly concerned with alibis. A large proportion of people wrongfully imprisoned have previous criminal records, as do many of their associates. Since these are the people with whom they spend their time, these are the people whom they will need to call as alibi witnesses. These may indeed be the only people who can substantiate their alibi.

We have already shown how easy it is for the prosecution to attack and discredit a witness of this sort (see p. 88 *re* Johnny Wandless in the Cross brothers case.) There may also be other problems facing the defendant most of whose alibi witnesses are of this type. Kenneth Cross summed up the situation when he said: 'Many of our alibi witnesses had records. If you have a past and most of your friends have records, you can be stuck for an alibi.' We have already discussed the problems of choosing the best witness in a situation of this sort. Even where honest witnesses are available, they are not necessarily the best ones to call. The witness with a record may give more accurate and more relevant testimony.

But this presupposes that you have some choice of witnesses. This is not always the case. In practice, your choice may be further cut down because not all the witnesses theoretically available to the defence want to appear in court. Ronald Barker describes the problems he had: 'I was sleeping-off a hangover in the hotel, and I went out to get a can of soup. They thought that was ridiculous for a start, not having soup in a hotel. I saw an elderly lady and a man paving the garden for her. She didn't want to go to court, he didn't really want to, and the police didn't particularly encourage them to. . . . Honest people are less used to the court, and more reluctant to go there.' The witnesses actually called at Barker's trial both had records, and for this reason the jury chose not to believe them.

Some people, as we have shown, have no alternative but to call witnesses of this kind. In this case, other witnesses were available. Why, then, were they not called? Barker thinks that the lawyers defending him believed he was guilty, and that the alibi witnesses were lying to protect him:[1] 'They thought I was guilty because of the depositions. They thought that respectable people telling lies in court would break down and crack in the box. But the two brothers had records, and they could deal with it. That's why they only called the crooked ones.'

It is not only honest witnesses who are reluctant to appear in court. Crooked ones, for very different reasons, may be equally unwilling. William Curbishley (see p. 78) called an alibi witness at his appeal who had not appeared at his trial. This man was afraid to come forward in case he, too, was charged with the offence. He said: 'I had no guarantee at all. If I'd been arrested and put on an identification parade and someone—a member of the public—had picked me out, made a perfectly genuine mistake, I'd have been arrested and charged no matter what alibi I had. I didn't want anything to do with it. It was self-preservation. It would have been much worse if it had been me doing fifteen years instead of Curbishley.'

Why, in these cases, were the 'more honest' or 'better' witnesses not subpoenaed anyway, willing or no? This may be because the defendant does not wish them to be called, and may conceal their existence, or at least the quality of their evidence, from his lawyers. This may be because he does not wish to involve his 'honest' friends with the courts; or because he does not wish to involve his friends with criminal records in the risk of appearing as witnesses and ending up as suspects.

Again, their lawyers may be of the opinion that an unwilling witness, forcibly summoned to court, may prove a bad witness for the defence.

One might add in this context that, for a lawyer defending a man with many criminal associates, one of his most difficult tasks will be this very selection of alibi witnesses. It is a situation in which, whatever line you take, it is impossible to be sure that it will not prove disastrous for your client in court.

In this situation, he often does not know whether or not the client is telling the truth about his alibi. If his client is a practising criminal, his alibi may well be that he was out committing another crime at the time. Even if the crime on which he was actually engaged was a less serious one, he may hope to be convicted of neither. He will therefore not admit the minor offence, has no adequate alibi, and gets convicted of a major one. This is what C. H. Rolph suggests may have happened in the case of Emery, Thompson and Powers, convicted of assaulting a policeman and causing him grievous bodily harm in the course of a robbery, but later pardoned. Rolph gives a detailed account of this case. He describes the alibi story as put up by Thompson and corroborated by the other two. They had, they said, been out to discuss business with a Mr Bloomfield that evening: 'So that evening at about 8 o'clock they drove out to have a talk with Mr Bloomfield and his wife at Ashford. There, Mrs Bloomfield (of whom not much is known except that she was a tireless maker of tea) said that her husband was out; and could they call back later? Then Powers suggested that they could fill in the time by going to look at a lorry for sale in Watford. On the way they stopped at two garages, ostensibly (and so far as Thompson knew) to buy petrol, but in reality, according to a later statement attributed to Emery, to size up one or other of the garages as a place to be robbed a few nights later.

'Thompson always maintained that he knew nothing of any plan to rob garages until he learnt of it in prison two years after his conviction at Northampton Assizes. In any case, the lorry at Watford proved unsuitable for their purpose, and they drove back to the Bloomfield's house at Ashford. Arriving there (opportunely and significantly) just in time to hear the six pips that preceded the radio ten o'clock news. Mr Bloomfield was "still not home from work"; and this time they settled down to wait for him, playing cards and drinking innumerable cups of tea. They waited for five hours! And at the trial, they were able to call a witness, an Ashford scrap-dealer, who had seen their car outside the Bloomfields' from 11.30 p.m. until after 3 a.m.

'This must all have seemed as odd to the jury as to most of us, this driving about to inspect eligible lorries after dark, this sleepless card-playing in the small hours, in the house of a man whose wife would get cups of tea for them, apparently, all night.'[2]

In the above account, Rolph suggests that this is not what the men were really doing that night. After they were pardoned, the Home Secretary said: 'The only perjury that occurred or which has come to light as the result of the inquiry, was that of the prisoners themselves. Indeed, I have it on the authority of the trial judge to say that, had they not perjured themselves so much during the course of the trial, they probably would not have been convicted. . . . It must be remembered that one alibi at least of one of the prisoners was that they were not concerned in the attack on the policeman because they were in fact on the way to steal a safe in Watford.'[3] At the hearing in the magistrate's court, the police alleged that Thompson, while being fingerprinted, had said: 'I've already told your governor we know nothing about it. We had been to Watford to do a peter [a safe].'[4] At his trial, Thompson denied that he had ever said this, and produced the alibi quoted above.

Evidence other than an alibi can be unusable for the same reason. In the case of Gerald O'Halloran, who got seven years for possessing gelignite and for assault on a police-officer, an important piece of evidence linking him to the crime was that his car was used in the committing of it. The morning after, his car was found abandoned near the scene of the crime, with documents in it relating to him. On the face of it, it seems unlikely that he would so carelessly have incriminated himself in this way, since he was a very experienced criminal with a string of convictions. His explanation was that the car had been stolen from him before the crime was committed. But he did not report this immediately to the police. Why not? And why did this explanation not stand up in court? The reason seems to have been that he was working some sort of fiddle against the company which was hiring him the car, and was also 'using a driving licence with intent to deceive'. He pleaded guilty to the latter charge in court. It would appear that he was reluctant to come into contact with the police at all as regards the car, because he wanted to conceal both these peccadilloes from them. Once in court, he admitted the offence regarding the driving licence, but gave contradictory evidence in his efforts to avoid examination of his dealings with the car-hire firm.[5]

Even where an alibi is given which appears to be largely true, it can be wrecked by the addition of untrue details which are exposed in court and discredit the entire alibi. This is what seems to have happened in the case of the man we shall call Timothy Riordan, who was convicted of robbery on rather shaky identification evidence. His defence was an alibi supported by his wife, a friend, and one of their neighbours. In addition, another alibi witness testified that they had collected their baby from her about 8.40 a.m. (the crime occurred some miles away on the other side of London at 12 noon and the criminal had been seen preparing for it early at 10.30 a.m.). But Mrs Riordan had claimed that this witness had also called at their home later that morning at 11 a.m. The baby-minder denied this, and said that when she had called at 11 o'clock, she had stayed in the hall and not gone upstairs. She added that Mrs Riordan had tried to persuade her to say that she had seen Riordan and his friend asleep upstairs. The judge pounced on this inconsistency in his summing-up: 'There are few more dramatic moments in a criminal trial than when an alibi, as some people put it, cracks wide open.' As one comment on the trial pointed out: 'In fact, all it shows is the possibility that [Mrs Riordan] tried to induce [the baby-minder] to strengthen it. Otherwise, it fits with Riordan's story.'

If a man can be shown to have produced a false alibi, the jury may cease to consider whether enough evidence has been brought to prove him guilty: he looks guilty. From their point of view, he must be guilty, or why should he fabricate or embroider his alibi? Sometimes a summing-up can rub this point in even where the alibi had not been discredited by the evidence. In one case of attempted robbery, the judge in his summing-up ridiculed alibi defences in general: 'An alibi may be a perfectly genuine defence. ... I have only had two of such cases in the whole of my career at the law. ... In each case I am bothered if the men didn't prove that they were in prison .... Well, that is the best possible alibi. ... Absolutely watertight. But generally speaking, people don't have such splendid alibis.

'There are two ways [of fixing an alibi]. ... One way is to get together some real pals amongst whom there may be some gullible fool who can be persuaded into saying he saw a particular thing: but very often they are not just gullible fools but dishonest persons who are prepared to give a highly circumstantial story as to what they were doing. . . . But a far better one is to get some of your friends and relatives to describe what really did happen, but it is on the wrong day.'[6] The defendant was, not surprisingly, convicted despite a strong alibi backed by several honest persons of good reputation. The Court of Appeal was very critical of the summing-up, but refused leave to appeal.

The people most in danger of being wrongfully imprisoned because defence witnesses are not believed are those with a criminal background. They are the most likely to have criminal associates whom they may be forced to call as witnesses. For many reasons (among them the ones we have just been discussing), these can rebound on the defence. Furthermore, defendants of this type are more likely to have been out committing another crime, or doing something else rather discreditable, at the time of the main offence. These people often tend to distrust the legal system, and so are likely to tell gratuitous lies in court. Because they are frequently stupid, it is unlikely they will get away with this. It is not unreasonable to postulate that the people who tend to become criminals may be the kind of people who tend to resort to lies in any situation.

Where the witness in question is a prosecution witness, then the problems encountered are very different. With the defence witnesses we have been discussing, they probably choose to lie or to tell the truth according to how their interests, or the interests of the associates, are best served. Where prosecution lies or exaggerations are concerned, it is not often that the witness stands to obtain any simple, tangible benefits from his act. (No doubt there are miscarriages of justice which occur as a result of evidence given for the prosecution by informers and accomplices, but we have not come across any amongst cases of acknowledged wrongful imprisonment.)

More common motives in the cases we have come across are a desire for revenge, malice, hysterical fear and anger induced by a frightening situation, and hurt pride. Defence lies are instrumental; prosecution lies are expressive.

According to C. G. L. Du Cann, Travers Humphreys said that 'he had never had a case of a man and had had many cases of a woman who from envy, hatred and malice, deliberately and falsely charged another person with crime, knowing that person to be innocent, and gave false evidence to support that false charge. Charges of sexual indecency by women, quite without foundation, were in his fifty years' experience of crime so frequent that he came to think of them as one of the commonplaces of crime. And his conclusion was that, in any sexual case, the evidence of the woman concerned should be "watched and probed" with the greatest care.'[7] Our experience bears out Travers Humphreys, both with regard to witnesses and with regard to the kind of crime. Even where women have made false accusations in non-sexual cases, the kind of hysteria and emotionalism which hangs over them is that commonly associated with repressed sexuality.

The law recognizes that there are problems in this area. A judge is required to warn the jury of the danger of convicting without corroborating evidence in cases involving sexual offences, because, false accusations are often made in this type of case as a result of fantasy, misunderstanding or spite. Notwithstanding these precautions, miscarriages of justice do occur. It is interesting to note that the two categories of evidence leading to wrongful conviction specifically stressed by the Donovan Committee in its report were (a) misidentification and (b) accusations made by the victim of an apparent sexual assault.[8]

In particular, they were referring to the type of case where intercourse or some other sexual activity took place with the consent of both parties, but where the woman later claims that she was forced into it. This is what seems to have happened in the case of a man we shall call Mr Stevenson, who was sentenced to four years' imprisonment for rape. The circumstances of the case were these: Mr Stevenson and the woman were neighbours, and apparently well known to each other. Stevenson took the woman into a house in the street where they both lived, and they had sexual intercourse. Stevenson claimed that she consented to this because she had had a quarrel with her husband and wanted to get her own back. Afterwards she became hysterical and tearful and said 'My husband will kill me if he finds out.' In this state, she ran to a neighbour and claimed that Stevenson had forced her into the act.

At the trial, there was little evidence to corroborate her story. The evidence of the neighbour was admitted on the exception to to the hearsay rule known as 'instant complaint', that is where the victim of an indecent assault, rape, etc., complains immediately afterwards to a witness, the witness can testify to this in court and this evidence can be regarded as corroboration of the victim's story.[9] The medical evidence was very slight, and inconclusive. Nevertheless, Stevenson was convicted. During the trial the woman said: 'Well, I was pregnant at the time; and I lost the baby through all this trouble.' Clearly, this influenced the judge when it came to sentence. He said: 'She was pregnant at the time, and as a result of what happened to her she had a miscarriage. You have done great harm to her. I do not take much account of your past record. In the main, these other offences were of quite a different character; but in the circumstances I think that the least sentence I can pass on you is that you will be imprisoned for four years.' This part of her story regarding the miscarriage was later proved to be inaccurate. The 'rape' took place on 10 August. She gave birth to a child on 16 May following, the birth being eight days' overdue. Gynaecologists commented that if the due date was 8 May, she could not have had a miscarriage after 10 August. Inquiry agents subsequently took a statement from another man that he had been the victim of a similar accusation by the same woman in the month previous to the 'rape', after which she tried to blackmail him.

Why did the police decide to prosecute Stevenson, when they so often choose not to do so when faced with accusations of this kind? It may well have been because he had a number of previous convictions for larceny and office-breaking. Although the judge explicitly excluded consideration of Stevenson's previous record when sentencing him, it may well have influenced the police when deciding whether to bring the prosecution in the first place. Once again, this time for apparently irrelevant reasons, the man with the criminal record appears to run a greater risk of wrongful imprisonment.

Although, as in many cases of this kind, the woman's motives seem to have been mixed, they are much more a means to a tangible end than is usual. Blackmail is easily comprehensible in these terms, and so also is a very real fear of her husband's reactions if he had found out about this act, and thought she had consented to it. But even in this relatively straightforward case, more complex emotions were at work. In particular, why did she state under cross-examination that she had had a miscarriage when she probably had not? Could this have been because an element of revenge was involved, since she wanted to make the incident look as nasty as possible in order to put Stevenson in the worst possible light?

In the Stevenson case, the woman's motives seem equally balanced between the instrumental and the simply malicious. In other cases, the malicious element seems to be dominant. Such a one is the case of a man we shall call Thomas White, who got ten years for rape.[10] White was driving in his van with his girl-friend, when they picked up an 18-year-old girl hitch-hiker. They drove into a quiet street so that White and the hitch-hiker could have intercourse in the back of the van. The girl said she was afraid of getting pregnant, so White rubbed some contraceptive cream on her. In the course of this, the girl undressed. Both these things would seem to show that she was originally a willing partner. They had intercourse, after which she claimed that White forced her to suck him off. He says this was voluntary, and that she was very good at it and had obviously done it a lot of times before. White then beat her on the bare buttocks with a cane which he normally kept for his dog. They then drove to the outskirts of the girl's home town, where they dropped her off.

On her way home, the girl passed the local police station, but she did not go in and complain at this stage. Nor did she tell her family of the incident when she arrived home. It was only the following day at work that she revealed to anyone what had happened. Later, she took her story to the police and complained that White had raped her. White and his girl-friend, who was charged as an accessory to the offence, both said she had consented throughout. The only corroborating evidence was that White acted guiltily under the pressure of the police investigation. He took the mattress and the kinky mirrors out of his van after the police called; he gave evasive answers to police questions; and he and his girl-friend tried to fake an alibi. Given what had happened in the van, it is hardly surprising that he acted in this way, even if no offence had been committed. Possibly this, seen in conjunction with the sore bottom, corroborated something, but scarcely a charge of rape.

Technically, this was regarded as providing corroborating evidence, but the crucial issue remains, who, in a case of this sort, is to be believed? It is simply one person's word against another. A jury is not likely to believe that a self-confessed kinky pervert like White would stop short of rape. He would not necessarily bother to gain the consent of his partner. Anyway, what partner would consent to such outrageous and painful sexual antics? If the only issue had been one of rape, then the jury might have disbelieved the girl when she said she hadn't consented to it. But they would be only too ready to believe that she had not consented to the other vile perversions; and by extension, that she had not consented to intercourse either.

After White and his girl-friend had been convicted, other evidence came to light which had not been available at the trial and which pointed to his being innocent. Investigation among her associates by an inquiry agent revealed that she often hitch-hiked home at night, and admitted to doing so that night. This contradicts her claim that White and the girl-friend forced her into the van after she had refused a lift from them. The inquiry also showed that she had taken methedrine earlier that night, though she had denied doing so in court. She was shown to be sexually experienced, and not the innocent girl who had been presented at the trial. At the time of the trial, she already had a conviction for dishonesty, and since has been convicted of attempting to steal money by false pretences and illegally possessing heroin. Even more damning, two and a half years after White was convicted, an anonymous letter was sent to the defence solicitors, which also contained two obscene photographs featuring the girl. They show her in a field, naked except for a suspender belt and stockings, sucking a man off. Either she was in the habit of doing voluntarily the 'repulsive' act she claimed White had forced upon her; or else she has been the victim of several such assaults. The covering letter commented: '[The girl] is a liar. She told lies in court about she was raped in a van. She told us all she made it up because of the meths and heroin. . . . I took these two photos out of her bag in the ladies. She's always doing this with men. The man in prison told the truth.'[10]

Why, if this was the girl's habitual behaviour, was she so bothered by the incident with White? There seem to be various possibilities. One is that there were rather special circumstances on this occasion which led her to feel resentful. She may have consented to intercourse, fellatio and even the beating, but it may have turned out more humiliating and painful than she bargained for. Even if it was exciting at the time, it may have appeared unpleasant in retrospect. A further possibility is that the whole experience came to appear unpleasant when she saw other people's reactions to her description of the events—a description that may originally have been a boast, not a complaint. This would explain her delay in making a complaint to the police. L. Kennedy makes the point that indecent assault, which would have seemed the more feasible charge, since 'consent is no defence to indecent assault which causes bodily harm', carries a much lighter penalty than rape: 'the maximum for the one is life, for the other it varies as to whether it is on a male [ten years] or on a female [2 years].' Once a complaint had been made, events may have taken on a momentum of their own. Kennedy says: 'It could be said that [the girl], humiliated by the unexpected presence of another woman and an unlooked-for beating, had every reason to feel malice; and that a charge of indecent assault, for which there was visible proof, grew imperceptibly into a charge of rape.'

Another possibility is that although she committed such acts regularly, possible under the influence of stimulants such as methedrine, that she equally regularly felt guilty afterwards. Since the effect of such stimulants can be to do away with people's normal inhibitions, they may well do things under their influence which they would normally feel restrained from doing. Their normal feeling of guilt after such acts may also be accentuated by the depression people may feel once the effects of the drug have worn off. Presumably her more regular lapses occurred with people she knew, and against whom she could not work off her guilt by making false complaints and accusations against them. But here was a complete stranger, in connection with whom no such restraints operated.

Either way, the more serious charge of rape rather than indecent assault was a more satisfactory way of projecting her feelings of guilt and getting her own back. If someone else alone is publicly blamed for an action in which you participated and about which you now feel guilty, then this restores you to the state of subjective innocence which you would have enjoyed if you had not taken part part in the activity at all.

Cases involving sexual offences are always difficult. Many of these cases involve children; and cases involving children present problems of their own. They may find it difficult to distinguish between fantasy and reality.[11] For various reasons, they are likely to tell lies in a more unpredictable way than adults. Children who have told lies often resist fanatically having to admit that they have lied. By themselves they find it hard to distinguish lies from truth, and yet they are very well aware that adults regard the telling of lies with strong moral disapprobation.[12] We have already discussed the problems created by the lack of accuracy of perception and memory in adults, especially with regard to cases of misidentification. Children experience these problems to a greater degree than adults, and in a wider variety of circumstances. Again, adults are susceptible to suggestion and rehearsing: children are even more vulnerable to pressures of this kind.

The law recognizes that there are difficulties in accepting children's evidence. If a judge satisfies himself that the child knows the meaning of an oath or affirmation, then the child will be allowed to give sworn evidence in court just like an adult. If a child is too young or immature to appreciate the meaning of the oath, but nevertheless knows the meaning of 'telling the truth', then the judge may allow the child to give unsworn testimony in court. In this case, the judge must instruct the jury not to convict solely on the unsworn evidence of the child. There must be corroborating evidence, and the unsworn testimony of another child is not regarded as 'corroboration'. We have already mentioned the rule that in cases involving sex offences the judge must warn the jury of the danger of convicting on the uncorroborated testimony of the victim. This rule applies equally where the victim is a child. There may be added difficulties where this is so because of the traumatic effect of the assault and its aftermath on the child. This may particularly be so where the child's parents and the authorities have made a great fuss about the incident.[13]

A typical case of what may happen where a child asserts that it has been indecently assaulted was that of the man whom we shall call James Connelly. In this case an 8-year-old girl claimed that she was assaulted, and said that Connelly was the man who assaulted her. She knew Connelly, since she was often in his house playing with his children. The alleged assault took place on one of these occasions, when Connelly was home sick from work. He says that he was bothered by the noise the children were making, and rather abruptly told them to clear off, and says that he never assaulted her.

The child's description of the man who assaulted her was rather vague and changeable. At first, she said it was a man with a beard. Later, in the magistrates' court, the mother said the girl had described the man as 'like father when he'd not had a shave'. By the time the case got to the appeal court, the man was being described as having a moustache. The vagueness of these descriptions is strange in view of the fact that the child was supposed to know Connelly. If on the other hand it was held that she did not know him, then presumably there would have been an identification parade instead of the rather unsatisfactory procedure that was in fact adopted. Connelly describes what happened: 'I was alone in the police station. The girl came into the room, with a woman police-officer. She was asked; "Is that him?" I was sitting down, she couldn't even see my face.' On the child's evidence and on her mother's evidence under the 'instant complaint' rule[14] and on some rather slender medical evidence which proved only that the child might have been assaulted, Connelly was convicted, and spent over a year in prison.

Connelly appealed, and at the Appeal Court the defence presented some new and crucial evidence to the effect that the girl had been assaulted by her own brother two years earlier. It so happened that the prosecution brief was originally given to the same barrister who had previously prosecuted her brother. He refused to accept the brief, and went to see the defence barrister. The police and the girl's mother knew of the earlier assault, but never mentioned this evidence in court. Only the chance intervention of the other barrister after the first trial brought the matter to light. It also turned out that the brother had assaulted other children, and that the local child-care officer had a dossier on the peculiar mores of this family. Two possibilities emerge from this. One is that the brother may have assaulted her again, but she was afraid to say so, and so pushed the blame on to a stranger. Or the mother may have put her up to it to keep the brother out of jail. The other possibility is that the girl had fantasies about being assaulted following the previous assault by her brother. Annoyed by her abrupt treatment by the accused, she may have pinned the fantasy on him.

At the trial, the girl denied several times that she had ever been assaulted before. At the appeal, the defence naturally wanted to lay stress on this point; but the judge refused to allow them to pursue it, and declared that the child had simply forgotton the previous offence, since it had occurred two years before, and that in the interests of the child these memories should not be revived.

The defendant's wife claims that the child had been coached in what to say by her mother, had been well-rehearsed before the trial, and seemed to 'enjoy going to court and being a little heroine'. The defendant and his wife are understandably resentful that during the trial the defence were unable to cross-examine the child as rigorously as they would have liked. As always in these cases, they were doubly restrained, both by deliberate intervention of the judge and by fear of offending the jury's sensibilities. In most cases, there are two considerations uppermost in everybody's mind and which affect the conduct of the trial. They are the need to protect the innocent from wrongful conviction, and the need to ensure that the guilty do not get off scot-free. In trials involving sex offences, however, a third consideration appears: the desire to spare the victim the need to relive a harrowing experience in the course of the trial. This can lead to a less than satisfactory examination of the facts. It can have two unsatisfactory results: the innocent may be wrongly convicted, and a guilty sex-criminal may escape conviction. The facts do not emerge either because, as in the case just discussed, there is no proper cross-examination of the key witness, or because a trial never takes place. This may happen because the defendant is persuaded to plead guilty, possibly to a lesser offence than the one with which he was originally charged, so that the victim may be spared the necessity of appearing in court at all. This may, as in the case of Henry Morgan (see p. 54) result in an innocent man pleading guilty to a lesser offence than the one with which he was originally threatened, but neither of which he committed; or of course it can result in the perpetrator of some enormity only pleading guilty to a much less serious offence. Another reason for no trial taking place is that the victim flatly refuses to come to court, and is consequently unwilling to assist the prosecution sufficiently for a charge to be brought.

People are sometimes brought to court for assaulting children when the whole thing is a fabrication, and no assault of any kind took place. One common instance of this is where a daughter is incited by her mother to accuse her father of assaulting her. The mother may want to get rid of her husband for some reason, and the daughter may herself bear a grudge against a strict father. Adults, too, can make imaginative accusations of this kind. Roy Dovaston was convicted of indecently assaulting a woman client in the estate agent's office where he worked as a clerk. The woman claimed that he tried for about ten minutes to commit an indecent act, and that she struggled and screamed the whole time. However, a house-painter and decorator working immediately outside the office said that he heard no screams and saw the woman leave in a calm state. A woman employee in the office confirmed that this was so. Dovaston spent five months in prison before his conviction was quashed at the Court of Appeal, where Lord Justice Widgery commented: 'This is a classic case in which a conviction was recorded on virtually uncorroborated evidence, and against a background of respectable witnesses whose testimony showed that the man was not guilty. . . . We regard this as quite a remarkable case. It is, in our view, quite impossible that this assault, or anything like it, should have happened without the witnesses having some idea that something had occurred.' It is difficult to see quite what motive the woman can have had, but the Appeal Court drew attention to the fact that Dovaston owed her money.[15]

In view of the comments of the Court of Appeal, it is hard to see on what evidence the jury based their guilty verdict. This unusually strong disagreement about a verdict between the Court of Appeal and the trial jury fits in with the findings of the Lord Chief Justice's survey of Queen's Bench judges for the American jury study. The survey indicated that the judges thought that juries convicted where they would have acquitted only in a very few cases, of which sexual offences formed the only coherent group.[16]

Bearing this in mind, it is tempting to recommend that cases involving sexual offences should not be tried before a jury at all. There seem to be three big disadvantages involved in a jury trying a case of this kind. Individually and collectively, they are likely to hold strong prejudices about this kind of case, and in most cases they will tend to be biased against the accused, whether he committed the crime or not, simply by virtue of his being accused of it. Secondly, because they are biased, they have great difficulty in weighing up the evidence unemotionally, and are prone to disregard the judges' warning about the desirability of corroborating evidence. Thirdly, if there were no jury that might be offended, the defence could cross-examine the victim much more thoroughly.

It is interesting to note in this context that though juries are more than eager to convict in most cases involving sexual offences, they are paradoxically ready to acquit in certain instances, notably where adolescents are accused of indecently assaulting a girl under 16, or having unlawful sexual intercourse with a girl between 13 and 16. Perhaps this is because they have learned rigorously to suppress any inclination to commit most sexual offences. But these peccadilloes are part of many people's youth, and so they are unwilling to regard them as crimes.

It is perhaps rather radical to suggest not taking sex cases before a jury. It seems to us that there are meanwhile some minor ways in which the system might be improved. The basic problem in all these cases is how to get the truth out of the victim without upsetting her too much. In the case of adult witnesses, what is probably needed is the encouragement of a more ruthless and rigorous cross-examination of the victim, possibly with the judge instructing the jury not to take umbrage at this. It might help the witness to be more frank without embarrassment if that part of the trial were held *in camera*. Such a course of action in the case of children would probably not be feasible or acceptable. It would not be feasible because there is no guarantee that this would elicit the truth from the child anyway. It would not be acceptable because such a hostile and public cross-examination might have a traumatic effect on the child. How then can one get the truth out of children? One method might be to have the child questioned in private by a person acceptable to the defence who is used to dealing with children in this way. An experienced and devious child psychologist would probably be the best person.

Up till now, we have been dealing with cases of an overtly sexual nature. We now come to a series of cases which do not involve explicit sexual assault, but which exhibit many features in common with sex cases. They seem to be mostly perpetrated by women on women.

The most obvious, and perhaps the most frequent crime in this category, is the sending of poison-pen letters. These are often full of sexual innuendoes, obscenities, and accusations of sexual misconduct, perversion and cruelty. There have been a number of cases in which one woman has falsely accused another of sending just such letters where she herself has written them: and this has sometimes led to the accused woman being imprisoned.

Just such a case was that of Mrs Rose Emma Gooding[17] who was accused by a neighbour, Miss Swan, of sending her obscene and libellous letters. She claimed to have seen Mrs Gooding push one of these letters under her door and an old man said he had seen Mrs Gooding's daughter posting a letter addressed to Miss Swan. Miss Swan complained to the police and Mrs Gooding was sentenced to fourteen days in prison for sending the letter. When she was released the police advised her to move out of Littlehampton to another town. Some time later, early in 1921, Miss Swan complained to the police that she had received further obscene letters. This time Mrs Gooding was sentenced to twelve months' imprisonment. She tried to appeal but the appeal was refused. Mrs Gooding now sent a petition to the Home Secretary saying she was innocent. The Director of Public Prosecutions, who was uneasy about the case, asked Scotland Yard to investigate. The Yard detectives carefully examined the blotters of the parties involved. Mrs Gooding's blotter was clean, but Miss Swan's blotter had the word 'local' on it in the handwriting of the letters. Miss Swan now alleged that Mrs Gooding had borrowed her blotter(!). Although Mrs Gooding was still in jail at this stage, many people in the district were still receiving obscene letters. Miss Swan claimed that Mrs Gooding's daughter was writing them. But even when the daughter was kept well away from the post office, the letters continued. The Director of Public Prosecutions referred the case back to the Court of Criminal Appeal, and instructed the prosecution to request that the court quash both of Mrs Gooding's two sentences and convictions. The Appeal Court did so unobtrusively, without looking in detail at the evidence. Mrs Gooding was released in July 1921 and awarded £250 compensation. The police now kept a careful watch on Miss Swan, and managed to sell her, and only her, secretly marked stamps through the local post office. In

1923, these stamps were found on some further obscene letters. Miss Swan later received twelve months' imprisonment and the letters ceased.

These cases happened some time ago, but accusations of this sort are still made, though they seem less likely to lead to mistaken imprisonment. Perhaps the police and the courts today are more alive to the psychological problems involved. The most recent case we have come across occurred in July 1971 in the backwoods of Wales. A Mrs Valmai Thomas was falsely accused of writing letters threatening to kill Rhiannon, the 3-year-old daughter of her neighbour, Mrs Averil Hughes, in a small Carmarthenshire village. The letters were very cruel and sadistic, and contained such phrases as: 'The little girl will only live if you get out or be murdered.' 'I will slash the child.' 'The agony of her death will be brutal.' Mrs Hughes claimed that the letters were left in the lavatory at her public house, and among crates outside the premises. She said that on 19 January at about 11 o'clock she was returning to the pub after being out when 'I went around the back and saw Valmai Thomas. I asked her what she was doing there and if she was the one sending the threatening letters.' Mrs Hughes claimed that Mrs Thomas replied: 'Prove it, bloody prove it.' Mrs Hughes said that Mrs Thomas then did a little jig and went away with a shopping basket over her head. Mrs Hughes's brother, Mr Graham Llewellyn, also received phone-calls threatening Mrs Hughes.

Mrs Thomas was brought to trial, but when she appeared in court the prosecution offered no evidence because forensic evidence then pointed to Mrs Hughes as the letter-writer. When confronted with the evidence of the handwriting expert Mrs Hughes was alleged to have said to the police: 'What can I say? I am sorry I wrote them.' Mrs Hughes was later tried and convicted of wilfully making a statement that she had found a letter threatening to kill her child, knowing it was false. In passing sentence the judge commented: 'You bore false witness against your neighbour. Your false evidence brought an innocent woman within the grasp of the law. There can be few offences more serious than yours. What you have done strikes at the very concept of justice that courts and juries strive to find. I do not know why you did it; nobody knows. But that you did do it is clear and I must treat this as seriously as it deserves.' (Mrs Thomas did in fact spend ten days in custody and had been ill as a result of the ordeal.)[18]

These bizarre false accusations do not always confine themselves to dirty and threatening letters. Sometimes people are falsely accused of carrying out the kind of obscene threats which are to be found in the letters. In 1946, Miss Kathryn Seaby was accused of throwing corrosive liquid in the face of a young nurse in the hospital of which she was deputy matron. It was thought that her reason for injuring the nurse in this way was jealous spite against a younger and more attractive woman. The girl alleged that Miss Seaby had earlier gone into her room, gone through her letters and damaged her possessions. Miss Seaby was found guilty and bound over on condition she go into a mental hospital for twelve months. She lost her job, spent her life savings on her defence, and was ruined and disgraced.

When she came out of the mental hospital, she tracked down her accuser, who was now a patient in a mental hospital herself. Miss Seaby's solicitor, who had always believed in her innocence, went to the hospital and found out why she was there. He learnt that she had a long record of making false accusations of being injured by other women while inflicting the injuries on herself. Following a Home Office inquiry, Miss Seaby was given a free pardon and compensated.[19]

Just as in the overtly sexual cases we discussed earlier, the motives in these cases are both complex and bizarre. In almost all of them, there seems to be a combination of a strong repression of forbidden sexual and aggressive impulses, which determine the form of the accusation, and a relatively trivial grudge against some acquaintance which determines who the victim will be.

In cases where the accusation concerns the sending of obscene or threatening letters, the repressed impulses find an especially tortuous expression. Where the letters contain obscene sexual accusations, the recipient accuses herself of the things which most horrify her and yet which she would possibly like to do. Yet in accusing another woman of writing the letters, she dissociates herself from the lewd notions in them, and foists these on someone else.

In cases where the letters are predominantly threatening to the recipient or her family, the motivation is basically similar. In the case of Mrs Hughes, defence counsel drew attention at the trial to the fact that Mrs Hughes 'had gone through great suffering to give birth to her only daughter, whom she loved dearly.' Mrs Hughes was 40 at the time of her daughter's birth, and 43 at the time of the trial. Before these offences, she had never been in any trouble. Perhaps in this combination of strong affection for her daughter, possible resentment at the suffering she had been through, one can see the origin of the odd threats to murder the child, which were projected on to the innocent Mrs Thomas.

Most of these offences seem to take place in small, closed communities: small towns like Littlehampton, a small Welsh village like Glynmoch, or the small, closed world of a hospital. In such communities, the inhabitants tend to know each other personally and intimately; and they may well have strong and shared, moral attitudes. In the village, this stems from the fact of the same few families living in close proximity for many years; in the hospital, from the intense, common occupational concern shared by those who live and work there. This kind of community presents the opportunity, and a heightened temptation, to someone who has an impulse publicly to play the role of victim or upholder of public morality. The victim, so long as she is not unmasked, will receive a satisfying and tangible show of public sympathy; and the upholder of public morals has the satisfaction of unleashing and personifying the collective conscience of her small world.

There are some cases of malicious false accusation where the interrelationship of crime and motive is much more straightforward. In the sex cases, both accusation and the accused are important. In the poison-pen cases, it is the accusation that is of greatest importance, while the person picked on is incidental. In the cases we will now discuss, the nature of the accusation is incidental: what is important is the person accused. The accusation is made because an opportunity has arisen through which a grudge against the accused can be expressed. Perhaps such a case was that of a man we shall call Patrick Boland, convicted of breaking into a bank and robbing it. The only evidence directly connecting him to the scene of the crime was a rather weak identification. The crime took place in Scotland, and so corroboration was needed if this evidence was to stand; it came, from a woman whom we shall call Mrs Fenton. She was a neighbour of Boland's, and gave evidence as to his coming and going from his house about the time the crime was committed. Her evidence damaged the alibi and showed that he could have committed the crime. Mrs Fenton's evidence was in conflict with that of other neutral witnesses, and at times contradictory.

In his petition to the Queen, Boland said of Mrs Fenton: 'It is believed and averred that Mrs Fenton is of unstable character, given to irrational fears and fantasies. She is believed to have feared being poisoned by a previous husband who was subsequently certified insane, and this episode (whether the fears were well- or ill-founded) has left her with a neurotic tendency to obsession, and in particular to fear. She has long been obsessed with the fact of the petitioner's previous criminal record; she objected to him as a neighbour, persuaded her uncle on this ground to come and live with her, fancies that the petitioner "made faces" at her, talked of leaving, and kept a watch on the petitioner in which it is believed the police were involved and which resulted in a dispute between her and her uncle. She suffers from a stammer. ... At and about the time of the petitioner's trial, she was particularly unbalanced as a result of bereavement. ... Two particular incidents, of which one was raised in evidence, indicate that Mrs Fenton is irrational, hostile to the petitioner, and dishonest. (1) She endeavoured to suggest that she had been intimidated prior to the petitioner's trial by a man who, she alleged, inflicted certain cuts on her arm and wrist and on her jaw. She attributed responsibility for this to the petitioner. . . . [A civil action was brought by the petitioner.] That action was settled by Mrs Fenton admitting that there were no grounds for the expressions complained of and tendering damages of £52·50. It is believed and averred that in making these objections Mrs Fenton was in any event irresponsible; but it is more particularly averred that she had not been attacked at all, and had inflicted the injuries herself, demonstrating at once her malice towards the petitioner and her unbalanced character. It is believed and averred that the police considered self-infliction probable or certain and took no steps in relation to the alleged assault, and the cuts were of a trivial nature indicating self-infliction. . . . (2) There is produced [that is, enclosed with the petition] a slip of paper and envelope . . . received by the petitioner's wife. The slip of paper bears what presumably purports to be a message from a man hired by the petitioner to commit the assault referred to at 1) above. No such assault occurred and no such man existed, as hereinbefore averred. The message is typed on the typewriter used by Mrs Fenton, and in particular used by her in typing a letter, also produced, dated 26 February 1968. Expert evidence of the identity of the machine used on these documents is available. It is believed and averred that the said slip of paper was sent by and the message on it typed by Mrs Fenton. Her motives in doing this are not wholly understood by the petitioner; but again the episode demonstrates Mrs Fenton's instability, dishonesty, and malice.'

Once again, this use of the courts almost as a direct weapon is much more prevalent among women. Because of relative physical weakness and social convention, women are inhibited from working off a grudge through direct aggression, as a man of similar instability and similarly frustrated might do.[20] Women also have a greater regard for conventional authority than men, and so are more likely to ask it to assist them in a dispute. (It must be remembered here that we have been discussing abnormal instances of this quite legitimate form of behaviour.)

People are not always wrongly accused as a result of the courts being used as a weapon in this way. This can also happen because the accused or some other party is seeking to protect the real culprit. This is what may have happened in the case of Alfred Weston, who was convicted of obtaining money by false pretences, and sentenced to eight years preventive detention in 1961.

At that time he was in partnership with a Miss Maltby who after the trial said: 'I believe Weston to be completely innocent. I knew his record when I went into business with him [Weston had fifteen previous convictions for eighty-one mainly trivial offences]. . . . I tried all I could to make him plead not guilty at the trial, but he pleaded guilty to keep me out of it.' Miss Maltby had always declared that the money was paid to her and not to Weston, that it was a business payment, and that he had received none of it. It is doubtful that there was ever any criminal intent to get the money by anybody. Weston alleges that he was advised by the police that the man who had been defrauded was deeply worried about the illness of his daughter and could avoid going to court if there was a guilty plea. He was also advised that such a plea would keep Miss Maltby out of the whole thing, and that almost certainly the sentence would be light. After his heavy sentence Weston tried to repudiate his plea of guilty at the Court of Appeal. The then Lord Chief Justice, Lord Parker, said that if a statement he had read by Miss Maltby was correct, Weston ought never to have pleaded guilty, but as he had done so the Court could not interfere with the conviction and sentence. He advised Weston to present a petition to the Home Office, adding: 'No doubt the Home Office will cause inquiries to be made to discover the truth, particularly of Miss Maltby's statement.' Weston presented a petition, but three months later the Home Secretary turned it down because he could find 'no grounds on which he would be justified in recommending any interference with the conviction or sentence or in taking any other action.' Mr Towndrow, Weston's solicitor, said that the Home Office in rejecting

Weston's petition, had claimed they had made a full investigation, but that in fact there had been no communication with Miss Maltby. His solicitors, feeling that there had been a miscarriage of justice, at this stage went to the unusual length of calling a press conference to publicise the case.[21]

This strange case of ill-thought-out gallantry also illustrates two points we stressed in earlier chapters. It shows the danger of being persuaded, for whatever reason, to plead guilty when you are innocent in the hope that later when the truth emerges you will be acquitted; and the inability of the Court of Appeal to overturn a conviction after a guilty plea.

A definite category of problem witnesses is that of recent immigrants to this country. One type of case which we have repeatedly come up against is that of a muddled affray concerning warring factions of Sikhs. These cases vary from the very serious, where someone may be killed or seriously injured, to minor fights. The problem in the former case is to find out who struck the most damaging blows; in the latter case, to find out whether the fight occurred at all or whether it was simply a put up job to discredit one or the other faction. In all these fights, Sikhs are the only people involved, and most of the witnesses are also Sikhs.

There are various specific problems that arise when these cases are investigated and come to court, many of which stem from the structure of Asian immigrant communities. They have very strong family and communal loyalties, which are what tend to lead to the feuds in the first place. A lot of trouble arises from the clash between the demands of these ties and loyalties and the rules and expectations of the English legal system. For those Asians who still live within small, traditional communities, many of whose members may even have come from the same village in India or Pakistan, and who may have little contact with people outside their community, it may be very difficult to comprehend the new and strange demands of a large, impersonal bureaucracy. The traditional Asian will see other Asians involved in the investigation and trial as still playing many roles—his brother-in-law, his neighbour, his local shopkeeper; the English legal system demands that he put most of these roles out of his mind, and consider only what the court considers relevant to the situation in question. The court demands that he take up the position of emotional neutrality towards these people implied in the phrase 'equality before the law', and this is strange and incomprehensible to them.

What are the problems arising from these clashes? The main one seems to be that Asians tend to commit perjury much more often than English people in the same situation. Relative to people who are more used to the impersonal demands of the system, what they say in court will be influenced less by what actually happened than by the expectations and relationships we have already mentioned. One of the Sikh affrays we described led to the death of one of the men concerned. Afterwards, four Sikhs, all named Singh, were convicted of murder, but later considerable doubt was expressed about the guilt of one of them, Joginder Singh, whilst it appears that yet another Singh, may have been implicated. Six years after the trial Jugtar Singh, another of the participants, said in a signed and witnessed statement to the secretary of 'Justice': 'You must understand that among Indians there are very strong family ties and duties which forced us to protect each other. We were frightened that Joginder, who was a brother-in-law of Swarn, was going to mention [the other Singh's] name at the trial. Gurdev and Swarn put pressure on me that if Joginder mentioned [the other Singh's] name, Gurdev and Swarn would bring in the names of Wali and Milka. Wali is my wife's brother, and Milka is Wali's wife's brother. So I said to Joginder: "If we are lucky enough, and as we haven't done anything, we will get justice." At this time, I did not know how these things worked. I was only thinking: "What will the opposite side say? As soon as they find out who was involved, they will put their names in as they have ours. . . ." '

This attitude towards giving evidence extends to fixing up false defences and false alibis when these are not necessary. This can seriously hamper the defence lawyers in conducting the case. This is what seems to have happened in the case of Thaman Singh, who following a fight among Sikhs in a pub in Bedford was convicted not just of taking part in an affray, as were all the others, but of the more serious charge of malicious wounding, for which he got eighteen months. There is a lot of evidence to suggest that he did not actually do the wounding; but he added to the morass of inconsistent accusations and counter-accusations by putting up a completely false defence. There was ample evidence that he took part in the fight, but he denied being there at all. One of the defence solicitors commented: '. . . It is a tragedy that Thaman Singh put up a false defence. This was not untypical of the Asians here. The results, however, of Thaman Singh's case and the preaching we have done in connection with it have at least persuaded a number of the Asians here that they might well suffer more if they do not tell their defending solicitors the truth.'

Another difficulty which arises with many Asians is that they do not speak English and therefore need an interpreter in court. Where there is a substantial local immigrant population, the court will often have a more or less permanent interpreter who has the requisite legal knowledge and linguistic proficiency. This may create problems in that in any case involving a dispute within the minority community, he may have ties to one group or another. Hence he may be tempted to slant his translations either in favour of, or against the defendant, depending on whether his family or community allegiance is to him or to the victim of the crime or to defence or to prosecution witnesses.

In nearly all the Sikh cases we have come across, allegations have been made either that the interpreter made mistakes or that he was biased. One case where an error in interpretation played a vital part in convicting two men for murder was the case of Joginder Singh and Swarn Singh (see p. 92). According to the judge's summing-up at their trial, one of the witnesses had said in his own language that these two men were watching the fight and had then struck the dying man after he had been knocked to the ground. This clear and decisive piece of evidence against them resulted in their conviction. Both men applied for leave to appeal but plainly had no grounds if this witness's evidence was true and had been accurately translated.

Five years later, Tom Sargant was asked to investigate Joginder's claim to innocence which had been pressed by an Urdu speaking prison officer who had befriended him. He obtained copies of all the depositions and statements and discovered that this witness had originally said that, when the victim way lying on the ground, Joginder and Swarn were 'standing by'. Luckily, the shorthand writer still had his notebook and remembered the case, and with the help of a Pakistani barrister it came to light that this vital piece of evidence had been mistranslated. There is an Urdu word which, with a very slight varying of inflection, alternatively means 'to strike' or 'to stand near'. The witness had been asked: 'What were Joginder and Swarn doing when the man was on the ground?' He had replied 'standing near' and it had been interpreted 'they struck him'.

An attempt was made by defence counsel to reconcile this with the previous evidence, but the judge let it go by and made no reference to it in his summing-up. Joginder and Swarn, who spoke no English, did not know what had happened and the staff and judges of the Court of Criminal Appeal at the time appear not to have thought it necessary, in the absence of a transcript of evidence, to study the depositions carefully enough to detect an error of this kind.

This discovery, together with statements made by the four convicted men and by other witnesses, pointing to the identity of the real murderer, was instrumental in persuading the Home Office to review the whole case. The Home Office made no admission of error but did agree to fix a release date in the near future though only after all four men had served seven years. Joginder and Swarn thus ended up serving seven years for murder when in fact no evidence has ever been produced of their having taken any active part in the attack. They have never been properly exonerated or received any compensation.

In another such case a relative of one of the men put in prison following a minor Sikh affray alleged not merely error but malice on the part of the interpreter. He told us: 'There is rivalry in the community—enough for one group to want to put down our group. The official interpreter is biased, he has had dealings with the other group. He was also against us because one of our group once protested against his taking bribes and had tried to get him dismissed. Therefore he tried to do him down. During the trial the interpretation of a Punjabi word for a knife was very important. He translated a chopper as a penknife.' At this trial the ambiguity of the interpreter's position was emphasised by the fact that one of the leading witnesses for the prosecution, and one of the leaders of the other Sikh faction, was a former interpreter for the police.

The temptations arising from a situation like this are obvious. The interpreter is in a position of power and influence *vis-a-vis* his community. There will be a strong temptation both for him to abuse this position and for other people to induce him to do so. People who are anyway used to exploiting a position that is supposed to be neutral but is of potential power, in order to further the interests of family or community, may be more easily persuaded to take a direct bribe. Accusations that this occurs are very common. Here is one such complaint, made by a Pakistani woman who had been a witness in a murder case: 'There should be English policemen who speak Urdu, and Pakistanis should not be used as they will take money to say anything. I really mean this, it is not fair to any of us the way that these matters are dealt with at the present time.' In this case it was alleged that the interpreter in the trial was bribed and biased, and that when new evidence came to light he hindered the police from investigating it.

Problems with interpreters are not limited to the major groups of immigrants in this country. Rather different difficulties occur in relation to languages rarely spoken in England. One problem that can arise is that the interpreter may not speak exactly the same dialect as the accused or some key witness, and an accidental distortion occurs in the hearing of the evidence. Alternatively, the interpreter may speak both languages adequately, but is uneducated or unfamiliar with court procedures, and hence unable to provide a translation adequate for the purpose of the court. These problems seem to have arisen in the case of an Algerian called Boukerou whom we interviewed. What happened in his case was that the first interpreter provided by the police was ideally suited to the case. He took Boukerou's initial statement, but was then taken as a prosecution witness, presumably to say what the statement was. A new interpreter was provided, but this one came from Beirut. He spoke both French and Arabic, but very differently from an Algerian. Boukerou's barrister later said of him (Boukerou): 'He can't explain himself clearly in any language.' This muddle may well have contributed to Boukerou's conviction on rather slender evidence.

Immigrants may not simply have problems arising from their lack of knowledge of the English language, but also because they are illiterate in any language, including their own. In the case of Joginder Singh, the judge in his summing-up commented: '. . . The prisoners and most of the witnesses you have heard are not Englishmen with the background and upbringing which we have; they are peasants from the Punjab, most of them, and some of them have been over here as many as ten years without learning much more of the language than enough to ask for a pint of beer. Most of them are illiterate, and so illiterate that they cannot even understand photographs. It is a type of illiteracy which it is difficult for us to understand here, but you saw it in the box.'

In view of all these disadvantages, it is unlikely that anyone in this position will have a trial as fair as an Englishman would. In addition to all this, these affray trials are frequently joint trials. We have already described the muddle and difficulties attendant on joint trials, and particularly to joint trials involving Asian immigrants (see p. 93).

West Indians, too, have family problems which get in the way of the court's finding out what actually happened. These problems, however, are almost the opposite of those we encountered in connection with Asians. Whereas the Indians have family relationships that are stronger and more extensive than those of English people, West Indians have much looser and less stable family ties. Where two or more members of a West Indian family are involved in a crime committed entirely or mainly by one of them, the guilty one may acquiesce in the conviction of an innocent member of his family. His subsequent behaviour may veer from complete self-incrimination in order to acquit his innocent relative, to a complete repudiation of him out of total self-interest. This may well reflect the ambivalent and wildly oscillating emotions present in many West Indian family relationships.

The case of Castin and Leathlan Townsend (p. 79) vividly illustrates this process. You will remember that Leathlan Townsend was convicted of a murder in which there was considerable doubt as to who did it. At one stage after the trial Castin made the following statement. He said: 'At this point a group of men in the party, approximately eight or nine in number, went for Leathlan. . . . The fight was like this, some were trying to push him out of the door and others were hitting him. They managed to cudgel him to the lounge door. I naturally decided to endeavour to rescue my brother. I pushed my way through the crowd of spectators up to the attackers, but found it impossible to get between them and Leathlan.

'I became desperate because I realised that if I didn't do something quickly, my brother was going to be seriously injured. I had a knife in my pocket. . . . I took it out and opened it. I started to push my way into the group of attackers. I had penetrated this group to an extent, I had the knife in my hand, and I plunged it into the first person nearest to me whom I know now to be Edwards, the deceased. . . . I do know that as a result of this Leathlan managed to get away. I did not intend to kill anybody, the only thing in my mind was to prevent Leathlan getting hurt.'

'During this entire incident, my brother did not attack anybody. . . . He never touched McKenzie [whom Castin also admits stabbing], nor Edwards. . . . In view of the pursuers, we decided to run to the police station for protection. I still had the knife. When we got to the police station, the crowd followed almost immediately.

'McKenzie, who was amongst them, pointed to my brother as the one that stabbed him. They arrested my brother straight away. They took my name and address when I asked for bail for my brother, then they let me go. I don't know why I did not own up, probably because I was scared. . . . I pleaded not guilty for the sake of both of us. I did not imagine that my brother would get convicted. It had also been in my mind that McKenzie had thought Leathlan stabbed him and not me, and that accordingly Leathlan had the knife. Therefore I felt that I would not get convicted either. I was then convicted at the trial of attempted grievous bodily harm because, according to Johnson, whilst in the street I urged my brother to attack him. . . .

'I have now made this statement because it has been on my conscience that my brother is serving a term of life imprisonment when he was totally innocent. I therefore hope this will finally clear his name.'

This statement was made to the secretary of 'Justice', who also made the following chronological comments on the case: 'Leathlan, when arrested, told the police that Castin told him that he had cut a few, and Leathlan later wrote to his wife and to Castin accusing him of the murder, and begging Castin to own up. He withdrew this charge after receiving a visit from Castin and two other brothers, in the course of which, so Leathlan alleges, they begged him not to accuse Castin as he had done the stabbing only to save Leathlan's life, and promised to look after his wife if he was found guilty.

'Leathlan's reason given at the trial for withdrawing the charge, was that he had written the letters for the sake of his wife who was threatening to commit suicide. But Leathlan's wife says that she never at any time made such a threat.

'Leathlan wrote to me after the dismissal of his appeal and I consulted his junior counsel . . . who provided me with a substantial memorandum on the case, suggesting it would be interesting if Castin could be persuaded to talk. I exchanged a number of letters with Leathlan, and he eventually came out with a clear statement that his brother had done it. Castin was then sent to Maidstone, where Leathlan already was, and I obtained permission from the Home Office to interview both the brothers together. After some rather tricky exchanges, Castin eventually confessed to the murder and gave me a brief account of how it had happened. I had specifically refused to give him any assurances. I discussed my notes of his confession with [junior counsel] who agreed that his account made sense. . . . After some delay, and obtaining the consent of Castin's solicitor, Leathlan's solicitor arranged for a full statement to be taken from Castin. I subsequently sent this to him, but he refused to sign it. Some time later, when I was looking for one of Castin's brothers, I found Castin at this house on home leave. I again pressed him to sign a statement but he said that he would soon be released and that it was a black thing in his life that he wanted to forget.

'A prisoner in Wormwood Scrubs who knew the dead man and the host at the party, has said that he knew that Castin was the guilty one. He had been with him for a short while in Maidstone, and while waiting for the doctor he challenged him as to why he did not own up and set his brother free. Castin replied "Why should I, I would only get more bird." '

Tom Sargant, Secretary of 'Justice', adds that "later, relations between the brothers deteriorated by reason of a quarrel over the beneficial ownership of a house which was in their joint names.' (Leathlan Townsend's release date was fixed for 1972, after nine years in prison.)

The wild swings of emotion between total self-interest and total self-abnegation, between total loyalty and total indifference, are very apparent in this account. Similar processes can be seen at work in the case of Ewart Hylton, who went to prison for a robbery his brother had committed. Ewart showed considerable generosity of attitude all the way through. Even after five weeks in Borstal after conviction at the Old Bailey, he remained silent while his elder brother Washington stayed free. Much later, Ewart said: 'After my arrest, I knew I was innocent, and because I was innocent, I expected to be freed at my trial. It never occurred to me at any time—because I knew I was innocent—to name my brother as the guilty party, although I knew he was.' Eventually, Washington was found guilty of another robbery, and asked for this case of robbery to be taken into consideration. Ewart was now released on bail from borstal, and later his conviction was quashed in the Court of Criminal Appeal. Mr Ralph Hewart, father of the brothers, said that 'Washington didn't come forward at the time because he thought Ewart would get off at his trial.'[22] One is forced to comment that neither did he come forward after Ewart was convicted.

It is not just the most recent immigrants to this country who have encountered problems of this kind in the English courts. In the mid-nineteenth century the Italians, and at the turn of the century the Ashkenazi Jews, both suffered in the same sort of way.

In 1864, an Italian immigrant, Serafino Pelizzioni, was wrongly convicted of murder after a big affray between a group of Italians and some Englishmen in which a man was stabbed to death. Pelizzioni was convicted as a result of his wrong identification by the victim before he died and by several other English witnesses. After his conviction, the leader of the Italian community investigated the case and tracked down the real murderer, Pelizzioni's cousin, Gregorio

Mogni. He was then put on trial for murder, and Pelizzioni, who under the rules of evidence at the time had not been allowed to speak at this own trial, was then for the first time allowed to give evidence. Mogni was convicted, and Pelizzioni exonerated. Belton Cobb describes the setting of the crime and the trial, and the prejudices involved, as follows: 'In the middle of the nineteenth century, the Hatton Garden district of London was the Italian colony. . . . By English standards, these Italians were a wild lot. . . . Even in London, most of these Italians carried knives. . . . A number of English people also went to the Golden Anchor [the pub where the murder occurred]. . . . They did not associate with the Italians. So it came about that the tap-room was given over to the Italians, while the bagatelle room accommodated the English. . . . Occasionally, the two parties got mixed, and there might be a row between them. . . . The majority of the Italians—particularly when a little drunk—did not know how to behave in a decent public house.'

The mutual mistrust and segregation of the two communities is a common feature of immigrant situations, including those involving the Asians and West Indians in Britain today. Mistrust can lead to bias on the part of the jury. Segregation reinforces the values of the closed community, and leads to their application in an English court of law, where they are inappropriate. Belton Cobb goes on to describe the trial: 'Perhaps [the jury] felt that half the witnesses must have either committed perjury or at least have sworn to what they believed rather than what they knew. If so, well, those for the prosecution were English, while most of those for the defence were Italian. And who was going to believe a lot of cut-throat Italians?' The Italians even suffered from the kind of identification difficulties we have already met with the Sikhs. Cobb now goes on to describe Mogni's trial at which both men appeared: 'Gregorio stood in the dock and Pelizzioni stepped into the witness-box, and everyone saw that the two men were as alike as two peas. Cousins? They could have been twin brothers. Other Italians, who were well-accustomed to the Italian cast of countenance, might have noticed distinguishing features; but to the unobservant English, they were both swarthy, both ferocious looking, and each had an enormous black moustache of precisely the same cut.'[23]

In the trial of Steinie Morrison (see p. 74), the factors we have described as prejudicing the trial of immigrants arise in the East End Jewish community of the early years of this century. Julian Symons discusses the community within which lived both the accused,

Steinie Morrison, and the murder victim, Leon Beron: 'Leon Beron lived in a very strange, small world: in the violently emotional —and sometimes physically violent—poverty-stricken tight enclave formed by foreign Jewish exiles in the East End of London. Some of these were political exiles, many were racial; most of them came from Eastern Europe; some drifted into crime, as some Poles became criminals in post-war England. They made little attempt to assimilate themselves into the country of their adoption, and often learnt no more than a few words of English. They talked with each other in Yiddish, French or Russian. Their lives were spent in restaurants run by people of their own kind, who served the food they liked, and allowed them to stay all day eating, drinking and arguing, as long as they spent a few coppers.'

When Steinie Morrison was tried for Beron's murder, this split the community into two factions. Symons describes the effect of this: 'Before the trial began in March, there had been several incidents which showed the excitement that the case caused among the East End community of Russian, Polish and Austrian Jews. There can be no doubt—although this was never admitted—that Morrison's criminal occupation was well known to most of the people who used the Warsaw restaurant. Passionate pro- and anti-Morrison factions formed, and under the stress of the enmities they engendered, some cracks began to appear in the police case. These cracks, damaging in themselves, must have been even more disturbing when considered as an earnest of what might happen when these volatile, eccentric, and nearly illiterate Jews were under cross-examination.'[24]

Once again, these intense communal pressures to lie for one side or the other were stronger than the lofty but abstract and impersonal demands of the court that the truth be told. One important potential witness was not called at the trial because he had previously told the police so many conflicting lies, depending on which faction had been putting pressure on him at the time: 'Rosen, who spoke no English, had said through an interpreter that he had seen Morrison and Beron together in the street at 1.30 a.m., and also that he had seen Morrison with a revolver. When Rosen retracted this evidence, he said that he lied in the first place and had since been threatened:

' "People have told me that what I have sworn I must keep to, and I must not put anything else in because I might get prison. The landlord's brother told me that. By the landlord I mean Beron, which was killed. . . . Some witnesses are threatening me that in the event of my saying different they will shoot me. It was the landlord's brother and Mr Deitch that threatened me that if I tell truth I shall get prison. Strangers also have threatened me in the restaurant. I can't be a witness as I haven't said the truth."

'So Rosen, also, could not be called at the trial. It should be said here that no suggestion is made that the police were in any way responsible for the original stories told by Eva Flitterman [another untruthful witness] and Rosen. Their task in extracting stories from people who had no regard for truth as an abstract principle, but simply thought in terms of the advantage that a particular tale would gain for themselves or their friends, was extraordinarily difficult.'[25]

Morrison, like some of the other immigrants we have described, ran a false alibi even though he was probably innocent. Mr Justice Darling in his summing-up dealt with this, and with the question of perjury generally in the context of an immigrant community: 'You may come to the conclusion that that is a fabricated alibi fabricated by or for him, and sworn to falsely by the Brodskys. . . . You may think it demolished and blown out of court. . . . But supposing that you do come to that conclusion he may not be proved to be guilty. . . . This man is a foreigner, those Brodskys are foreigners, apparently Polish Jews; they are Polish Jews or Russian Jews. He was a Jew when he was writing that letter to the Home Secretary; he said that he was a Hebrew then and that his name was Petropavloff. Ask yourselves, do you or do you not know that it is very common among people of certain classes and of certain nationalities, if they have got a good case, not to rest upon that good case? If you have ever talked to anybody who has administered justice in India you will know that there, if they have got a good case, they are not content to rest upon the good case, because they are convinced that perjured evidence will be brought against them, and that in order to overthrow the perjured evidence, which they suspect will be brought against them, they themselves produce perjured evidence. . . . Gentlemen, I make that observation, as you see, in favour of the prisoner, to suggest to you this: that if you come to the conclusion that this alibi is false, you should not judge it then as strictly against him as if it had been produced by an Englishman.'[26]

One factor linking such problem witnesses as women, children and immigrants is that they are relatively helpless and powerless people. As a result of this, they have rather special attitudes towards authority. Women are unable to settle disputes in which they are involved in as direct a way as men can. They are therefore tempted to bring in authority as a weapon on their side. Children see authority as a mysterious and capricious power that has to be placated.[27] Immigrants share something of both these attitudes. This could be because their past experience of authority amply justifies this suspicion; or because they find themselves in a strange country and a situation which they do not understand. In such a situation it is only natural to fall back on the customs and loyalties they have always known, and to try and apply them to manipulate the new authority.

The reasons why immigrants often do not get as fair a trial as an Englishman would often have their roots in social factors whose remedy is outside the scope of this book. Nevertheless, there are certain adjustments which could be made to the legal system to improve the position of the immigrant in court.

The position of the interpreter is a point at which a defect is clearly visible, on which many discontents are focused, and which is easily remediable. Firstly, the defence should have an automatic right to object to a particular interpreter, much as it can object to a particular juror. It should have this right to object not simply at the beginning, but also during the course of the trial. There are two main grounds on which the defence might object. One reason might be that the interpreter turns out to be inadequate or inappropriate, perhaps because he does not know the relevant dialect well enough. The other reason is that the interpreter may turn out to have connections with the people on trial, and to be biased either for or against them. This may particularly be true of people not appointed as official interpreters by the court, but who interpose themselves between defendants or witnesses and the lawyers. There would seem to be a good case for excluding them from the court altogether.

One solution to the problem might be to appoint interpreters entirely from outside the community. These might be Englishmen who have a fluent knowledge of various Indian languages which they have acquired by living and working in India.[28] There are many Englishmen who have worked in the Indian courts or legal systems who would be suited for these posts, more especially since one of their admitted virtues was impartiality.

Some immigrants have suggested to us that there is a case for constituting a court that can hear cases in languages other than English. Increasing latitude currently seems to be given to the use of Welsh in courts, although only a tiny minority even of Welsh people can speak the language. There are now probably more people in

Britain speaking Asian languages (such as Hindi, Urdu, Punjabi or Gujarati) than there are speaking Welsh, and this is certainly true of monoglot speakers. Furthermore, the numbers of such people are increasing, whereas the number of Welsh-speakers is declining. It would seem rational to give these languages equal status with English in certain contexts. Certainly there are enough lawyers with a knowledge of these languages available to constitute a court able to hear a case almost entirely through such a medium, with monoglot English-speaking witnesses' evidence being translated into the vernacular.

Nevertheless, in the long run we do not feel that this system would be in the best interests of the immigrants themselves. The overwhelming drawback would be that the setting up of a court would delay the time when the immigrant would know he was receiving the same justice, meted out in the same way as an Englishman. Also, such concessions to separatism would result in an undesirable fragmentation of the legal system. The experience of the Jewish and Italian communities probably shows that in the long run the conditions that lead to a demand for separate legal facilities disappear anyway.

Meanwhile, the problem of the immigrant communities remains. Clearly, some attempt must be made to ensure that the courts understand their special difficulties. Mr Justice Darling's summing-up in the Morrison case, quoted above, shows that some judges are well aware of and sympathetic to the problems of an immigrant defendant. But not all judges can be expected to have such insight. Perhaps the Home Office should issue a memorandum to judges and lawyers taking part in trials involving immigrants instructing them in the special problems they are likely to face.

Chapter 6

How They Got Off

Arthur Thompson (see p. 36): I appealed, and then I was just called one day into the Governor's office and told that the appeal had been dismissed and that my sentence would now start. So I'd actually been in prison $4\frac{1}{2}$ months, and none of the $4\frac{1}{2}$ months I did counted.

Q: How did you eventually get out?
A: We eventually got out by one of the men who was involved in the actual attack sending a petition to the Home Secretary and the petition being investigated and found to be true, and Superintendent Lewis was put in charge of the case, and he investigated it thoroughly and he found out we were completely innocent.
Q: Now the men who actually did it, did they know that you three were doing time for what they had done?
A: I'm not quite sure, I couldn't say that.
Q: How did they find out?
A: How did they find out? Well, actually, I found out who they were and got a message through to one of them, and he then came forward.
Q: How did you find out who they were?
A: Oh, a complete fluke.
Q: Unless this fluke had happened, you would presumably have served your full sentence?
A: We would have served our full sentence, yes.

What can you do if your appeal fails? The 'Justice' Report on *Home Office Reviews of Criminal Convictions* describes four critical stages in the existing procedure for applying to the Home Secretary:

1. The initiation of the process by the preparation and presentation of the petition.
2. The sifting and selection of those petitions which merit some further investigation from those which are obviously without merit.

F

3. The control and nature of the investigation into those complaints which justify it.

4. The appropriate action that should follow such investigation.'

As to the preparation of petitions, most prisoners are at a severe disadvantage. They rarely have the knowledge, the resources or the expertise to do it satisfactorily themselves, and it is unlikely that a lawyer will be available to do it for them. Legal aid is not available at this stage. There are various persons and organizations to whom such people frequently turn, and we shall be discussing these later. But because these are unofficial bodies, who have many other tasks to perform, there is no guarantee that they will be able to give the matter the attention it deserves.

Most petitions, though, are prepared by the prisoner alone, are inarticulate and ill-thought out, and do not put forward the grounds for his complaint in a way that would encourage investigation. How many of these petitions are there? The 'Justice' report quoted above states that '. . . in the first six months of 1967, an average of some sixty-six petitions a week were received in the Criminal Department of the Home Office directly from prisoners themselves and in addition a substantial number of representations were received on behalf of prisoners from relatives, friends and MPs. Of these, an average of 40 per cent required some investigation by the Department, though not all these cases were of equal difficulty. Consideration of these cases accounts for the time of about twelve of the Department's officials.[1]

The Home Office has published a detailed description of how these petitions are dealt with: 'All these petitions, many of which are very long and complex, for naturally it is the more difficult and doubtful cases that produce the largest proportion of petitions—have to be carefully read and examined. A large number can be set aside at once as mere repetitions of pleas already urged—some convicts petition five or six times a year. . . . A few are obviously frivolous; but there remain a great mass of petitions which put forward pleas which are, *prima facie*, reasonable and have to be considered on their merits.

'In the case of summary convictions, if there appears to be any *prima facie* ground for inquiry, the first step is usually to obtain from the magistrates a report of the evidence, and it is the practice in most cases, in applying for the evidence, at the same time to forward the petition and to ask for the magistrate's opinion. Sometimes, however, it appears better to obtain in the first instance a report from the police, especially in cases occurring in the Metropolitan Police District, where the Secretary of State is the police authority.

'In the case of petitions from prisoners convicted at quarter-sessions and assizes, where there appear to be *prima facie* grounds for consideration, the first step is to obtain a report of the evidence. The evidence given at the trial is preferred, if it is available either [from the court's records] or in a good newspaper report. . . . The evidence in the reports of the trial or in the depositions is read and examined, and usually at this stage a *precis* of the case is prepared or minutes written showing whether there is any substantial grounds for inquiry or for reference to the judge, or whether, as often happens, the petition either misrepresents the evidence given or contains only statements which are irrelevant to the question of the prisoner's guilt and innocence and may, therefore, be at once dismissed.

'In deciding on the review of the evidence whether any further action is to be taken it has to be borne in mind that the Home Office is not a Court of Appeal, but that it merely advises the Crown in the exercise of the prerogative of mercy; and that it is useless to attempt to re-try at the Home Office, on paper, cases already heard in open court before a jury. The Home Office cannot hear counsel, does not see the witnesses, and cannot judge of their demeanour, and has no means of arriving at the truth by the method of cross-examination, and therefore any attempted re-trial of a case would necessarily be inferior in every way to the original trial. Moreover, if the Home Office, standing in these points, in a position of inferiority to the Court, were on slight pretexts to criticize verdicts and attempt to reopen cases, it would soon lose the co-operation of the judicial Bench, which is essential to the carrying out of its functions as the adviser to the Crown in the matter of prerogative. It requires, therefore, very strong grounds indeed to induce the Home Office to take any action in a case where the plea urged is innocence and no fresh evidence is available beyond that already submitted at the trial. . . .

'. . . In spite of some exceptions, the broad principle remains that a case will not be reopened merely in order to reconsider evidence which has already been fully examined at the trial. If the plea is that the verdict is wrong, and if no material evidence is offered, nor any means suggested by which new evidence can be obtained, the petition will, in ordinary circumstances, be refused.

'On the other hand, if new evidence is offered, that appears to be material, or if (in a case that on the reported evidence seems open to serious doubt) any means suggests itself of obtaining new evidence, steps are taken for further investigation. Sometimes the judge is referred to before an inquiry is made; sometimes the inquiries are completed first and the judge is consulted at a later stage. The inquiries are necessarily in most cases made through the police (in difficult cases, in the country, a specially selected officer from Scotland Yard is sometimes sent down to investigate): but in a few important cases, inquiries have been specially entrusted to members of the Treasury Solicitor's staff or a stipendiary magistrate has been asked to examine witnesses and report.'

Obviously a lot of Home Office time and effort goes into the examination and investigation of these petitions. But as has been said above, and as we shall further show, they can very rarely act on this. In the nature of things, there cannot be a great deal of contact between the prisoner and the Home Office official investigating his petition. There is therefore no way in which the prisoner can know what is being done about his petition, and he may therefore get very despondent and feel nothing is being done. Thompson, quoted earlier, said: 'The petitions that are sent into the Home Secretary are very poorly looked into. Possibly one in ten thousand has any luck. But I'm quite sure that more than one in ten thousand justifies looking into. I found that it didn't make no difference who I objected to or who I spoke to, or how many petitions I sent in. When I spoke to the visiting magistrates who are supposed to listen to you, they didn't listen to you in any way at all. They just walked round the prison. All they wanted to do was just see that it was clean. They wasn't the least interested in the prisoners or anything like that. They never give you no time at all.'

The 'Justice' report quoted above comments on the danger of this situation: 'It is vitally important that the petitioner is not left with the impression that his complaints have been ignored by an impassive authoritarian establishment. Unfortunately, no matter how conscientiously his case may in fact have been dealt with, he is frequently left with a contrary impression. After despatching his petition he will not normally hear anything for many months. Eventually he will receive an impersonal notification that it has been rejected. No reasons will be given to the petitioner who petitions unaided, although in the case where he has received the assistance of a person or a body in a position to exert pressure, some explanation for the decision may be obtained. The petitioner will not be told what inquiries have been made, and he will have been given no opportunity of challenging the reports submitted against his complaint. To a man who is already suffering from a sense of injustice, the result may well be frustration and bitterness.

These feelings of disillusionment and alienation are only too visible in ex-PC Luckhurst: 'I think in my particular case that it is definitely a case that we have myself, one ordinary person, on one side, and on the other side we have through the various decisions and statements that have been made over the last two or three years, we have, from the highest to the lowest—the Home Office, the Lord Chief Justice, the police chiefs, and various other offices—well, all these people have shown in their own way that I am wrong. I have tried to prove I am right. I am convinced that one of the reasons why it is extremely difficult for me to prove my case is because it will be a very very big decision for somebody to take to say that I, the small man, am right and the whole machine is wrong. And because of this—that they just never will say that, even if it were proved, that it was not me. I should think the only way that it would be absolutely proved that I was the innocent man is if somebody came along and admitted the offence, and then I sometimes wonder if they would simply take his word for it or whether he would have to prove as hard that he was the offender as I've tried to prove that I'm not the offender. This sounds ridiculous but I think they would be reluctant to let me off the hook.'

What are the Home Secretary's powers, and under what conditions does he exercise them?

1. He may grant a free pardon. (Technically it is the Queen who does this.) This effectively nullifies conviction and sentence.
2. He may refer the case back to the Court of Appeal. As in an ordinary appeal, the Court of Appeal may then quash conviction and sentence, order a new trial, or dismiss the appeal.
3. The Home Secretary may grant 'special' remission of part of a prisoner's sentence.

How does the Home Secretary decide whether to invoke any of these powers? The 'Justice' report comments: 'The overriding factor governing the exercise of the powers available to the Home Secretary is a proper concern to avoid even the appearance of interfering with the independence of the judiciary. Home Secretaries have accordingly taken a very restrictive view of the proper scope for executive intervention—a matter which has been dealt with before a competent court is not normally considered to be reviewable. As a consequence, a Home Secretary will only intervene in cases where evidence is presented by the petitioner which was not available to the courts which dealt with the case. A further principle which arises from reluctance to interfere with the decision of a properly constituted court is that the Home Secretary will not grant a pardon unless the petitioner can establish his innocence beyond doubt; it is not sufficient at this stage (although it is sufficient at the trial and on appeal) for him to raise a reasonable doubt as to his guilt. At the level of executive review, the onus of proof is effectively reversed. In cases where the petitioner fails to convince the Home Secretary of his innocence, but establishes that a serious doubt exists as to his guilt, he may be granted some remission of his sentence, or released on licence if the sentence is appropriate. . . . The more complicated cases in which evidence accepted by the jury at the trial has to be balanced against any new evidence, are referred back to the Court of Appeal.'[2]

'Justice's' view of this seems to be confirmed by official statements made on the subject. The Mars-Jones Report of Inquiry says: 'Where the conviction was on indictment, it is open to the Home Secretary to refer the case to the Court of Criminal Appeal, under Section 19 of the Criminal Appeal Act, 1907. In the case of summary convictions, such as those with which this inquiry is concerned, it is not possible to refer to the Court of Criminal Appeal and the duty of the officers concerned in the Criminal Department [of the Home Office] is to consider whether the new evidence conclusively establishes the complainant's innocence, and to advise the minister accordingly. If the new evidence falls short of this, it is no part of their duty to weigh it against that given in court and try to determine whether, if the new evidence had been available to the court, the decision might have been different. Exceptionally, where the new evidence, while not conclusively establishing the applicant's innocence, raises very strong doubt, whether he was in fact guilty, and he is still serving his sentence, the Home Secretary may, after consultation with the court, recommend the remission of the balance of sentence.'[3]

As the 'Justice' committee graphically puts it, petitions of the kind we have been discussing fall into 'a kind of "no man's land" between the courts and the executive where there appears to be a reluctance on the part of either to accept any responsibility to correct an apparent injustice or to investigate a complaint'. This is not a simple question of buck-passing. It is a fundamental constitutional tradition that the executive and the judiciary are separate and do not interfere in each others' sphere of responsibility. In particular, the government always seeks to preserve the independence of the judiciary. We are therefore sometimes faced with a situation in which the judges will not intervene with a verdict because they regard it as the jury's responsibility, and the Home Office will not do so because they regard it as the judges' responsibility. There is often no way out of this impasse, though sometimes the judges, when faced with a particularly tricky case, will not on their own responsibility allow the appeal, but indicate that their attitude would be different if the Home Office were to refer the case to them (see p. 114).

We have discussed the formal machinery by which a man whose appeal has been dismissed may have his case reviewed. But to whom does he turn for help to prepare his petition, to see it through the machinery, and, if necessary, to apply extra pressure on the machinery from outside?

The prisoner's first need when he goes to jail is for somebody outside who still believes in his innocence and who will both keep his morale up and prod the authorities. The first person to whom prisoners seem to turn under these circumstances is—Mother. Mothers may not have much legal or organizational expertise, but their total commitment to their sons often seems to make up for this. Wives and fathers may have their doubts, and be less effective as a result, but mothers seem to have an unshakable faith in the innocence of their offspring. The Cross brothers' solicitor said to us: 'Their mother was very consistent. She was the main instigation—wouldn't let the case rest. I was never certain of their guilt, especially after listening to their mother.' Kenneth Cross said:' When they close your appeal you think, that's it. Nothing you can do then. But me mother wrote to different people.'

Harold Dunsmore, convicted of 'unlawfully having in his possession a cigarette lighter, a ring and a watch' and sent to Borstal for two years, was suddenly released after eight months, and the rest of his sentence remitted, almost entirely as a result of his mother's efforts to prove his innocence. Mrs Dunsmore said: 'It was over a week after his trial before we knew what had happened. We didn't know nothing. Soon as we heard, I says, put in for an appeal, and he did, and I went to the Appeal Court—and the judges, they don't take notice of what you say there, talk about falling asleep. They didn't listen to a word he said. After that, I didn't know what to do for the best. I wrote to our MP, but I didn't know at the time you could go and see him. He wrote back and said that there hadn't been any miscarriage of justice. So I write to the paper. I was sure something could be done because he was innocent. My old man said, it's not worth your while bothering, but I said, I don't care, I can't leave it. I said, I'll try and try and try till I do, I can't sleep till I've got him out, knowing he was innocent. I'll tell you what started me off, they put him in Wormwood Scrubs with murderers and all people like that. As a mother, it just comes natural if it's your own son, especially if you know he's innocent.' Mrs Dunsmore had not merely tried to raise help for her son after the appeal, she also collected all the defence evidence for the appeal hearing. This is a job normally done by a solicitor, but her son was not granted legal aid and they couldn't afford a lawyer. She located the man from whom her son had said he had bought the watch. He confirmed Harold Dunsmore's account and agreed to appear as a witness. She also found the man, William Warrington, who had owned the ring inscribed 'WW' and had sold it to Dunsmore. He gave Mrs Dunsmore a letter supporting Harold Dunsmore's story.

But neither the petitioner not his mother can achieve very much on their own. There are two directions in which they can turn. There are those individuals and organizations part of whose job it is to look into cases of this kind. In this category come MPs, possibly the defence lawyers, and organizations such as 'Justice', the National Council for Civil Liberties, the Lay Legal Complaints Tribunals, the Citizens Advice Bureaux and even the Council for Human Rights at Strasbourg. Alternatively, you can seek publicity, usually through the press.

In nearly all the cases we have examined, either the prisoner or his relatives had been in contact with their local MP, who frequently played an important part in their case. The important power that MPs have is that they can bring to the attention of the minister problems involving their constituents. If an MP takes up a case and writes to a minister, then the minister will personally look into the affair, and it will not simply be left to a civil servant. This kind of work is an essential part of the MP's role as the representative of his con- stituents.[4] An MP may visit his constituent in prison, may advise him and his family of their rights and of the procedures open to them, and he may even be able to have the case reopened and thoroughly investigated. In the case of Ron Avard (see p. 57) the investigation which led to his release from Rampton was the result of six months' hard pressure by his MP, William Price. This was decisive for Avard; for the MP, it is a routine, though important, part of his work. The importance of the MP's role was stressed by Tom Sargant in a memo sent to the Donovan Committee on Criminal Appeals: 'At present the plight of the wrongly convicted prisoner after appeal is a desperate one. All the forces of authority are against him, and no one is interested in helping him. He can write a hundred letters, produce cogent arguments and significant evidence, but unless he has a sympathetic and energetic MP working on his behalf no one will tell him why his petition has been rejected and no one will come to see him.'[5]

Lawyers are under no obligation to continue with their interest in a client's case after they have ceased being paid. Most accused persons cannot afford to retain a lawyer after the failure of their appeal, and legal aid is not available at this stage. But there are some lawyers who continue to take such an interest where they feel their client has suffered a serious miscarriage of justice. Such lawyers may contact the Home Office or local MPs or even the press in order to get their ex-client's case reopened. They may even conduct further investigations on his behalf, sometimes with the assistance of inquiry agents, and often at the expense of considerable time and money. There are certain firms of solicitors who have repeatedly come to our notice as exerting themselves on behalf of their ex-clients in this way. If either of the authors of this book were to be faced with a false criminal charge, they would now know which firm of solicitors to engage.

We have already mentioned a number of organizations concerned with this kind of case. Of these, the most efficient and impartial seems to us to be 'Justice', the British section of the International Commission of Jurists. 'Justice' has no particular political axe to grind, but consists of lawyers and laymen of a great variety of political persuasions. It stresses in its constitution its aim to 'uphold and strengthen the principles of the rule of law in the territories for which the British Parliament is directly or ultimately responsible: in particular to assist in the administration of justice and in the preservation of the fundamental liberties of the individual'. It proceeds by way of the appointment of expert and representative committees which examine areas of potential injustice and recommend reforms. It has never set out to investigate and take up individual cases and has very limited resources for doing so, but it was inevitable that as its assistance and purposes became more widely known, victims of injustice, both civil and criminal, should turn to it for help in increasing number. It is from these requests for assistance and the efforts to do something about those which seemed to have special merit that the reports of 'Justice' have gained much of their detailed knowledge and authority. Some idea of the scope of its activities with regard to wrongful imprisonment can be gained from Tom Sargant's memorandum to the Donovan Committee on Criminal Appeals: 'In the course of the past five years, I have received well over a thousand letters from prisoners complaining about aspects of their trials and convictions. Some have asked for help with their appeals. A larger number have approached me, only after their applications for leave to appeal have been dismissed. A substantial number running into hundreds have claimed that they have either wholly or in part been wrongly convicted.'

An alternative method of drawing attention to one's case is publicity—which generally means getting it discussed in the newspapers. When Mrs Dunsmore's son was wrongly convicted, the first thing she did was reach for one Sunday newspaper after another: 'When he got sentenced to two years' Borstal, I wrote to the *News of the World*, the John Hilton Bureau, but they said what was he doing in London with only £6 in his pocket? So I thought, I'll write to the other one, but the *Sunday Mirror* wouldn't take it up. *The People* took up the case and traced it all back. Everybody took it up after the fuss in the paper.'

The People report of the case that they investigated reads:

'It was then that Mrs Dunsmore sought the help of *The People*. In the past few weeks *People* investigators have taken statements from all the available witnesses.

'In particular Mr Warrington gave further information about the sale of the ring. His wife, too, made a statement confirming the transaction. And Mr Duke provided vital new evidence about the watch.

'He said he had given the watch to his cousin, Mr Alfred Dale, to pawn. Dale gave the pawn-ticket to Duke, who sold it to Dunsmore. Then Dunsmore redeemed the watch.

'In two important ways, the *People* investigators were able to confirm John Duke's evidence.

'Firstly, they took a statement from Mrs Gladys Duke, John's mother. She said: "I was busy about the kitchen one day in August. There I saw John give Harold a pawn-ticket for 50p. I asked him what it was for, and he said it was for the watch. I was annoyed at him giving it away, and told him off about it."

'THE PAWNBROKER

'Secondly, an investigator established that a watch *had* been pledged by Dale with a pawn-broker in Carlton Road, and that it *had* been redeemed early in September—almost exactly as Dunsmore and Duke had said.

'All this evidence could have been obtained by the police—if they had sought it. It is more than a pity that it was left to *The People* to secure it.

'There remains the cigarette lighter.

'Dunsmore had told the deputy chairman of London Sessions that he found it during a walk with his brother John. Now, *The People* has secured a statement from him corroborating his brother's evidence.

'HE MUST ACT

'What, then, is left of the case against Harold Dunsmore?

'*The People* put that question last week to an experienced barrister. "If all this evidence had been given," he replied, "I feel sure that Dunsmore's appeal would have succeeded."

'It is now for the Home Secretary to act. He can and should clear Harold Dunsmore of the charge on which he was mistakenly convicted.

'Justice demands no less.'

That report was dated 1 March 1964. Two months later the Home Office issued the following statement: 'At Bow Street Magistrate's Court on 2 October 1963, Harold Graham Dunsmore was found guilty of unlawfully having in his possession a cigarette lighter, a ring and a watch.

'He appealed to the County of London Sessions against this conviction, but the appeal was dismissed. On 20 November 1963, at London Sessions, he was sentenced to Borstal training.

'Following the publication on 1 March 1964 of an article in *The People* newspaper suggesting the existence of fresh evidence which was not before the courts, the Home Secretary asked the Metropolitan Police to make further inquiries into the circumstances of Mr Dunsmore's conviction.

'These inquiries have established that Mr Dunsmore was in fact in lawful possession of two of the articles which formed the subject of the charge on which he was convicted.

'In these circumstances the Home Secretary decided to recommend the remission of the remainder of Mr Dunsmore's sentence. He was released today.'

The People was happy to agree with this assessment of its role. It reported that 'there were heartfelt thanks too from Harold Dunsmore and his family' and that Dunsmore's MP, Lt-Col. J. K. Cordeaux, 'paid a tribute to *The People* for producing the new evidence which "certainly put the whole case in a very different light".'[6]

Newspapers are always on the lookout for cases of this kind. They provide marvellous copy—this is the sort of thing that makes newspapers sell, especially Sunday newspapers. They also provide concrete backing for the newspaper's constantly reiterated image of itself as 'protector of the small man' from scandalous outrage, whether bureaucratic or sexual. The Sunday newspapers especially seem to run this kind of story, perhaps because they can afford to devote more space to items not of immediate topical importance. The Sunday newspaper, which is both in concept and in format a kind of half-way house between a *news*-paper and a magazine, is the most widely-used, and currently perhaps the best vehicle for this kind of story. Whatever their original motives were, newspapers have come to perform a genuine public service in this way. If a newspaper can combine the provision of this public service with getting a good story, then it may put a very large amount of time and effort into it—far more than would be the case with a television or radio programme. We have noticed that people seem far more inclined to turn to the newspapers: perhaps this is the reason why, for instance, a great deal of time was spent on the case of Curbishley and Stupple (see p. 78) in an effort to find and publish the new evidence which might get the case reopened. The *Sunday Mirror* reported its own efforts, paying special attention to its own public spirit: 'Last January the *Sunday Mirror* laid before the Home Secretary a thick dossier of new evidence brought to light in more than two years of investigations by 34-year-old author and journalist Jeremy Hornsby and the newspaper's own staff.

'The facts were also laid before the public in a *Sunday Mirror* campaign to have the conviction of Curbishley and Stupple urgently reconsidered.

'Now, after a probe into the information by his legal experts, the Home Secretary has decided that it warrants reopening the whole case in the courts. Accordingly, Mr Callaghan has:

Exercised his powers under the 1968 Criminal Appeals Act to refer the case to the Court of Appeal for further consideration.

Sent the *Sunday Mirror* dossier, together with issues of the paper containing the facts, to the Registrar of Appeals.

Informed Curbishley in Wormwood Scrubs and Stupple at Gartree Prison near Market Harborough, Leicestershire, through their prison governors.

Telephoned the news to their local MPs in the last Parliament, both members of the Labour government, who had asked him to look into the new information.

Written to the Editor of the *Sunday Mirror* "to thank you again for the information" and to emphasise that it was "after careful consideration" that he made his decision.

'The law states that "where a person has been convicted on indictment . . . the Secretary of State may, if he thinks fit at any time . . . refer the whole case to the Court of Appeal and the case shall then be treated for all purposes as an appeal to the Court by that person."

'But as both former MPs agreed last night, such action is seldom taken.

'The Courts had earlier refused both Curbishley and Stupple leave to appeal.

'Mr Robert Mellish, the Housing Minister, and Stupple's former MP in Bermondsey, said: "In my twenty-four years in Parliament I have only known of one previous instance in which a constituent had his case referred back to the Court in this way, and his sentence was revoked. It is quite apparent that the Home Secretary has been impressed, as I was, by the case made out for these men, and substantiated by the *Sunday Mirror* campaign. All involved in it can be proud indeed."

'Attorney-General Sir Elwyn Jones was Curbishley's MP at West Ham South. He said: "I am very pleased at the Home Office decision. This is a rare thing. I am well aware of the interest that your paper has taken, and I know how grateful the Curbishley family are."

'Curbishley himself has already sent his thanks to the journalist who took up his case. "The hope that eventually somebody would help has been my lifeline", he wrote from his cell at Wormwood

Scrubs. "The fact that you have all shown such concern and determination to help me has dissolved virtually all the cynicism and bitterness that enveloped me. This will not only be a victory for me, or you, or justice, or truth, if I am freed—but for all other innocent persons who may be in prison at this moment. This should give them the inspiration to fight and hope." [7]

The press can only take up a limited number of cases. But they must receive a very large number of appeals for help of this kind. In Dunsmore's case, his mother tried three Sunday newspapers before she found one willing to take up the case. In Curbishley's case, his solicitor, who always believed he was innocent, happened to know the journalist who went on to do the investigations. Therefore, unless your case is in some way especially interesting, or unless you are fortunate enough to have contacts with the press, you will have to draw attention to yourself in some specific way. One thing you can do is to get some person or people of high standing publicly to express doubts about your case. Lord Longford performed this service for Michael John Davies, convicted of the Clapham Common murder. The case of Colin Temple, convicted of rape, was strongly taken up by the headmaster of his approved school, who said 'I must show the boys in my care that protecting the innocent is every bit as important as punishing the wrongdoer', and by the Right Reverend Andrew Herron, Moderator of the General Assembly of the Church of Scotland, who called for the case to be reopened. Distinguished pressure leads to press publicity: the *Daily Record* promised on its front page to continue its 'relentless probe' into this rape case until justice was done. The *Observer*, reporting the campaign, noted: 'Mr David Lambie, Labour MP for Central Ayrshire, has raised the matter in the House of Commons in an adjournment debate, and is organizing a petition throughout Scotland in collaboration with Mr Alexander Munro, the headmaster of the approved school. Pupils at the school have been washing cars to contribute to a "Temple Defence Fund", and the son of a cat burglar has written a letter to the Queen.' [8]

If you have the money to start with, of course it's a lot easier. Dennis Stafford and Michael Luvaglio, prosperous businessmen convicted of murder, were able to mount a highly efficient publicity campaign to bring their case to the attention of the media. As a result, a great deal of newspaper space has been devoted to the case; a lengthy television programme was made about them; and a book has been published analysing the case. [9] Part of the strength of their claims lay in the fact that they were backed by a number of honest and reputable forensic experts—a pathologist who re-examined the medical evidence, a consultant motor engineer to have another look at a vital car crash, and a statistician and computer expert who tested whether the crime could have been committed in the way the prosecution alleged.

If you have neither money nor the backing of influential people, and if there is nothing immediately interesting or remarkable about your case, then more primitive means of attracting the attention of the press can be resorted to. Ronald Barker (see p. oo) said: 'I knew I'd carry on fighting before I went to jail. I knew before the trial I'd be convicted from the evidence. I would have convicted if I'd been on the jury. I knew I'd go on hunger strike because there was no other way of drawing attention to my case. I decided to go on hunger strike at once to force an inquiry. They didn't take any notice for the first few days because people do go on hunger strike. After nine days they sent me to the prison hospital, and after eleven days they began to force-feed me through tubes. I stayed on hunger strike all the time I was in prison. I did 375 days of hunger strike. I drank water because I didn't want to do myself an injury. I was co-operative in prison except for not eating. I didn't fight against being force-fed by tubes, Even so, they messed me around, so I resisted force-feeding for a time and struggled. They put me in a cell on my own to make sure I was not eating other people's food. They put me in the "strip" cells with no bedding in the cell except for a mattress at certain times. I was in a sort of canvas—I can only describe it as a miniskirt. They claimed I was mentally disturbed and that they needed to isolate me and keep me away from the prison's belongings.

'After about thirty days or so, there was a piece in the paper about me. My uncle had been round and told everybody he could. My first appeal against conviction was refused by the single judge. So I immediately appealed to the three judges. There was a lot of publicity by now, and it had got back to the Court. Later I was granted leave to appeal, not on the evidence but on the fuss, though they obviously couldn't admit this. They granted me a re-trial, and I was acquitted at the assizes. There were some new alibi witnesses, but most people reckoned that even if these witnesses had been at my original trial it would have made no difference. The fuss was the key thing.' At the re-trial, the judge warned the jury: 'I would be cautious if I were you, about concluding that the accused is innocent from his having gone on hunger strike or from his having maintained for over a year that he has been wrongly convicted.'[10]

Pressure of the various kinds we have been discussing usually results either in the reopening of the case, which may or may not lead to an acquittal, or in the parties concerned giving up. But occasionally, if the matter appears to be particularly grave, if all other channels have been exhausted, and if pressure from different sources is insistent and prolonged, a public inquiry may be set up. These are necessarily rare both because they take up so much of everybody's time and resources, and also because if they were at all usual they would effectively set up a parallel legal system which would undermine the authority of the existing one.

The most interesting of these inquiries from our point of view have been the Scott-Henderson and Brabin inquiries into the case of Timothy John Evans, and that section of the Mars-Jones inquiry which deals with the cases of Tisdall, Kingston and Hill-Burton. The advantages of such inquiries are, firstly, the resources in time and manpower available to them, which allow them to undertake a very thorough investigation of the case; secondly, their procedural rules are different from those of the courts, and they can therefore re-examine a particularly tricky case in a new way which may well throw new light upon the case. In particular, they are not bound by the admissibility rules which apply to evidence given in court. These advantages are apparent in the inquiries mentioned. In the Brabin inquiry, Mr Justice Brabin was left with 800,000 words of transcript to read from 100 witnesses who gave evidence over thirty-two days, and another 800,000 words in documents. The Mars-Jones inquiry lasted forty-six days, and evidence was heard from sixty-eight witnesses. These were both much longer, more thorough and much more expensive than the original trials.

As to the possible advantages of greater freedom of inquiry and looser procedural rules, Mars-Jones in his report said: 'I spent some ten days investigating the incident and the surrounding circumstances. . . . On such part of the evidence placed before me as would have been admissible in a criminal trial, a properly-directed jury would be bound to acquit the three young men. There can be no possible doubt of that.

'Although at first sight the conviction of the three young men and the affirmation of that conviction on appeal was a formidable vindication of the police officers involved, there was a considerable body of evidence to be investigated which was not available to either court. This was no fault of the persons responsible for the conduct of the prosecution or the defence before the magistrates' court or the appeal committee. They simply did not know and could not have known of its existence. The bulk of this additional evidence tended to confirm the account of the incident given by the three young men. Much of it, of course, would not have been admissible in a criminal trial.'[11]

There are concomitant disadvantages to these inquiries. Because so much evidence is taken, and because it is not bound by clear rules of admissibility or procedure, the decision as to what is or what is not true or relevant must necessarily be an arbitrary one. Also, it is in the nature of the system that these inquiries take place a long time after the events they are investigating. The Brabin inquiry into Evans's case took place sixteen years after the murders were committed. Mars-Jones said: 'To establish anything with this degree of certainty after the lapse of five years has proved an extremely difficult task. This lapse of time had obviously placed a strain upon the recollection of everyone concerned.'[12]

One way of getting a new and different hearing of your case is to bring a civil action which will necessitate going over the same ground as was covered at your criminal trial. This was the last and most effective course followed by Alfred Hinds, whose repeated attempts to draw attention to his case and get it reheard earned him the nickname '57 Varieties Hinds'. In 1953, Hinds was convicted of complicity in robbing Maples furniture store. He was sentenced to twelve years' preventive detention. Lord Goddard, the then Lord Chief Justice, congratulated Detective Chief Superintendent Herbert Sparks, Head of the Flying Squad, for his work on the case. In 1964, the *Sunday Pictorial* published extracts from ex-Chief Superintendent Sparks's autobiography largely concerned with Hinds's case. In these, he asserted that not only had Hinds been found guilty of the crime, but that he was guilty of it, and was lying when he claimed otherwise. Hinds immediately sued him for libel in the High Court. A jury decided that Sparks had libelled Hinds, and awarded £1,300 damages. As Mr Justice Edmund Davies put it, this libel action had 'handed him on a plate' the chance to get his case reheard.

At the civil trial, Hinds was able to call a lot of new evidence which had not been available at the criminal trial. He called new scientific evidence, and new alibi witnesses including Christine Keeler's stepfather.

Not unnaturally, Sparks decided to appeal against this verdict, but had to abandon the appeal because he ran out of money. He had been sued personally, and not the newspaper.

Hinds, who had been out on parole under the hostel system, and going to work daily on condition that he return nightly to Pentonville, was now in effect set free. In view of the unique circumstances, the Home Secretary also referred the case to the Court of Criminal Appeal. This put them in something of a quandary, since they were now faced with two jury verdicts, one of which said he did it, and one of which said he didn't. The Court failed to act as Hinds had hoped and refused to quash his conviction. Hinds felt that 'the Court had merely to emulate Pontius Pilate and shed all responsibility by pointing to the libel case verdict. Failing this, they could have recourse to the new re-trial legislation.'[13] However the Court of Appeal chose to wash its hands of the matter in quite another fashion.

It would no longer be possible for Hinds to get his case reheard in this way. The Civil Evidence Act, 1968, provides that if a libel action hinges on the issue of whether someone did or did not commit a certain crime, then the fact that he has been found guilty or acquitted of it in a previous court is accepted as conclusive proof of the matter.[14]

Nevertheless, there are still other ways in which people can use the civil courts to get their case reheard. Henry Scudder, for instance, sued his solicitors for negligence (see p. 102), and got what was in effect a re-consideration of the issues involved in his case. In many complex fraud cases there is simultaneously a civil and a criminal action. There have been cases where a man has been convicted of fraud in the criminal court, and yet has won his case in the civil court on the same evidence and using the same documents. Civil actions may be initiated by the defendant against a prosecution witness, or by the apparent victims of the fraud, hoping to get their money back.[15]

Up till now, we have been discussing cases where people have gone on fighting, often with the powerful help of outside agencies; and when they have got off, it has been largely as a result of these efforts. There are also a few cases where the effort is to some extent organized by the authorities themselves. Such a one was the case of Leonard Davey, who pleaded guilty to possessing Indian hemp and was sentenced to six months' imprisonment. Davey was on his way to Wormwood Scrubs to start his sentence when the Scotland Yard laboratory boffins reported: 'This is grass-seed, not Indian hemp.'

Davey, a hot-dog salesman was bailed immediately he arrived at the prison, and was later exonerated. He said: 'It's a bit of a liberty, isn't it, mate, but I'm not complaining. The police have been good to me over this. They made a genuine mistake. I don't want to cause trouble for anybody.' When asked why he pleaded guilty, he said: 'The police told me it was Indian hemp I had in a small package. I didn't know what it was so I took their word for it and pleaded guilty. Fortunately someone bothered to check the stuff or else I would be down the line now. A man asked me to collect the package from another man in a shop in Camden Road. I picked up a small packet wrapped in tissue paper from a Greek in the shop. The police came in and arrested me while I was still there. I didn't know what the packet was, but I never use dope myself and I hadn't suspected that.'[16] Another man got off on the same sort of charge for possessing drugs which turned out to be spinach.

Another drugs case of a different kind is that of Walter Pinter who had pleaded guilty to unlawfully possessing drinamyl tablets. He said at the time that he had bought them in a cafe, but later told a policeman who had nothing to do with the case that he had in fact obtained the tablets on prescription from a doctor. Police investigation showed this to be correct and he was awarded a Queen's pardon. The chairman, Ewen Montagu, in a characteristic observation, said: 'This is an interesting commentary on the suggestion we have to listen to so often that the police are only interested in convictions and plant these articles on defendants.'[17]

We have already discussed the role of police investigation in the case of Trevarthen and Cunliffe (see p. 120).

But in most of the cases we have come across, eventual exoneration has been neither due to the efforts of the defendants nor to those of the authorities. It has been due to chance, in one way or another. As we have pointed out earlier, this seems a strong indication that there are many more cases of wrongful imprisonment which are not brought to light.

The random occurrence that seems most frequently to crop up is that the real culprit confesses to the crime. This is not to say that this happens often or systematically. It is fair to assume that in many cases the person who has really committed the crime is only too pleased to find someone else blamed. In many other cases the culprit may not know that someone else has been convicted of his offence.

There appear to be three main categories of people who do

eventually confess. One is when, for one reason or another, the real culprit appears to be smitten with a bad conscience. Albert Chapman was convicted of driving a van knowing it had been taken without the consent of the owner, and assaulting a police officer. He said: 'I got nine months for that and eighteen months' disqualification. So I went to Leeds [prison]. I was in Leeds about a week and I was in the prison library and a bloke went in that I knew and he come up to me and said; "What are you doing here?" So I told him all about it, so he says: "Oh, they've brought a bloke back that's admitted doing yours." And what had happened—the day that the van got stolen, the bloke who had done it, he had got away, run away, he got away from the police, and the same night, Friday night, he'd done something else and he got caught for that, and the following morning, Saturday, he got six months. When he were in the open prison at Thorpwell, he'd read it in the paper—Bradford man gets, you know, Chicago-style attack, all a load of rubbish, and he'd read it in the paper and he'd told the governor of his open prison, and they'd got in touch with Bradford police.' Desmond Joyce, solicitor for Roy Roberts who made this confession, said in court when Roberts subsequently pleaded guilty that his client had told him: 'I put myself in his position and I had to tell the truth.' Roberts's confession was believed, and Chapman was exonerated.

The second category is that of people whose confessions emerge as a result of police investigation of other offences. This is what happened in the case of the Cross brothers. Their solicitor said: 'The case was reopened about a year after the Crosses were convicted. Three youths were apprehended and during police questioning stated that they had done it and one of them produced the watch that had been taken in the robbery. None of the property had ever been recovered from the Crosses.' Kenneth Cross added to this: 'There was a police detective called Paul Cottingham. He was concerned in our job and he helped question us but he wasn't one of the main ones. If it wasn't for Paul Cottingham, we'd still be inside. He was concerned with the arrest of the other three, and as soon as he'd found out what they'd done, he went straight up to the head of Nottingham CID, McCulloch, who went to the Home Office in London on the same day.'

The suddenness of this chance discovery took everyone by surprise, including Kenneth Cross who had by now resigned himself to seeing out his sentence. 'One day the jailer came in and threw all my things into a blanket and put them in a heap outside the door.

He said: "The governor wants to see you straight away", and I thought: "What've I done now?" and then the governor said: "We've got orders from the Home Office and you're to be released straight away." Dartmoor wasn't ready for my release. They usually give people clothing on release, but there was nothing ready for me. I made some good friends in prison, and they all yelled out: "What've you done?" They released me from Dartmoor at 4 o'clock, they took me in a Land Rover to Plymouth and put me straight on a train.'

Our third category is that of people who confess because they seem to have nothing more to lose. They may be in jail doing a long stretch for something else, and are unlikely to have the sentence increased. When convicted of another crime, they may ask for this offence to be taken into consideration along with a string of others. They may confess when they are at death's door, for medical or (in the past) judicial reasons.[18] Gerald Morris said of the man who later confessed to his crime: 'He was arrested in Cardiff on a job, burgling an office. He asked to have taken into consideration fifteen other charges including the Swansea garage. The authorities checked back and found out about me, and so a Home Office investigation was set up. I'd seen him earlier in prison when he was doing six months for assault. We were there together for about five months but I had no idea he was connected with this crime. He never said anything, even though he knew about my case.' (In fairness it should be added that the other man claimed he did not know of Morris's conviction, and that he had confessed to the charge while on remand for another. The judge said to him at his subsequent trial: 'It is strange that I should pay tribute to you, but as a result of your candour a person who was apparently wrongly convicted is now going to be freed.')

There are various other ways in which chance new evidence has come to light and got somebody out of a difficult position.

A man whom we shall call Short was held in prison for, as was thought, committing a series of indecent assaults and attempted rapes. One of the women had identified him as her assailant and another had identified his clothing. Luckily for Short, the crimes, which were of a distinctive type, went on happening while he was in prison—five similar assaults were committed by a man answering to the same description as Short, even down to his clothing. It was quite impossible that Short could have had anything to do with them, and so he was released. This recent case recalls the classic one of

Adolf Beck, which was instrumental in getting the Court of Criminal Appeal set up. On two separate occasions Beck was imprisoned for committing a series of frauds on women. A large number of the victims identified him as the man who had defrauded them. More frauds of the same kind occurred while Beck was in prison on the second occasion, and the real culprit was eventually caught.[19]

James Ritchie was also wrongly accused of indecent assault, and was jailed for nine months. In his case, the victim was never convinced that the police had caught the right man, although Ritchie had confessed to the crime. He said to the police, 'if the lady says I did it, I done it.' After the jury found Ritchie guilty, his victim was not satisfied that justice had been done. She searched the streets for her attacker, and six days later found him. The man was later arrested, and admitted the attack and assaults on other women. Ritchie's conviction was quashed by the Appeal Court.[20]

Patrick Michael Breen was found guilty of murder and sentenced to life imprisonment. The victim, a 15-year-old girl, disappeared on 18 October, and was not found until sixteen days later. The essence of the prosecution case was that Breen was the last person to see her alive, and that he strangled her—that is the case depended on no one else having picked her up after Breen had been seen with her. In jail, when they were both queuing to see the governor, Breen met a new witness who had known the girl since childhood. He said that on the evening she disappeared, he saw her in a cinema with a man who looked by his clothes and his crew-cut like an American serviceman. As the witness left the cinema, he said he saw Breen in the street. This witness had not given his evidence before because he was in prison both at the time of the committal proceedings and at the time of the trial. On the basis of this new evidence, the three judges gave leave for Breen to appeal.[21]

It might be worth noting here that in a number of cases, wrongly imprisoned men have found out whilst they were in prison who really committed their crime. When this has happened, they have usually been able to get in contact with the man concerned, who is often in jail himself. Sometimes the real culprit is induced to confess in this way.[22]

One further possibility is where the prisoner is able to prove that the crime of which he has been convicted was never committed. This occasionally happens in certain cases connected with sex and fraud.

We have been discussing various ways in which wrongly convicted persons have been able to prove their innocence. But we have also come across instances where the same procedures have been followed and have not worked, though in some cases some other chance has later exonerated the prisoner. Once again, this leads us to believe that the proven cases of wrongful imprisonment we have examined are simply the tip of an iceberg of wrongly convicted persons.

We have shown that a persistent proclamation of innocence can, as for instance in the case of Ronald Barker, lead to eventual exoneration. In practice, most people are inhibited from pursuing their case in this way. Kenneth Cross said: 'You get resigned after a while and you do your time. Prison's full of people who say they're innocent. You keep your mouth shut, or people think you're a crank. I talked to the deputy governor at Lincoln and he said: "It's no concern of mine. You're here for five years and you do five years." Then when I went to Dartmoor I didn't think no more about it.' Arthur Thompson reinforces this point: 'Well, when you're in prison, everyone is guilty. I might have told one or two, perhaps three people altogether all the time I was there. I've just never wasted my time telling people I was innocent. Everyone, well, 10 per cent of people, have got various grievances. They're not actually innocent, but the way the evidence has been put against them, they're not guilty as charged. So therefore you're getting various petitions and different people saying they're innocent, and that, but I only spoke to one particular person that I walked round with. He was a person much older than myself, and always used to more or less bolster up my confidence, always kept saying it would come right, and eventually it did come right. It was a complete fluke of one in a million.'

There are times when the wrongly imprisoned man happens to meet someone who knows the real culprit. But this does not necessarily mean that the real culprit will be willing to confess, and if he doesn't want to, then the contact between the two men may not want to incriminate him. Kenneth Cross said: 'When I was in Lincoln gaol I met a man from Warsop who told me that he knew we hadn't done it, and said he knew who had. I felt you couldn't ask him to give evidence—it would have put him in such a difficult position as it was a particular mate of his—Warsop's such a small place. Anyway, he would probably just refuse to say it in court. It bucked me up no end knowing that someone believed me.'

In Ronald Barker's case, Barker's co-accused, Ross, knew who his real accomplice was, but refused to name him. The man knew that Barker was in prison for what he had done, but wouldn't come forward. Later, Ross wrote in letters that Barker was not involved, but wouldn't tell the whole story in the Appeal Court because it might have revealed perjury by his alibi witnesses. When asked at the Appeal Court, Ross admitted he did it, and said that Barker was not involved. But he still declared his original alibi was true, and would not say who had done it.

Even where the guilty person can be induced to confess, there is no guarantee he will be believed. Thomas Hall (see p. 27) was able to contact the man who had committed his crime, and got him to admit to it. Frank Maughan, the real culprit, said: 'I never saw Whitfield [Hall's co-accused] again until I was sent on remand to Durham prison for an offence at Whitley Bay. When I was on remand I was greatly surprised to find that a man called Hall was also charged with Whitfield for breaking into Tate's, which was impossible because only me and Whitfield was involved. One day in the prison, when I was still on remand, but after Whitfield and Hall had been sentenced, Hall saw me in the cookhouse passageway. He said to me: "Harry tells me that you were the one that did the job with him which I've been found guilty of." I told him that as soon as somebody come up to see me, I would admit it, as it was wrong that he should be in prison for a thing what I'd done. The reason why I didn't admit it before is because I didn't think it possible that he would be found guilty of a crime he did not commit.' This confession was not believed, and Hall only proved his innocence much later by producing a number of new alibi witnesses.

It is difficult in this case to see why the confession was not believed. But in cases where the person confessing has little to lose, it is perhaps understandable that the authorities should be suspicious. The kinds of people likely to arouse this suspicion are: people who are already doing a long stretch of imprisonment for another crime, and would be unlikely to have very much added to their sentence; people convicted of another crime, and who ask that this, among many others, should be taken into consideration—as one police inspector put it: 'Young criminals quite often ask old lags to take offences into consideration for them.' A third category is that of first offenders who confess to a crime of which a hardened criminal has been convicted. They will get a much shorter sentence than he got, and might agree to undergo this for a consideration. (This may be what happened in the case of Seamus O'Toole, see p. 60).

We have earlier urged various reforms and changes in the legal system which would reduce the number of people wrongfully imprisoned and who remain in prison, their appeal refused or dismissed. But in whatever way any legal system is operated, mistakes will always be made, and there will always be cases that slip through the net. What can be done to rescue people in this position?

Firstly, there should be some provision for legal aid and advice for people preparing petitions for the Home Office. Obviously the danger of this is that all prisoners would want to take advantage of this scheme: some sort of appropriate sifting machinery would be needed.

Secondly, the Home Office's investigators at the moment are office-bound, and any investigations in the field have to be left to the police. We feel that the Home Office should have a unit which is able to undertake field investigations of petitions. This could perhaps be staffed by retired police officers. They would have the requisite experience and known integrity in this field, and would enjoy the confidence of the serving police, yet at the same time they would have no axe to grind. They would not have been in the case earlier, and would not resent being taken away from what the police regard as more essential duties.

Perhaps the onus of proof for gaining a free pardon should still lie with the petitioner, but this would still leave a lot of cases where the petitioner, although he has not proved his innocence, has been able to show that there is considerable doubt about his guilt. For cases like these, perhaps the already existing system of remission could be formalized and adapted to ensure that such men are released, even if their conviction has not been set aside.

Chapter 7

Consequences

For the person wrongly imprisoned, as for the person rightly so, there are essentially three aspects to his punishment. There is the time he actually spends in prison. He loses his liberty, and he loses his earnings for that time. Secondly, he will suffer other direct and tangible losses. He may have to pay his legal costs, or part of them; his family may be reduced to poverty while he is in jail. This may, but does not often, break up the marriage. He will almost certainly lose the job he was holding at the time he went to prison. Thirdly, there are the more indirect and intangible consequences of conviction. He may lose his reputation among his family, his acquaintances, and potential employers. By being labelled a criminal, he may be forced into becoming one: he may no longer be able to make a good living honestly, because people may be unwilling to employ him. His confidence in himself may be undermined.

Obviously, we are more interested in the way these punishments may affect the wrongly imprisoned man. For various reasons, they may be heavier, and affect him more, simply because he is innocent. Also it must not be thought that these punishments can easily be compensated for or reversed when he is finally exonerated. It is easier to label someone a criminal than to unlabel him.

For the man wrongly imprisoned, the main burden he suffers is the time actually spent in jail.[1] But the length of the original sentence will also contribute to this, since he has no reason to think that he will not serve the full sentence. To serve the first six months of a ten-year sentence is perhaps rather worse than to serve the first six months of a one-year sentence. Ironically, the innocent man may get a longer sentence than if he was really guilty of the offence. If he continues to insist he is innocent, he will not be able to plead mitigating circumstances, and may not wish to show remorse for a crime he has not committed. Ronald Barker said: 'I wouldn't disclose my antecedents or pay retribution. I wasn't willing to ask for leniency for something I hadn't done. I had a good army record, but I didn't want mitigation. So I got a longer sentence.' The probation officer's reports on the Cross brothers presented to the court before sentencing also imply that this is the case. That on Kenneth reads: 'His denial of the present charge prevents any assessment of the degree of culpability or reasons for involvement. If he is guilty, I can find nothing to offer in mitigation.' That on Peter and John reads: 'His complete denial of this offence precludes any attempt to relate my inquiries to it. If he is guilty, his conduct is completely incomprehensible. He was not short of money, and I have discovered nothing which might explain why he might involve himself in such a risky and ill-conceived crime.'

When he is in prison, the man's reactions may vary largely according to temperament and whether he has been in prison before. At one extreme, there is the man who, although wrongly convicted this time, takes the attitude: 'I think quite big mistakes happen quite often, but people say: Ah well, I'll appeal, but I've done five others like this anyway, so it's poetical justice'—as one man in this position put it, adding: 'I don't feel bitter, I put it down as a game really.'

But even men who have been in prison before, and who aren't particularly dismayed by the prospect of it in itself, may not be quite so light-hearted about the distinction between prison when you have committed the crime, and prison when you haven't. One such man, who got off when the real culprit confessed, told us: 'I've gone in before. I've been guilty. I know I've got time for what I've done, but when you get time for something you haven't done, you walk up the wall. You know there's somebody done it, you know.' In a similar case in America, Jerome and Barbara Frank quote a wrongly imprisoned man, Caruso, as saying: 'When you're guilty and in prison, you're OK. You can get a good night's sleep. But I was innocent and I kept thinking about that, and I didn't sleep so good.'[2]

Some people, understandably, are affected much more seriously. One such was Edward Hogg, who said of his experience: 'It was terrible in prison. I have never been in a place like it before. It was a dirty place. I thought that it was not right that I should be there, but I honestly did not expect to get out. . . . I shared a cell with two others—one in for breaking and entering, and the other for taking and driving away a motor car.'[3] Naturally prison is unpleasant; but this seems much worse if you feel you are there unjustly.

One of the things about prison is that it gives you so much time to brood about this very injustice. Kenneth Cross said of his experience: 'You go through several periods. First of all, you're appealing, and you think, I'm in England, things like this don't happen here. Then one day the governor flings open the door and says: "Your appeal's been refused. . . ." But you appeal again. Then he says: "Your second appeal's been refused, and you've lost forty days' remission"—forty days for having the cheek to appeal. Nothing you can do then. When they close the appeal, you think, that's it. For a few weeks then, you're in a very depressed state. In Dartmoor, I would sit in my cell and think, did I do it? You almost believe you did it. Perhaps I had a blackout and did it. Perhaps our Pete and John have done it with a third person and I'm just dragged in. In Dartmoor at one stage I was obsessed with the thought that my brothers had done it. I spoke to our Pete after, and he had had the same thoughts—that our John and I had done this . . .' For Kenneth Cross, the enormity of what had happened led him to doubt three of the basic assumptions of his life: his own memory, his trust in his brothers, and his sense of what was possible and impossible. Fortunately, he had the intelligence and strength of character not to be overwhelmed by these doubts, but to use his spare time constructively. He said: 'In prison, I did a hell of a lot of reading, mainly modern history. I even had my lights left on late at night to read. I did a correspondence course, too.'

For some, the ordinary unpleasantness of prison is compounded still further. Ron Avard didn't understand what was happening to him, nor what he was in for. His mother said: 'He used to be very depressed. Mum, could you try and get me home. Oh no, son, I said, I can't. I said, turn round, son. He said, what am I here for, Mum? I said, you know, don't you? He said no. I said, well, you know, rape. He said, what's that?'

For Thompson, there was the ever-present possibility that the victim of the attack might die, and that he might be hung: 'If he'd have died within twelve months of us being found guilty, they say we would have hung.'

Q: How did it feel?
Thompson: It's terrible, just unbelievable. It's something you didn't have to think about at all. It was already a nightmare serving seven years without having to think of that. Sometimes you'd think, well, it would be a quick ending or something like that. But even when I was released, for two or three years afterwards I still

had various nightmares. It was always one thing. Always screaming at my mother, asking her to release me. Just always the same thing.

Wallace, in a similar position, wrote in his diary: 'The most appalling shock of all came when the governor visited me and announced that the date for my execution had been fixed.'[4] Wallace's conviction was quashed by the Court of Appeal.

Anyone involved in a trial of any size will have to face substantial legal costs. For many people, and certainly for most of the people with whom we are concerned, most or all of these costs were met by the legal aid scheme.

But there were people who were judged to be earning too much money, or to have too much put by in a capital sum, to be granted the whole of their legal costs. Some were required to pay all of them. None of these people was rich, and for some of them it turned out to be a heavy burden. Many people subsequently proved innocent are very bitter about this. In most criminal trials, even if one is acquitted, one will probably have to pay at least some of one's costs. It is by no means usual for the judge to award costs to a successful defendant. Even when costs are awarded, they may not be fully adequate. Ben Hugman (see p. 67) said: 'At the Old Bailey the judge threw out the case and directed the jury to find us not guilty, and awarded costs to the defence. But that still left us £420 out of pocket, because we were told we had hired a more expensive counsel than the case warranted.'

Just how high the cost of proving your innocence can be is shown by the case of a man whom we shall call Denmark. He received legal aid at his original trial, but was forced to pay privately for his appeal. He received a lawyer's bill itemized as follows:

QC's fee: £674·40
Junior counsel's fee: £429
Solicitor's costs: £362·50
Total: £1,365·90.

The parents of this young man were not well-off, and were forced to sell their house for £1,400 in order to meet the bill.

Even if all legal costs are met by the State, wrongful imprisonment can still involve you in substantial financial loss. Gerald Morris (see p. 27) said: 'On earnings alone I lost £1,500 through being in jail. [He spent twelve months in jail.] I'd been a self-employed plasterer on £30–£40 a week. I lost my business, my tools, equipment, site and money, and when I came out I had to start from scratch again. I lost my car, which was on hire-purchase. My wife had to go on National Assistance while I was away. My wife, who was pregnant at the time, was thrown out of our house because it was in my name.' This case is a very typical one.

In spite of all this, it is worth noting that in most of the cases we looked at, people showed a strong degree of resilience. After release, they were on the whole able to take up their old lives again. They did find jobs again. Many of them were not married. Where they were, their wives generally stood by them.[5] There are, of course, exceptions to this. William Thomas Davies claims that his wrongful conviction broke up his marriage and cost him £1,800 in pay: 'My life is in ruins. . . . Before I was jailed, I was earning £30 a week [as a long-distance lorry-driver] and we were a happy family. Now my marriage has broken up and I have started divorce proceedings.'

The people likely to be worst hit are those middle-class and professional people whose job depends on their maintaining a reputation of unblemished respectability. For these people, who have careers rather than a series of jobs, a break in the continuity of their career can mean the permanent loss of financial prospects, promotion and a pension, as well as what was anyway lost while they were in jail. A case in point is that of Major Peter Cory, who spent eight months in prison through a court-martial conviction which was later quashed. He was 40 at the time of the conviction, had been in the Army for twenty years, and would have stayed there until he was 55. He would have been entitled to a substantial pension. As a result of the case, he had to resign from the Army, and took a job as a site inspector with a building firm. His Army career was at an end, and his pension much less than it would have been. He said: 'My whole life has been in the Army, but I had no alternative but to resign and start a new life.'[6]

A lot of people of this type cannot go back to their old jobs. Even where they can do so, they often feel that they must resign, for the time being at least, because of the disgrace surrounding them. Philip Berry (see p. 101), a lecturer in a drama college, said: 'I resigned from the position that I held, which involved contact with, amongst other things, a number of schools, because I felt that my exposure in public would create embarrassment, even with people who were altogether reassuring. I still felt that it was unfair to hold that position with that particular case still sort of echoing around me. I am still working at the same place, but I'm no longer in that position.'

The 'costs' of imprisonment can take a less tangible form. The man accused of indecently assaulting a little girl (see p. 138). was very much affected by his case. His wife said: 'We won't have the children's friends at home any more. The doors are always kept shut, and he has quite a phobia about other children.' Ron Avard spent three years in Rampton on a false charge of raping children. When he came home, he was, in the words of his mother, a 'nervous wreck'. 'He's coming round now, he laughs a lot, but you should have seen him when he first come home, first fortnight. He's getting more like his old self now, you know, jolly and talks and that, but he can't forget. It's left him a wreck. He can't get up and down stairs any more, because he was on the flat in Rampton. It's left him a nervous wreck, but he'll get over it in time. I don't think he could have stayed there much longer, as he says they deteriorate there. He'd have become much worse.' The experience left Ron permanently uneasy with women and girls.

Ron: They told me not to talk to any married women or girls or anybody like that. When I come home, well I can't even talk to my little nieces, and I'm scared to pick them up, you see. It's shocked me to death, hasn't it? Yes, it shocked me to death when they said 'don't talk to anybody'.
Mrs Avard: Well, of course, they've got to warn them, haven't they?
Ron: That's what put the wind up me, that's why I don't touch them. I touch her now and stroke her, but wouldn't pick her up, or the little one, because it's frightened me nerves that bad, you know, hasn't it, Mum?
Mrs Avard: Yes, he won't go outside without me.

Ron is frightened of girls in this way perhaps because he associates them with punishment, with Rampton, and hence with feeling guilt at a crime he never committed. He still has a series of confused memories associating girls, Rampton and punishment: 'So one of the boys says, well, why don't you go to the dance? I said, Oh no, might be a death-trap, you see. Well these boys and gentlemen take cigarettes, you see, and the boys they nick these cigarettes and they put them down the girls' blouses—I don't like saying that, it's dirty. Anyway, Denis come back and said to me, why didn't you go off to the dance? I said Oh no, no, it would be a death-trap.

'So the staff is there watching on the other side. Anyway, then if you kiss in the hall they start the feet or the chains. They wait till you get back to the ward, you see, and then they give you the chain or the spoon, you see. Many times I've seen that being done. People with black eyes and that.'

Nevertheless, Ron's recollections of Rampton vividly recall other people's reminiscences about other 'total' institutions,[7] notably their public schools. He even justifies what is undergone by the inmates in much the same terms as these other loyal sufferers:

Ron: Well, I think, honestly speaking myself, well, it's done me good, ain't it?

Mrs Avard: Well in a sense it's made you manage, hasn't it? You know, cater for yourself.

Ron: Yes.

Mrs Avard: You've learnt the hard way.

Something else that prisons have in common with public schools is that the label they pin on you can greatly affect your chances in later life. The fact of having been to jail is a proof in the eyes of society that you have been tried and convicted of a crime of a certain degree of seriousness. Whether or not a person is labelled as a criminal is dependent not on what they have done, but on what they can be publicly displayed to have done. The whole ceremony of conviction and sentence is designed to draw attention to the fact that this man is guilty of this crime, and what a wicked person he is.[8] Some of our wrongfully imprisoned persons were very well aware of this. One of them felt labelled 'guilty' by the very process of investigation and trial: 'When they took me in they charged me with a crime, threw me in a cell with the other fellows, brought me out early next morning to be photographed and fingerprinted. When they told me what I was going for I turned round and I said to the men who were taking me in, I said, "Don't take photographs of me because I'm innocent, and don't take my fingerprints." They said: "Why?" I said: "Because I'm not guilty." I was taken into the court, never done a wrong action in my life, to man, beast nor child, and charged with a cruel thing of assaulting a girl. When I got to the court and they asked me if I was guilty or not guilty, I stood to attention as smart as I could and cried "Not Guilty!"'

This man even felt polluted by being put on an ID parade: 'Well to be on an identification parade and to think that you're going to be picked out, it's a terrible ordeal. Because as soon as you get in that parade with the other fellows, and you know that the police have taken you down and have brought them fellows in from off the street they haven't taken them down—as soon as you stand on that parade, you're guilty. You feel guilty. You feel every eye that's come into that place is on nobody but yourself, and you feel terrible and disgusted with yourself for having done such a thing that they're going to blame you for which you have not done.'

The presence of the press at the trial is an important element in this public denunciation. The court reports are a staple element of all newspapers—but especially local newspapers—and special facilities are provided for the press in courtrooms. Once this process has been gone through, it is very difficult to reverse, even if you are later shown to be innocent. There is no public pardoning ceremony equivalent to the public sentencing ceremony. Arthur Thompson, for instance, together with Leonard Emery and James Powers, received one of the most publicized pardons in recent years. Here is his description of how he received his pardon:

Q: Was there a sort of retrial at which you were exonerated, or what?
Thompson: Oh no, no, we were just given the Queen's pardon. We were just let out, we were just told at 7 o'clock at night that the Queen had pardoned us and we would be released the following morning.

This was a spectacular case, which for various reasons did hit the headlines. But in view of the very unspectacular nature of pardons, as described by Thompson, it is really not surprising that far fewer of them hit the headlines—or indeed get reported at all—than do trials.

We were able to find out details of many of our cases because they were sensational enought to be reported in the national press. If they reach this level of publicity at all, then the pardon is likely to get at least as much, and probably a lot more publicity than the original conviction. People who have committed boring crimes may well receive spectacular pardons. But there were a number of people whom we knew, from the list supplied to us by the Home Office, had received pardons, but whose cases did not seem to have been reported in the national press. We knew the dates on which these people had been convicted, on which the decision was made to pardon them, and on which the pardon was granted. We therefore searched in the relevant local newspapers for reports of any of these

G

three events. There were eighteen cases of men whose conviction or pardon had been reported in their local newspaper, but not in the nationals. In fourteen of these cases the man's conviction alone was reported, usually in some detail. In only four cases were both conviction and pardon reported, and there were no cases in which the pardon alone was reported. Of the four cases where both were reported, in three cases the conviction and the pardon got roughly equal treatment, both in terms of headlines and column inches. In the other case, the pardon received far more publicity than the conviction, because of its spectacular nature. We were very surprised at the nature of this imbalance, since we had expected if anything an imbalance in the other direction; pardons are much rarer than convictions, and, one would have thought, make better copy. But, as we have already noted, there are always reporters on the spot to report convictions, and there is no corresponding way in which they can pick up the news of a pardon—unless the news of the pardon comes up in court. This was what happened with each of the four pardons which actually got reported. In two of the cases, those who received the pardons were remanded after conviction for a medical report, during the course of which it was found that they had not committed the crime. When they came back to court, the court drew public attention to the fact that they had been pardoned. In one case, the pardoning of one man led to the trial of a prosecution witness for perjury. In the fourth case, the man concerned was being tried for another offence at the time when he received his pardon, and his lawyers made use of this fact in court.

We have already shown that being in prison can affect people's lives in a direct and damaging way. But the fact of being labelled 'a convict' can have additional, less tangible, but equally important effects. It can lead to doubt and mistrust by your family; your friends and neighbours may shun you; you may have difficulty getting a job. These consequences are not inevitable. They depend very much on the expectations and attitudes of your family and friends, and on the level of your job aspirations. We did talk to some people whose lives had been crushed in this way. But on the whole we were surprised at the lack of lasting social effect of this labelling.[9] In retrospect, this perhaps does not seem so surprising. Many of the people we spoke to already had criminal records, and sometimes these were very long and very bad records. Several others, who had no record themselves, moved in circles where a criminal record was fairly usual, and where it was no bar to social acceptance. Nor was a conviction much of a problem when it came to getting the kind of employment they wanted. What sort of jobs did these people have immediately before they were convicted? Typical jobs were: gardener, miner, dresser, labourer, merchant seaman, lorry-driver, porter, docker, butcher's assistant, window-cleaner, scrap-metal dealer, night-watchman, cowman and caretaker. Many were unemployed or on casual work. What stands out about this list is the lack, not only of respectable career jobs, but of skilled or even steady working-class jobs, Many of the people we spoke to simply returned to the kind of job they had always been used to after they came out of prison, and at this level found their conviction no hindrance in finding work.[10]

The people who really suffered from prison labelling were people who had always thought of themselves, and been thought of in the community, as highly respectable. Only a few people really cracked up because of their experience. None of these had any previous convictions or had been in any sort of trouble before, and they all belonged to what might be termed the respectable working class. One of these people described the effects of his wrongful conviction on him and his wife: 'All I know is, that he did the job and confessed, but I myself went through eight weeks of hell, backwards and forwards with a hundred pounds on my head all the time, getting snubbed by every person under the sun on the streets around where I lived. I was forced to come up here to live. It's worried my wife, it worried her beyond all control, but she couldn't do nothing. Every time I've sat down in a chair and for ever after, as I'd sit, she'd say: "Get up and get for a walk—or something like that, forget what has happened"—but if I live to be a hundred I'll never forget.'

The same man went on to describe the ostracism he had suffered from friends and neighbours even though someone else had confessed to the crime and he was completely exonerated: 'With me being in bed sick, and my wife downstairs, sick, neighbours kept coming in to see if they could give us a little bit of a hand, or do a little job, or did she want a cup of tea, or did I want anything, or to help her doing a bit of cleaning up. But after all that was over, and I'd been convicted of this serious crime, and my name was in the local paper, that they got a man for assault and robbery with violence—then everybody turned against me and my house, and my children, and everyone, and now I don't want to have nothing to do with them. I was called a dirty, black, filthy . . . I'll cut that out, by not just one person. Women on the street when they saw me come up the street, they'd get hold of their kiddies' hands and pull them into the house and say "Don't go near him, love", and young lads, when I'd been working in the front garden, have come and shouted foul stuff over the fence at me, but I've stood it all because I had to. I've been told to forget all about it, and walk with my head up, but I can never walk with my head up as long as I've that Town Hall to pass. I think that the people, at bottom of them, they are still not forward, they don't speak to me as a friend—normal. In fact, some of them say: "Now did you really do that job, Harry? We believe you did, you know, we believe so." I say, how can I do it when there's a young lad confessed to it? "Aye, he could have been bribed to say so."

'As far as neighbours go, I don't tolerate them. I keep entirely on my own. I don't want nobody to know none of my business. And I will not have a policeman up my path.'

A startling illustration of how unwilling people can be to believe that a man is innocent when once he has been found guilty—even though he has since been pardoned—was given us when we inquired for a man at a pub where he had been a regular customer. The publican said: 'I wouldn't bother to go and look for him if I were you. He did it all right. He's as guilty as hell.' This was despite the fact that the pardon had received extensive publicity in both local and national press. The man himself said: 'There are still people whispering against me. There's a rumour going around that I paid £200 to the man who confessed. I'm afraid to breathe in this town.'

Wallace (see p. 69) gives in his diary[11] a poignant illustration of how hard these pressures can hit a man: 'I think I must definitely abandon the idea of returning to a Liverpool agency, as the ill-feeling against me is evidently stronger than I expected. . . . I find all my neighbours are against me. . . . I met old Blank. The pompous old ass evidently did not want to speak to me, and after passing the time of day, he drew in to gaze at a shop window. I suppose this feeling against me will persist, and I may never live it down. . . . My nerves are all shattered after the ordeal. Today I have been very much depressed, full of grief and tears.'[12] Wallace had been a door-to-door insurance salesman, and the firm had to move him to an indoor office job after his conviction was quashed. His health broke down, and he died less than two years after his release.

Even those who might most reasonably be expected to believe in one's innocence sometimes find it hard to know what to think. Mrs Avard found herself forced to believe that Ron was guilty because the police and the courts said so: 'I was getting his dinner, you know, and getting him such a lovely dinner on the Monday, him and Dad, and a gentleman knocks on the back door. Oh, Mrs Avard, do come quick, he says, to the police station, your boy's in serious trouble. I can't come, I said, I'm getting his tea. Well, he says, he'll never come home again. I said, well I thought to myself, a lady can't do anything like that, I'd better get the tea. My husband came about quarter past six and I said, I don't know what's wrong, duck, something terrible's happened. So just then the police constable who picked him up came. He said, Mr Avard, can you come quick, I'll take you in my car. Of course, Dad didn't know what to think. He said, no, I'll go in my own car. This was quarter past six. Well, he went. It was quarter to nine, Dad hadn't come. Nearly nine o'clock he came home. Well the tea was ready. He said, I don't want no tea, so I said why? So he said, oh, Ron's done a terrible thing. Oh dear, I said, oh dear. He said, but I don't believe it. But, he said, I read all the copy of it down in the police station. Oh, I said, I don't know. I said, I can't take that in, duck. He said, nor me. But any rate, I said, they picked him up. I don't know, he must have done. I didn't know what to think.'

Q: Did you believe he was guilty at all?
Mrs Avard: Yes, wouldn't you have done? I did. I thought, well, he'd never been brought up like that. He's never been brought up to anything like that. He didn't know sex and he didn't know anything, you know, and we never talked about it, and he was always one for going to mass. I said to Dad, what's gone wrong, Dad, with him, and he said, oh no. He sat down there on that Monday night, he come in, he broke his heart. He sat in that chair, I couldn't get him to bed. He said, to think I've brought children up like that, to think one's turned out like that. He said, I can't believe it. I said, I can't, but then, if you've been picked up, I said, I don't know. . . . Mind you, I should still have gone to see him whether he'd done it or not, but I was pleased to think after two years that they gradually broke the news to me that it wasn't him. I don't know where my thoughts were at times, I'm sure.

We have shown that for most of these people, the prison label didn't materially affect their job prospects, because the prospects were never very good anyway. But for those with intelligence and ambition, it could be a hindrance. Kenneth Cross, an intelligent and educated man, said: 'When I was nicked, I was about to become a dust suppression officer, but that fell through. When I came out, I took up as a ripper [coal-miner], where I had left off. The mines management are very understanding. Where you come from, a punch-up's a serious thing, but here, it's neither here nor there, if no one gets hurt. But I think it hindered me a few years ago. I was on a shortlist for a National Coal Board course on industrial relations—there were three ways you could do it, three years full time at university, two years full time, or eighteen months practical course. Lads that were at school with me and got chucked out for being stupid, they got on it, and I didn't. Nobody had anything against me before, but they all knew about this, this affair got all the publicity.' Kenneth Cross is now a colliery deputy, and responsible for safety in the pit.

Another man, a college lecturer, felt that his prospects were no longer as good as they once might have been: 'I find that people who are colleagues and—I won't call them friends—but colleagues and people who have wished me well, and indeed, wished me well during the trials, their attitude has changed slightly because they feel now, I think—this is sheer conjecture—but one has the feeling that now I'm out of the mess, they're having second thoughts and thinking, well, how did he ever get into it? There's a sort of cooling of sympathy, if you like, and I think that the actual damage done to one personally in feeling and professionally in both present and future reputation is quite considerable.'

Respectability, and the self-respect that comes with it, may make people more vulnerable to an experience of this sort, but it also has its strengths. These were demonstrated by ex-PC Luckhurst: 'When it comes to recovering after the experience of being convicted and imprisoned and so on, it's been a very strange thing in my case [how straightforward it was], I think because I have never really regarded myself as a convicted person. I have never regarded the imprisonment as being proper or lawful, and it hasn't been a case where I've come back from the prison as a person who'd done some horrible crime who's been brought back and put into society to lead a new life. It was simply a case of coming back to continue where I left off before. I had always, I believe, led a proper, law-abiding life, and it was simply a case of coming back and carrying on in the same way. This is one of the reasons I've been able to carry on so easily since I came back, because there was nothing to live down.'

In Luckhurst's case, there has never been a pardon, and his conviction has never been quashed, but the publicity given to his case has had the effect of reinstating him in society. This is the kind of effect that should result from the publicity given to a pardon—but then, as we have shown, pardons seldom get this amount of publicity. Luckhurst said: 'Well, since I came home, we've been very fortunate in having a certain amount of publicity from television and news-papers and so on. I think it's become quite clear to a large amount of the community that I didn't commit any offence. There's no reason why I should hide anything, and I've been accepted as just somebody who lives here; just somebody who carries on the same as everybody else. I meet the local people in the local pub, and so on. I carry on a normal life now, and it's rarely discussed. I just carry on as a normal workman living here and nobody ever worries about it—nobody doubts my integrity or anything of that kind at all. . . .'

Q: Did you find it easy to get a job again?
Luckhurst: The strange thing was that it was easier than I thought it would be. I was given to understand at the local ministry that certain jobs would be barred to me because of my conviction, but I found that the jobs that I'd been interviewed for, I'd been accepted straightaway as being a person suitable for the job, despite the past, which I've always admitted right from the very outset. I've always told a prospective employer of my past, and he's simply disregarded it. They usually know something of it, because it's quite big local news, and it's never been held against me. The first job I had when I came back was in some way con-nected with the fact that I'd appeared on television, and the employer interviewed me after that. I kept that job for a period, and for various reasons I decided to leave, though in no way con-nected with this case. I simply went after another job. I went to see two or three people about a job, and each time I was accepted as just a person who wanted a job, and I was regarded as suitable or unsuitable because of my past experience in that particular job.'

Where someone suffers the experience of being wrongfully imprisoned, this may push him into committing later offences which otherwise he would probably never have been involved with. And if he comes up before the courts again as a result of this, his sentence may be all the heavier because his previous wrongful conviction is taken as constituting a criminal record. Edward Hogg was sent to a detention centre for three months after being convicted of stealing an axe and attempting to commit sexual offences with chickens. He had in fact not committed these offences; later, another man confessed to them and Hogg was granted a free pardon. Later, Hogg admitted stealing £4 from his mother and was prosecuted. When the recorder was told of his previous convictions, he sent him for borstal training, which in the absence of previous convictions would have been an incredibly harsh penalty for such a trivial offence. It was shortly after this second conviction that Hogg was exonerated of the earlier offences. Accordingly he appealed against sentence, and the Court of Appeal set aside his sentence and put him on probation instead. The Lord Chief Justice, Lord Parker, said that Hogg had felt a measure of resentment at having served his detention sentence. He later left home and picked up with a girl, and on a visit to his mother's house he stole £4 because he and the girl were desperate. This antagonized his mother at the time, and only sometime later were they reconciled.[13]

When we looked for John Cross, one of the Cross brothers, we found that he was now serving four years' imprisonment for taking part in a fight and causing grievous bodily harm. He had been in trouble for fighting before, but his mother felt this was a very harsh sentence nevertheless. She said: 'We thought he'd get three or six months, or even just told off. I'm sure it was this that went against him.' This, of course, is just surmise, because Cross, unlike Hogg, had been exonerated before this later conviction came up.

We have come across many cases of people wrongfully imprisoned, and very few where they have been compensated for it. These were people who had received Queen's pardons. We came across only two cases of people who had received compensation after their conviction had been quashed by the Court of Appeal after referral by the Home Secretary; none where the Home Secretary had agreed to remit their sentence because their conviction was seen to be doubtful. By no means all the people who received free pardons also received compensation.

The attitude of the Home Office to such payments was summed up by Mr Ennals, then Under-Secretary at the Home Office, in answer to a question by Mr Lyons, MP for Bradford East:

Ennals: Under present practice *ex gratia* payments from public funds are not normally made to persons acquitted by the courts unless there has been negligence or misconduct by the police or some public authority or official.

The Home Secretary was aware of hardship caused to people wrongly charged, but it would be wrong to attempt to discriminate between people acquitted. He did not feel able to modify the existing practice.

Lyons: Doesn't this mean that people who through no fault of their own have been convicted and spent a substantial time in prison have no remedy whatsoever? Is not this a denial of natural justice?[14]

This bears out our own observation with regard to cases coming through the Appeal Court. By implication, this also indicates why it is so difficult even for those people who have free pardons to get compensation. The only recent cases we have located where substantial compensation has been paid by the Home Office have been:

Arthur Thompson	27 months in prison	£400	1956
Leonard Emery	27 months	£300	1956
James Powers	27 months	£300	1956
Danny O'Leary	7 months (borstal)	£200 (offered)	1963
Kenneth Cross	8 months	£1,400	1965
Peter Cross	8 months	£1,850	1965
John Cross	8 months	£1,600	1965
Ronald Avard	42 months	£4,000	1969
Gerald Morris	10 months	£1,500	1970

In none of these cases was negligence alleged. The one common factor seems to be that all these people suffered substantial terms of wrongful imprisonment, and the Home Secretary seems to have admitted some liability for this, even in the absence of negligence on the part of the Crown's servants. Where negligence is involved, people seem to do rather better. Tisdall, Hill-Burton and Kingston, whose cases were examined by the Mars-Jones inquiry, received substantial compensation even though they spent only a month in prison.

How did these people feel about the amounts they had received? Arthur Thompson said: 'Sometime in January we was released after serving twenty-seven months in prison. My total compensation for this was £400. This I would think was not 20 per cent of what it cost my family to prove my innocence. . . . If you lose two years of your life between twenty-eight and thirty, what money can recompense that? Unbelievable to lose two years of your life at that stage of your life.'

Kenneth Cross said: 'I got least of all, and I got five years. I got £1,400 odd. Peter got most of all because he'd never been in trouble all his life, and I had. The amounts we got bore no relation to our wages, because Peter got most of all and he was the lowest paid. But it was ridiculous, £1,400 for a year—I could have earned at least £26 a week at that time, and really it was only my wages back— and they deducted all sorts of things, like insurance stamps, from the compensation money. Soskice said to our solicitor that there couldn't be compensation really unless we could prove malice on the part of the police. As it was, it was decided by an independent assessor, and it was take it or leave it.'

Danny O'Leary said: 'I faced the prospect of nearly three years in Borstal. The £200 does not even cover my loss of earnings.'

Any compensation is obviously better than no compensation. The mother of Harold Dunsmore (see p. 167) said: 'Such a little thing, you get picked up, you get eight months inside, you don't get a penny for it. It wouldn't be so bad if you got paid.' Nevertheless, the compensation paid, when it is paid, is obviously nothing like enough. A bare repayment of wages lost is, as we have shown, scarcely sufficient compensation for the damage likely to be suffered.[15] Curiously, the amounts paid out recently by the Home Office seem to be rather less than was the case in the past. Here are some payments made in Victorian and Edwardian times:

Oscar Slater—£6,000
Adolph Beck—£5,000
William Habron—£500
William Henry Barber—£5,000
Edmund Galley—£1,000

It must be remembered that some of these men served very long terms of imprisonment, and that some of these moneys were voted by special Acts of Parliament. On the other hand, the value of money has fallen very considerably since that time. Also we as a country, and as individuals, are considerably wealthier, and the earnings and standard of life that you lose by being put in jail are correspondingly greater.[16]

The Home Office awards also suffer by comparison with sums awarded by other institutions and by the civil courts. Major Peter Cory was initially offered £7,500 as an *ex gratia* payment by the War Office for his eight months in jail following a wrongful cashiering by a court-martial in Kenya. He said: 'I regard £55,000 as adequate compensation. I have spent about £2,500 to clear my name. I have sold my car and my insurance policy, and borrowed money to fight the case and keep my boys Tim and Simon at boarding-school.'[17] The civil courts make even more generous awards against the police or prosecution witnesses on charges of false accusation, without imprisonment being involved at all. The couple in the 'kiss in the car' case were awarded £5,200 damages. Eric Allum and George Hislop were awarded £4,000 each and costs for false imprisonment and malicious prosecution after they had been accused of attempting to steal or drive away a car, and later acquitted. It was alleged in this case that the police had planted the car keys on the accused. A law student who had been convicted of indecent exposure and fined £10 later had his appeal allowed and the conviction quashed. He then sued the police officer concerned for damages for false imprisonment and malicious prosecution. He was awarded £999·22½. This consisted of: £25 for false imprisonment, and £863·22½ for the malicious prosecution. He was also compensated for his costs in the other courts, agreed at £363·22½, and costs for his High Court action. Sometimes these cases are settled out of court. A schoolteacher acquitted of a charge of spitting at a policeman received £750 compensation from the police, and his companion at the time £300. In the cases connected with Detective-Sergeant Challenor, two men and two boys who were arrested and accused of carrying bricks at a political demonstration received £1,600 between them.

Why were the awards and damages so much higher in these other cases? There appear to be two main reasons. One is that they reflect the indignation of the jury, the courts or the public at some recognizably culpable act for which some identifiable person can be blamed. This amount reflects his punishment as well as the victim's compensation. On the other hand, because the onus is on the plaintiff to prove negligence, these cases are very difficult to win, and certainly to make a profit out of. But, secondly, these amounts also include compensation for those intangible losses, such as reputation, which we have discussed earlier in the chapter, and which seem to be omitted when the Home Office works out its particular brand of compensation. Admittedly, the people concerned in these cases—a solicitor's clerk, a lecturer, a schoolteacher, a barrister and a businessman—had higher social status, and therefore more to lose by way of reputation from a criminal conviction, than most of the people we have been considering. This does not affect the principle that money should be granted for loss of reputation, though it might affect the actual amounts concerned. Also it must be stressed that none of the people who sued the police had served a prison sentence, as had all the people we have been discussing.

There are three simple ways in which this situation could be improved. Firstly, some sort of commission should be set up whose job would be to look into and assess for compensation all cases of wrongful imprisonment, and not simply those terminated by a pardon. The Commission's attitude to granting compensation should be more generous than is the case at present. This is not to say that compensation would have to be granted in every case, but we feel that most cases of wrongful imprisonment merit some compensation.

Secondly, the basis on which compensation should be assessed is the harm done to the person so imprisoned, and not whether malice or negligence was involved. In this case, we feel that the State should accept absolute liability for what might be termed legal injuries. The issue of culpability is irrelevant. If it is felt to be relevant, it should be taken up in the civil courts.

Thirdly, great publicity should be ensured for pardons. A man's exoneration should be at least as well publicized as his conviction. One way to do this might be to adopt the French system, where a man who is pardoned can choose five newspapers in which a notice of his pardon will appear at the expense of the State.

Chapter 8

The French System

The process of penal investigation and trial in France is very different from that in England. It is often classified as 'inquisitorial' as opposed to the 'accusatorial' or 'contradictory' British system; but these labels are not particularly helpful. What is often understood by the label 'inquisitorial' is that the examining magistrate plays a vital role in the process; and this is certainly true in France. As a result of this thorough and often prolonged official investigation taking place at an early stage in the process of bringing a suspect to trial, the other stages of investigation and trial are seen in a very different light to similar processes in England. Many of the basic concepts, for example of the rights of the suspect, are different; and investigation and trial are conducted in a manner very different from investigation and trial in England. Where wrongful imprisonment is concerned, therefore, although many of the basic causes (for example misidentification, false confessions and statements) are the same, the reasons why they are permitted to take effect, and the stages at which they may do so, are often different from the English ones.

There are three principal stages in the bringing to trial of a suspect in France. Firstly, there is a preliminary inquiry (*enquête préliminaire*). This is conducted by the police, and it involves the search for the culprit and the evidence of his guilt. This search is conducted in secret. Officially, the police are not allowed to arrest or interrogate a suspect at this stage. In fact, they do do this, but it must be 'voluntary' on the suspect's part—the police have no legal right to force him to submit to questioning except in cases of *crime flagrant*. They may, however, indicate that it might be better for him should he acquiesce; and many confessions are obtained at this stage of the investigation. These will be discussed more fully below.

Secondly comes the *instruction préparatoire* conducted by the *juge d'instruction* or examining magistrate. When the police officially arrest the suspect the rule is that they should bring him before the examining magistrate within forty-eight hours. This rule is not always complied with. A well known case of this kind was that of a barman of the Champ-Elysées, who was kept in custody for almost a week without seeing the magistrate. He was arrested by two *gendarmes* who came to his house in a Paris suburb early one morning with a warrant from an investigating magistrate. They themselves knew nothing about the case. After spending twenty-four hours in different cells in and around Paris, he was transferred to the Santé prison where he was the eighth in a cell built for four. During these wanderings, he did see a magistrate once. The magistrate asked his name, but when the barman asked what he was charged with, said: 'You must see my colleague about that.' On the third day in the Santé his complaint reached the prison governor, who allowed him to send telegraphs to his lawyers. Three days later, he was suddenly released. The details of the case emerged later. What had happened was that the car number of his brother in Nice had been noted in connection with a minor crime. At the *Préfecture* the car number had been attributed to the barman rather than his brother, and the machinery of arrest set in motion. He was arrested on a Thursday morning; on Saturday, he got permission to communicate with his lawyer, who in turn got in touch with the examining magistrate concerned. The magistrate apparently did not want his weekend interrupted, and replied that he must wait until Monday. The barman therefore spent six days wrongfully imprisoned in a way which simply should not be possible under French law. It is hard to suppose that his case is unique, however.[1]

Once the suspect has arrived before the magistrate, the investigation of the case and the search for evidence goes on, though no longer in secret. During this stage of the investigation, the suspect may or may not be kept in custody, depending on whether the offence of which he is suspected is bailable or non-bailable, which in turn depends on how serious it is. At this stage, the suspect is stringently protected from malpractice. His lawyers may be present at all interrogations and confrontations; they have access to the dossier being built up against him. If he is kept in custody, the suspect does not undergo prison treatment. Subject to remaining in custody, he may as far as possible carry on his normal life; he may conduct his business from the remand centre, and receive visits, food and clothes. For his part, the examining magistrate has wide powers:

to arrest, to search, to seize private property, to read correspondence. The examining magistrate's investigation establishes whether or not there is a case to bring to trial.

Should the magistrate decide there is a case to answer, then the process carries on to the third stage, the *instruction définitive*—that is to say, the trial. This may take place in the *tribunal correctionnel* or *tribunal de police* if the offence is a minor one; in the *cour d'assises* if it is more serious. A case cannot be referred directly by the magistrate to the *cour d'assises*; it can only reach there via a court of first instance, which may make a recommendation of *renvoi* or *mise en accusation*.

These several stages of judgment might be thought in themselves to provide some safeguard against mistakes happening. But this is not necessarily so. Maître René Floriot, a leading defence lawyer in France, says: 'There are two stages of jurisdiction in France, the tribunal and the court, which hear the same case one after the other; of these two, the court takes the opposite view to that of the first-stage judges in one case out of every four. The conseillers at the court always have the last word, but that does not necessarily mean that they are always right. In other words, when a first judgment is reversed, it is certain that at least one of the two judgments was wrong . . . and not necessarily the first one. We are forced to the conclusion that a mistaken judgment has been made either provisionally, which is not so bad, or conclusively, which is far worse, in a quarter of all cases.'[2] (Me Floriot makes the proviso that these figures apply to civil and criminal cases, but that mistakes are far less likely to happen in criminal ones, because the magistrate there has much more chance of getting at the truth than a civil magistrate.)

The cause of wrongful imprisonment in France which has given rise to most public outcry is that of prolonged detention while the magistrate is conducting his investigations, when the case in the end is dropped, or when it is finally decided that there is no case to answer. This is to some extent equivalent to the problem which arises in England when bail is refused to someone who is finally acquitted, or at least not imprisoned, at his trial, but who may nevertheless have spent weeks or even months in prison. In France, the problem was until recently much worse than that: there were cases where people spent literally years in prison awaiting the completion of investigations. One such was Marie Besnard. In 1949, a local gossip wrote to the police saying that she had poisoned her husband. Every member of Mme Besnard's family and circle who had died in the past twenty-five years was exhumed: all the bodies were found to contain arsenic. Marie Besnard was arrested and put in prison while experts made their investigations. They finally submitted their report in July 1960. It was found that the arsenic in the bodies could have been absorbed from the cemetery soil in which they lay. During these years, whenever the case had come up for trial at the *cour d'assises*, it was referred back to the magistrate for further investigations. Marie Besnard was finally acquitted in 1961.[3]

A new law was brought in in July 1970 which attempts to minimize the danger of excessive detention of this kind. *Détention provisoire* can now be ordered only under certain conditions, even if the offence is non-bailable: if it is the only way to ensure that vital evidence is not destroyed; to prevent pressure being put on witnesses, or conspiracy between accomplices; when it is the only way to protect public order; to protect the accused; to make sure he remains within the reach of justice; to prevent the recurrence of crimes. If the magistrate wishes to make an order for detention, he must specifically refer to whichever of the necessary conditions is relevant in this particular case. Otherwise, *controle judiciaire* may now be applied. This involves the imposition of certain conditions on the subject (for example, he must report every day to a police station, must remain within certain bounds, must not leave his residence) subject to which he may remain free. Where detention is imposed, it may not in the first instance exceed four months. At the end of this period, it can be renewed by the magistrate, for not longer than four months. (It is worth noting that, for a *guilty* man, a long period of *détention provisoire* may be very welcome. He will anyway only be liable for detention if his offence is punishable by imprisonment; and any time spent in detention, under conditions considerably better than in prison, will be deducted from any sentence eventually passed on him.)

To the British observer, it may seem positively monstrous that, even under the new law, it should be regarded as normal for a person to be kept in prison while investigations are going on to find if a case can be made out. But the comment has been made that '. . . in France, it would be thought more than unfair, it would be thought most grossly improper, if the inquiry were conducted *ex parte*— without the presence of the person principally interested, the person, that is, against whom there were reasonable grounds of suspicion that he had committed the offence. . . . That an official should be allowed to gather together evidence against a citizen and construct a case against him without his knowledge and without a right in this to make representation to the official and to put forward his own view of the situation from the start—that would generally be judged in France to be monstrous.'[4]

There are various obvious advantages to the innocent suspect in the examining magistrate's investigation. He would seem to be safeguarded against several of the anomalies which we have noted as leading to wrongful imprisonment in England. One is the failure on the part of the police to check out alibis (though this ought not to happen in England either). Another is where mistakes are made because the jury, in an English court, simply cannot sort out the facts of what happened, as in the several affray cases we discussed. The examining magistrate is able to sort out what happened before the case comes for trial; in a case that would lead to a large and muddled joint trial in England, he may rule one or more of the accused out at this stage. Also, there should be no question of false confession being coerced out of the suspect by the magistrate: the suspect's rights to legal protection during his interrogations have already been described.

And yet there is no doubt that people *are* wrongly convicted in France on the basis of false confessions. This is what happened in the case of Jean Deshayes, who made a detailed confession to a murder in the course of robbery with violence which he did not commit—he was in no way involved in the crime. The confession was made to the police, and Deshayes reaffirmed it and signed it when formally accused by the examining magnistrate. Some time later, he wanted to retract, and accused the police of having beaten him up in order to obtain the confession. The magistrate replied, reasonably enough: 'You couldn't have known the details through being beaten up.' There seemed no reply to this; Deshayes was found guilty, and sentenced to ten years' hard labour. He did not appeal. This all took place in 1948, and Deshayes would have served his full sentence had it not been for a conversation overheard by chance in a café in 1952, which led to the discovery of the real culprits. These then confessed to everything, and Deshayes was freed.

If, as Deshayes alleged, the confession had been forced out of him by the police, why did he confirm it when faced with the magistrate, and not take the opportunity to deny it at once now that he was no longer faced with the prospect of intimidation?

Me Floriot comments on this case: 'This appears to be a strong objection. In fact, it is a weak one. Most people accused of crime are ignorant of the legal system, and think that after they have been interrogated by the *juge d'instruction* they will be handed back to the police. If they have already been beaten up, they will not dare to retract their confessions before the magistrate for fear of being beaten up again.'[5] As far as the police are concerned, the suspect is so over-protected once he comes before the examining magistrate that they feel it is highly unlikely that he would ever confess to anything at that stage. They therefore have a strong incentive to do all they can to extract any requisite confession themselves. Public opinion is exercised by this situation, but it is hard to see quite what can be done, given that confessions are generally acknowledged to be desirable evidence.

We have already shown that the extraction of a false confession need not necessarily involve the use of physical violence. Indeed, as was pointed out, the use of physical violence would not explain Deshayes's apparent knowledge of the detail of 'his' crime. But, as in the case of Henry Morgan or Ron Avard, if someone is sufficiently bewildered and demoralized, it is not hard to get him to say practically anything you want—and this, if we are to believe the reconstruction of his interrogation which emerged at Deshayes's trial, is what happened in this case. It turned out that the officer who originally questioned him, and who assumed he was guilty, had been one of the first on the scene, and knew all about the trial. The interrogation went something like this:

Q: How many rooms are there in the house?
A: I don't know.
Q: You know as well as I do that there are two.
A: Yes, there are two.
Q: And where was the stove in the first room?
A: I don't know.
Q: You know very well that it's on the right. . . .[6]

Even where a confession is not somehow extracted by the police—and it should be recognized that, under the system as it now stands, the temptations for them to try too hard are very strong—there may be other reasons for making false confessions. The system of *détention provisoire* holds out a very specific inducement to confess to respectable citizens who, rightly or wrongly, may find themselves caught in the net. This is the possibility of getting it all over quickly and getting back home without a scandal—the implication being 'You help us and we'll help you'. They may have the mistaken idea that if they confess—'yes, all right, I did it'—then everything will pass easily and no one need know they have been in detention. This idea, of course, *is* mistaken; once you confess, then the last thing anyone is likely to do is to send you home and let the whole business blow over.

Although the suspect is well-protected from possible involuntary indiscretion during the magistrate's investigations, witnesses are not. If a witness incriminates himself in a way that his lawyer would never have permitted, had he been the suspect and therefore had a lawyer present, then there is nothing to prevent him becoming the suspect in his turn—too late. The case of Gaston Dominici shows how this may work. He was the old peasant patriarch who was finally convicted of the murder of Sir John and Lady Drummond and their daughter Elizabeth while on a camping holiday in the South of France. When investigations were first made into the crime, the prime suspect was Gustave Dominici, Gaston's son; another possible suspect was one of his grandsons. After prolonged interrogation, Gaston broke down and said that his father had committed the crime, and that he had also confessed to Clovis, Gustave's brother. The old Gaston was immediately put under guard, and to the guard he made the interesting statement that Gustave had committed the crime, but that 'I'm confessing to preserve the honour of my grandchildren. Going to prison won't make any difference to me, so long as they leave me my dog.'[7] He made a rather muddled and unsatisfactory confession to the magistrate— without benefit of a lawyer, since all this time he was treated as a witness and not as the suspect—and on the basis of this confession, together with the accusations of his two sons—one of whom later retracted—he was convicted.[8]

We have mentioned the theory that, at a certain point, the police switch their energies from finding a suspect, and concentrate on proving that the suspect they have in mind did it. In some ways, the French system would seem to reinforce this narrowing-down process. While one suspect is being interrogated by the examining magistrate, human nature and police work-loads being what they are, it is unlikely that the police will be out looking for other possible suspects. The investigation by the magistrate is devoted to examining the case against the person under interrogation. But he is handed over at a very early stage in the investigations—the case against him need by no means be as complete as that which British police need to present to court, if they are to stand a chance of winning it. If it were, there would be no need for long delays while the case is examined. This is what seems to have happened in the case of a *gendarme*, Jules Barrault: '. . . the badly-burned body of a bank manager, Georges Segretin was found in the wreck of his car in an area called the blue woods, near Bourges. A post-mortem showed that he had been beaten to death before the car was set on fire. Police interviewed everybody who had been seeing the manager—and all clients with a large overdraft. The *gendarme* was known to have had a row with the manager only three days before his death. Jules had an overdraft of more than £500—he borrowed it to buy a new car—and he lied about it when Flying Squad detectives came down from Paris. He also lied about a gallon can of oil he bought the night of the murder. An empty can was found ten yards from the wrecked car. It was thought to be the one bought by the *gendarme*.

'Villagers spoke of seeing the *gendarme* and his friend, the 29-year-old wife of a photographer, acting strangely on the day of the killing. The case against the *gendarme* was convincing. Flying Squad Commissioner Michel Nocquet, sent from Paris, arrested Jules and the woman and closed the dossier. The woman was released after seven days. But the accused *gendarme* stayed in jail.

'Then the case took a surprising twist. Commissioner Nocquet received a mysterious letter. The signature was an illegible scrawl. But the contents stated plainly that the *gendarme* was innocent. Jules was freed, and Nocquet was obliged to admit his mistake and reopen the case. Finally the Commissioner tracked down a 45-year-old smallholder who admitted sending the letter—and said that he killed the bank manager because he refused him a £150 advance.'[9] One can't help feeling that perhaps Commissioner Nocquet was too easily satisfied in the first place, and that it is altogether the simplest way to hand the case on to the *juge d'instruction* and close the case—from the police point of view, anyway.

The *juge d'instruction* is of course very dependent on the police, since it is they who must conduct all his investigations for him. This may make him unwilling to alienate them by hauling them over the coals too often for rough handling of suspects. But it may also mean that, since in both cases there is a positive advantage in successful arrests and convictions—career chances are often advanced in this way—the *juge* has a positive interest in not restraining them too much, especially if the result is sometimes a confession convenient to all. The desire for a successful prosecution is only natural both in the police, and in a career prosecutor. As was admitted in the Mars-Jones report, the number of arrests made is important in obtaining promotion in the English police force; but this in no way affects the judicial process. The job of the judge and the prosecution in an English court is not to obtain a conviction at all costs, but to see that justice is done. The prospects of counsel are not necessarily enhanced by a string of successful prosecuting briefs—though they may be by a similar string of successful defence briefs. Anyway, barristers are as likely to defend as to prosecute; these are not separate careers as they are in France.

There are two different directions which a lawyer can take in France. He may decide to become a defence lawyer. In that case, he will specialize in defending; this is a career in itself. Or he may choose to join the civil service in the office of the public prosecutor. This is the branch which may eventually lead to the judiciary. Misgivings have frequently been voiced about this conjunction. One commentator says: 'The whole mentality of a public prosecutor is necessarily different from that of a judge, and a man who had, for decades, exclusively performed the task of prosecuting can hardly be expected to become an absolutely impartial judge.'[10]

The defendant, too, in a French trial, is in a very different situation from the defendant in England. To say that in England one is innocent till proved guilty, and in France, guilty unless one can prove one's innocence, is to be both simplistic and inaccurate. But there is no doubt that the fact of having been committed for trial in France after a very thorough official investigation has been carried out, is considered far more indicative of probable guilt than is a similar committal from a magistrates' court to a higher court in Britain. This is a natural consequence of the different emphases placed on different stages of the investigation and prosecution procedure in the two countries. In France, for instance, a large part of the evidence has been presented and accepted at official level, and in the presence of the prisoner and his lawyers, before the trial stage is ever reached. It is all present in the dossier which lies before the president of the court all through the trial. Any evidence heard in court is simply a rehearsal of points already heard and contained in this dossier, which remains, visible to the jury as to everyone else in court, a very solid reminder of the weight of evidence already marshalled against the prisoner.

Because all this evidence is already known to the judges, and has, theoretically at least, been collected under stringently controlled conditions, many of the formalities and rules which seem to turn an English trial into some kind of elaborate game as much as a detailed examination of each and every fact, simply do not exist in a French trial. Many of these rules, of course, tend to protect the defendant (though not all, as we have shown in the chapter on Trial Proceedings).

In France, the prisoner's record, if he has one, is before the court from the beginning. We have already discussed the effect this may have (see p. 82). As far as the French are concerned, a man's propensity to commit certain types of crime is relevant to the matter in hand (though it should be remembered that this can be introduced as evidence in England if the purpose is to show system). On the other hand, it is quite possible for the police to pick someone up on no evidence other than that he seems a likely culprit, for the *juge d'instruction* to concur with this opinion, and for a jury to convict because they consider the prisoner capable of committing such a crime, rather than because he has conclusively been proved to have committed it.

The duty of exposing the prisoner's past life and previous record falls to the presiding judge; and if it does not prejudice the jury in the way just described, it may prejudice them in the opposite direction. Professor Hamson says: 'It is felt that the presiding judge has an impossible task. There falls upon him, by custom rather than by reason of any precise text of law, the duty of examining the accused in court immediately after the formal indictment has been read out. In this examination the previous life of the prisoner, including his criminal past if he has one, is rehearsed: often to the evident and great prejudice of the prisoner. This examination is capable of giving rise to an unseemly wrangle between the prisoner and the president on matters of little apparent relevance to the issue to be tried that day. The president seems to be compelled at the outset to depart from his office and easily conveys the improper and quite false impression that he is more prejudiced and more vehement against the prisoner than the prosecution itself.'[11] One result of this apparent weighting of the court against the accused is that juries may react in the opposite direction, and acquit because they think the defence has not had a fair chance.

Another rule which does not exist in France is the prisoner's right to silence. He must testify in court, though he may refuse to answer specific questions—though this is usually quite as prejudicial to his cause as any answer he might have given. Again, given the fact that he has participated in the magistrate's investigation, the right to silence in court would be an anomaly, as would any of the exclusion rules of evidence operating in England. Nothing which is relevant to the case is excluded in France.

Mᵉ Floriot, speaking from long experience, is of the opinion that perjury is at the bottom of almost all judicial errors in France. In connection with this, he particularly regrets the absence of the right to cross-examination in French courts, especially when it comes to ascertaining whether or not a witness is speaking the truth. As things stand, defence lawyers may only question witnesses on their statements if and as the presiding judge permits. 'I have often heard presidents say, "That's enough, maitre, the witness is on oath." A lot of use that is. I must admit that I attach very little importance to the oath. If the witness is dishonest, the raising of his right hand while pronouncing the sacramental "I swear" is not going to stop him making a false statement. If he is honest, he will tell the truth as best he can, but that is not to say he will be infallible. That is why I think the defence should have complete freedom to put any questions which may seem useful, in order to make sure that the person giving evidence is not mistaken. In this instance, the Anglo-Saxon system is undoubtedly better than ours.'[12] Presumably, once again bearing in mind that theoretically the *juge d'instruction* has already found out the real truth of the affair and that the trial is nothing more than a rehearsal of it, cross-examination should be superfluous. Once again, theory does not appear to coincide with practice. (Nevertheless perjury seems to be taken much more seriously in France than in England when it is found out: perjurers may not only be punished by the State, but ordered to pay compensation for the harm they have done. For a fuller discussion of this, see below.

One question in which the defence is at a material disadvantage in France is the matter of expert witnesses. If there is forensic work of any kind to be done (analysis of bloodstains or handwriting, for example) then one of the body of State-approved experts will be hired to do the job. He is not a prosecution witness to be countered, if necessary, by a similar defence witness; he is an official witness. Should the defence disagree with his findings, it can always demand another expert opinion, but this may not be granted. If this request is refused, the defence can turn to other experts, who may usefully combat the official report. But these will have less facilities than the official expert—they may not, for instance, have access to the clothing for analysis—and their opinions will not carry as much weight with the judges. Under a recent ruling, one official—that is, State-credited—expert may not give evidence for the defence against another who has already made the official report; so that the pool of experts available to the defence is smaller than that available to the State. This may be particularly serious in a small town, where the number of suitably-qualified people is small, and all are accredited to the State.

Juries in France are in a very different position from their opposite numbers in England. In some ways, they are credited with much greater powers of discernment. As has already been mentioned, admissibility rules are much wider in France. Hearsay evidence, for example, is not excluded for fear that the jury will not know what weight to accord it. They may therefore have a far greater body of evidence to consider than an English jury; and they will not have the benefit of the judge's summing-up to help them, since in France the judge does not sum-up. In addition to this, they must pass a verdict not only on fact, but on law, and also on sentence.

But in the handling of this evidence, and in the making of these decisions, they are allowed far less freedom than an English jury. They do not go out to cogitate in some sort of vacuum, with what degree of logic or emotion we not not know, eventually to bring in—who knows how?—their verdict. Instead, they are given a number of questions by the presiding judge, relating to both fact and law, to which they must answer 'yes' or 'no'. The more complex the case, the more questions they will have to answer. Moreover, they are assisted in this relatively limited task by the three judges, who retire with them (there are seven members of a French jury).

In what way does the French jury system work differently from the British? It is generally acknowledged that in England, juries are far more inclined to acquit when they should probably convict, than vice versa. In France, Me Floriot at least seems to feel that they do not apply the benefit of the doubt as often as they ought to. 'If [the judge] feels that a doubt exists, even the smallest doubt, he should give the suspect the benefit of it and acquit. This would not be a miscarriage of justice, since the suspect's innocence is far from being upheld during the trial—on the contrary, it is strongly contested. If this rule of the benefit of the doubt were to be systematically applied, then judges would run no risk of making judicial errors in criminal cases. Unfortunately, the rule is as often broken as it should be stringently enforced. Judges and juries do not like the idea that a guilty man should get off scot-free. And the circumstances which seem to cast doubt on the case are outweighed by the often much more detailed charges which tell against the suspect.'[13] (But it should be remembered that this is a career defence counsel speaking.)

In such cases, French juries may have resort to a device which is denied to their English counterparts: that is, to impose a sentence which is too light if the accused is guilty, but much too heavy—which in fact should not be imposed at all—if he is innocent. This is what happened in the case of Deshayes discussed earlier. Having been found guilty of a brutal murder committed in the furtherance of robbery, Deshayes was condemned to ten years' hard labour—a light sentence as French sentences go if he was guilty, and one which reflected the jury's doubts. These later turned out to have been fully justified. Floriot comments: 'These verdicts are quite common in cases where a doubt remains. Are they the result of some kind of bargain struck between those who wanted to convict, and those who were hoping to acquit? Some kind of attempt not to be too extreme? Whatever the reason, the solution is an appalling one.'[14]

Once he has been found guilty of a criminal offence, the only hope for an innocent man is that he will be granted a *pourvoi en cassation*, that is, that his case will be referred to the *cour de cassation*—the Supreme Court which sits in Paris. The *cour de cassation* is limited to the consideration of points of law. It does not pass judgment on fact; it does not evaluate responsibility or decide on punishment; it is not, in other words, a third stage of judgment. Its functions are much narrower than those of our own Court of Appeal. If it finds that the law has been wrongly applied, then the judgment is nullified, and the case is sent back to a lower court for retrial.

If his offence is a trivial one, and there is no point of law which can be taken up by the *cour de cassation*, then that is the end of the road for the prisoner. If the offence of which he was accused is a serious one, however, and therefore incurred a serious punishment, there rests the possibility of a *pourvoi en révision*, that is, a reconsideration of the case on the facts, carrying with it the possibility of acquittal.

There are four sets of circumstances which may lead to the revision of a case. Firstly, if a person has been found guilty of murder, and the victim is found to be still alive.[15] Secondly, if two people have, in two separate trials, been found guilty of the same offence, under circumstances such that one of these findings must be wrong. Thirdly, if after the trial one of the witnesses is found guilty of perjury. Fourthly, if some new evidence can be produced after the trial which seems to show that the accused was not guilty. M. Gilbert Marc, a judge at the *Tribunal de grande instance* at Le Havre, comments that this provision is the most important one from the practical point of view. But the rarity of revision being granted can be shown by the experience of Me Floriot, who says: 'I have been concerned with criminal law for more than forty years, and people have often asked me to try and obtain a revision of their case. I have personally never come across any new evidence which would enable me to do so. Those of my colleagues who have been more fortunate then myself—and you can count them on the fingers of one hand—have never succeeded more than once in their career.'[16] Given French pre-trial investigative procedures, this is perhaps less surprising than it would be in England, where the production of new evidence, though difficult, is nevertheless not an unusual reason for the granting of an appeal. (It seems, for instance, unlikely that Thomas Hall (p. 27) would ever have been brought to trial in France.)

As in England, there are in France cases where there is a strong element of doubt, recognized by all, and yet which do not appear to fall within any of the categories which render reconsideration possible. Such a one is the case of Jean-Marie Deveaux, who was sentenced to twenty years' imprisonment in 1963 for murdering the little daughter of his employers. He was convicted largely on the basis of a confession he made to the police, which he retracted in the course of his trial (see p. 221 for discussion of such cases). He ceaselessly proclaimed his innocence, refused a pardon which would have set him free, on the grounds that he never committed the crime and so could not be pardoned for it, went on two hunger strikes and attempted suicide in a bid to get his case reopened and obtain an acquittal. In April 1968 M. Louis Joxe, then Minister of Justice, supported an appeal for a revision on the ground that the code of criminal procedure had been infringed. The *cour de cassation* threw out the appeal six months later. In March 1969, M. René Capitant, a new Minister of Justice, asked the *Procureur Général* of the *cour de cassation* to denounce before the court the verdict of the court which sentenced Deveaux, on the same grounds, of infringement of criminal procedure.[17] Once again we see the familiar spectacle of a Court of Appeal trying to find a legal pretext for reconsidering a case where a mistake of fact has occurred.

As in England, one possibility in France when a really doubtful situation crops up is the granting of remission, which accomplishes the essential, and gets the suspected innocent out of prison (always supposing that, unlike Deveaux, he will take the opportunity offered). This is what happened in the case of Gaston Dominici. His sentence was remitted after a few years of imprisonment, although further inquiries into the affair had failed to produce any solid new evidence in his favour (largely because his son retracted a confession he had made).

One aspect where the French system is very different from the British, and in many ways seems far superior to the British, is with regard to compensation. The French seem as a whole far more concerned with indemnification, an attitude which embraces the compensation both of those who have suffered wrongful detention or imprisonment and of those who have suffered a loss at the hands of criminals. In general, the attitude is that restitution and compensation are a matter of right, and are therefore legislated for (though this does not mean that everyone automatically receives compensation).

The process of indemnification may be included at any criminal trial, in which two separate actions may be brought, for punishment and for reparations; the former, by the State, the latter, a civil actions, by the *partie civile*. The civil action by the victim of the crime will of course only be brought when actual damage has been suffered—that is, not in cases of attempted crime. The victim can choose to prosecute purely in the civil court or in both courts. If he chooses to bring a criminal prosecution before the State has done so, this decision automatically sets in motion the State's machinery. If the *partie civile* is successful, then any sums awarded in damages will be paid out by the prisoner or his relatives.

Article 149 of the law of 17 July 1970 (the same law which imposed limits on the length of *détention provisoire*) states that an indemnity may be granted to a person who has been kept in detention where the investigation has shown that there is no case to answer or has resulted in an acquittal and where the detention has caused '*un préjudice manifestement anormal et d'une particulière gravité.* (Before the introduction of this law, there was no provision for indemnifying the victims of such detention.) This compensation is by no means automatically granted should a lengthy *détention provisoire* be followed by a decision that there is no case to answer, or that the case be dropped: it will only be granted where the accused was plainly innocent, not where he was granted the benefit of the doubt. This would be the equivalent to compensation for bail in England, if it existed.

More relevant to this inquiry, if a verdict is set aside and the accused is judged to have suffered wrongful imprisonment, then the court which makes this judgment may decree that the State should compensate the victim. The compensation may take two forms, 'moral' and monetary. The moral compensation is concerned with damage to the victim's reputation, and consists of the insertion of the complete revision judgment in the *Journal Officiel*, and extracts from it in five newspapers of the prisoner's choice, at the State's expense. Monetary compensation is not automatic, and may be withheld particularly if the accused in some way helped cause the judicial error, for instance by making a false confession. M. Gilbert Marc, already quoted above, comments: 'This exclusion of any damages if the fault is partly the prisoner's is altogether exceptional in French law, and in some ways recalls the common law theory of "contributory negligence". It is even more open to criticism since experience proves . . . that one of the most frequent causes of judicial error is the fact that the accused, who in France effectively cannot refuse to submit to interrogation, sometimes thinks it preferable to dissemble the truth, which is often unpleasant, and put up a story which shows him in a more favourable light but which runs the greater risk of being easily disproved.' (This is what happened to Jules Barrault, the unfortunate *gendarme* (see above).) It recalls some of our own findings with regard to false alibis, for example, the case of Emery Thompson and Powers, who presumably would have stood little chance of compensation in France on the grounds that their own lies helped to convict them in the first place.

Such indemnities, if they are allotted, are paid out by the State on the demand of the victim of the error or his dependants. If the error can be traced to any particular course, for example, a false denunciation, or a perjured witness, then the State can in its turn reclaim from these parties the amounts paid out. It is also open to the victim to bring his own action against the witness for perjury or false denunciation. In the case of perjury, it is worth noting that it can only be deemed to have taken place if it was committed in the *cour d'assises*, and not merely before the magistrate, the idea being that there should be every incentive for a person who has lied to the magistrate to retract and tell the truth at the trial, without fear of being prosecuted for perjury. An action for false denunciation must prove malice on the part of the accuser. The denunciation must also have been made spontaneously—for example, someone who has been wrongfully imprisoned cannot bring a successful action for false denunciation against someone who has made the accusation simply because he wanted to turn suspicion away from himself. The kind of thing which would be considered malicious is the writing of the kind of letter which originally got Marie Besnard into such trouble. If the action succeeds, there is a penalty of between six months' and five years' imprisonment, and a fine of 500–15,000 francs.

It is also possible to bring an action against the police or the Bench, but for this to succeed either some definite infringement of the code or gross professional negligence must be proved. In rejecting one such action, the court of Douai pointed out that, if such actions were to be brought (and to succeed) every time a case was abandoned, there was shown to be no case, or an acquittal took place, then public servants would simply be afraid to do their work.

The picture which emerges in France is that of the paramount importance of the State—and a State characterized by a certain rigidity and impersonality. In the case of the barman mentioned earlier, for example, the machine simply went grinding on without anyone really knowing what was supposed to be happening. Once the wheels are set in motion, it can be hard to stop them.

Again, when it comes to the questioning of suspects by the examining magistrate, it is the convenience of the State which seems to be paramount. It is certainly easier for everyone—except the suspect—if he is kept in custody during the investigation. One might take a more charitable view if only the protection which the system theoretically affords the suspect, could be seen to *be* afforded him. But it would appear that the narrowing-down process, for example—a process which some people have thought might become less apparent in an examining-magistrate system—seems rather to be emphasized: the suspect is physically brought in at such an early stage in the investigation (much earlier, for instance, than in Scotland, where the police have to present the procurator-fiscal with a strong case against the suspect before he can be brought in). And false confessions and statements *are* made, and the wrong person *is* sometimes brought to trial.

It is not the system itself, so much as the assumption that it will work according to plan, which seems to cause most of the mistakes. The French presumably have confidence in the procedure they have created. But the gap between theory and practice seems very wide, and this can be dangerous, since it is not taken into account. Failures in the system are not sufficiently envisaged nor provided for.

No one, for instance, seems to have taken account of possible police reaction when framing rules which must be very frustrating to them. How far is the police brutality which admittedly goes on, a function of feeling that the system is weighted against them, and that there is no other course open to them?[18]

Again, the fact that the defence is denied at the final trial certain rights which are granted to it in England (for example, secrecy with regard to any previous record, the right to cross-examine) assumes that the prior investigation will have discovered the truth of the matter. Another corollary of this assumption is the extreme difficulty of getting a case re-examined on the facts. Since these facts are supposed to have been ascertained for the judge before the case comes to trial (rather than being presented to the judge for the first time *at* the trial, which is the case in England) it is presumably supposed that they will have been correctly ascertained. This means that the most important figure in the whole process is the *juge d'instruction*, the examining magistrate. It is essential that he be both thorough and impartial. But, as has been shown, the temptations to co-operate with the police in obtaining confessions and convictions are very strong. This is of course not to say that most examining magistrates are *not* impartial; simply that they are in a difficult position.

The difficulty of obtaining a revision on fact, or because a verdict was given 'against the weight of the evidence', seems ironic, since the French method of putting the case to the jury allows a far more detailed knowledge of how the verdict was arrived at than the English. This is both because the judges retire with the jury and because of the 'questions' method of delivering individual verdicts on points of fact and law. If, for instance, the jury answers 'no' to all questions about the facts of his guilt and then delivers a guilty verdict against the accused, then this is clearly against the weight of evidence (should it ever happen; but this is the extreme case). Indeed, we feel that this method might be partially adopted in England. The English jury is effectively presented with the questions relevant to the facts of the case, and the law affecting them, in the judge's summing-up. It might be a good idea for transcripts of this to be available to the jury, with the separate points requiring an answer marked clearly. This would give a definite guide to the Appeal Court when considering whether a verdict was arrived at correctly. A particularly contrary verdict, shown up in this way, might even be grounds for appeal.

There are two other aspects of the French system which we feel might with advantage be adopted in England. One of these is the method of dealing with people remanded in custody before the trial. It seems sensible not to treat these people in the same way as if they had already been found guilty. Prison, after all, is a punishment; why should those who have not yet been tried be punished? Deprivation of liberty here is for quite another purpose. It might also be a good idea to specify that any time spent on remand awaiting trial should be deducted from any sentence passed at the trial. This is a practice already followed by many judges and magistrates; why not give it the force of law?

The other way in which we might usefully borrow ideas from the French is in compensation. We are anyway moving towards the system of the criminal indemnifying the victims of his crime. But in general French attitudes towards compensation and indemnification seem altogether more sensible than ours. The system of 'moral' compensation, where inserts are made in five newspapers of the victim's choice and at the State's expense announcing his innocence seems an excellent one, and we feel it should be adopted in England. So should the concept that everyone who has suffered wrongful imprisonment may be entitled to have his case routinely assessed for compensation. This need not be automatic, any more than it is in France; but every case should at least be heard on its merits.

Chapter 9

The American Experience

Wrongful imprisonment in America is like so many aspects of American society on a much larger scale than anything experienced in Britain or the other Western European countries. More people are wrongly convicted, sometimes under bizarre or outrageous circumstances, they are often convicted of particularly serious crimes such as murder or armed robbery, and they receive correspondingly heavy sentences. The error has sometimes remained undetected or unredressed for ten, fifteen or even twenty years and an innocent man has remained in gaol for this length of time. Because such cases are so plentiful and often so tragic they have been the subject of many books of case histories and legal comment, notably Edwin M. Borchard's *Convicting the Innocent*, Jerome and Barbara Frank's *Not Guilty*, and Edward D. Radin's *The Innocents*. In these and other books are listed details of over 200 cases of proven wrongful imprisonment resulting from mistaken convictions for criminal offences in the State or Federal courts.

These cases provide the material on which this chapter and its conclusions about American society and American legal procedures is based. The cases do not, however, provide a representative picture of wrongful imprisonment in America, or even of proven wrongful imprisonment. The authors of these studies have selected their cases for publication in such a way as (*a*) to lay greater stress on the more serious cases involving grave crimes and long sentences (there are undoubtedly many proven cases of wrongful imprisonment for petty thefts or minor assaults resulting in a pardon or a quashing of conviction but these do not enter anthologies of cases in proportion to their number); (*b*) to exclude certain types of sex cases presumably on the grounds it might offend the American reader or censor. It is curiously like American television. Violence and brutality are permitted, sometimes in great length and detail, but not sex.[1] Borchard explicitly states in the introduction to his study: '. . . there are a few cases including cases of alleged rape of a type *intentionally omitted* from this collection where the issue of guilt turns mainly upon the veracity of the prosecuting witness and of the accused.'[2] Consequently, these cases cannot be regarded as a random sample of proven cases of wrongful imprisonment in America. They are indeed only the tip of the tip of the iceberg and the tip of the tip is probably not typical of the tip, leave alone of the iceberg. Nonetheless, an analysis of these cases does reveal some interesting patterns, and points to systematic similarities and differences between the British and the American experience.

The 200 or so cases listed by the American authors are probably drawn disproportionately from the more serious cases of wrongful imprisonment that have occurred in America. These are the ones most likely to be noticed and recorded. But even if this is a complete list of the serious cases and the unnoticed and unrecorded cases are more trivial, it is evident that miscarriages of justice are much more frequent and far more drastic in their effects in America than in England.[3] Of these American cases, ten men served over twenty or more years in prison for crimes they did not commit, seven served fifteen to twenty years, sixteen served ten to fifteen years, and twenty-three served five to ten years. In England no *proven* case of wrongful conviction in the last twenty years has result in a man serving four or more years. To find cases comparable with the American ones it is necessary to go back to the time of Queen Victoria and such cases as that of Adolf Beck who was twice wrongly convicted of larceny by fraud and served a total of nine years in jail. Even at that time, such cases were rare and when the error was discovered it resulted in an immense public outcry. Indeed the controversy following the Beck case (and its Scottish counterpart, the case of Oscar Slater) resulted in the setting up of the Court of Criminal Appeal (and its Scottish equivalent). In America, by contrast, such cases have always been common and remain common and are generally treated as routine errors of the legal system.[4] It is also noteworthy that a large number of the American cases listed, involve the wrongful imprisonment of men and women with no previous convictions, with no criminal associates and from an entirely respectable background. These cases are again more likely to gain publicity, but it is remarkable that the large number that are recorded should exist at all.[5]

The reasons for the prevalence of wrongful imprisonment in America are to be sought in American society, in general, and particularly in its values rather than in any peculiarities of the

H   225

American legal system, though certain aspects of American (State and Federal) law and court procedure are a contributing factor. In the first place America has more wrongful imprisonment because it has more rightful imprisonment. There is far more serious crime in America than in England and hence far more trials, far more verdicts, and far more people sent to jail and for longer stretches. More mistakes occur simply because there are more occasions on which a mistake could be made. In particular murder, rape, and robbery, which are rare crimes in England, are relatively common in America[6] (though even there they are a small proportion of all crime).[7] Many American cities have more murders every year than the whole of Britain and in few of them is it safe to walk about at night.[8] These are crimes which carry very heavy sentences (sixty-four of those listed as wrongly imprisoned received a sentence of life imprisonment and a further eighteen received sentences of twenty years or more. Of these, sixteen had been sentenced to death but their execution was fortunately commuted to imprisonment or postponed).[9] They are also crimes for which the crucial evidence on which conviction is based is often unreliable—notably identification evidence in a case of robbery or murder for gain.

Much of the wrongful imprisonment in America stems from similar causes to those suggested for England, there being more of it simply because there is more crime. Factors such as misidentification,[10] false confessions by the mentally defective[11] and by those hoping for leniency,[12] perjury by the family of the accused[13] or of other suspects,[14] perjury by women[15] and children,[16] especially in sex cases, dying declarations,[17] mistakes made during joint trials[18] and during the trials of immigrants and others with language difficulties[19] all occur in America as in Britain, only on a larger scale. The sequence of events in individual cases is often strikingly similar to our earlier detailed descriptions of British cases and provides some degree of confirmation of our hypotheses about how such errors occur. Even so there are often bizarre twists to some of the American cases that put them outside the range of British experience.

Misidentification is in America as in England a common cause of wrong convictions. Indeed this was the key evidence in over half the listed American cases and in over 80 per cent of the robberies, and in nearly all the cheque frauds. (Cheque frauds are more common in America than in England because cheques are more widely used and misused and the police in America are more ready to prosecute.[20] In such cases evidence of identification is often sufficient to convict

226

even where it is contradicted by the evidence of handwriting experts. The British police are often unwilling to take up the case of a bounced cheque unless there have been enough of them in a neighbourhood to show 'system', and instead tend to leave the victim to seek redress for himself.) In many of these cases there was no corroborating evidence whatsoever and a good deal of strong evidence for the defence, but nevertheless a jury was willing to convict. In fifty cases there was but one eyewitness for the prosecution and in general the number of errors made was inversely proportional to the number of eyewitnesses, that is, the more eyewitnesses the fewer mistakes.[21] In many cases of single witness identification the identifying witness has been the victim of the crime—indeed Professor Borchard comments: 'Perhaps the major source of these tragic errors is an identification of the accused by the victim of a crime of violence. . . . Juries seem disposed more readily to credit the veracity and reliability of the victims of an outrage than any amount of contrary evidence by or on behalf of the accused whether by way of alibi, character witnesses, or other testimony. These cases illustrate the fact that the emotional balance of the victim or eyewitness is so disturbed by his extraordinary experience that his powers of perception become distorted and his identification is frequently most untrustworthy.'[22]

The American experience reinforces our view that proper procedures are essential in the handling of identification evidence. Errors seem to have been fewer where identification parades were held (these are called line-ups or show-ups in America) provided the rules were correctly adhered to, than where identification followed a confrontation of eyewitness and accused in the police station, in court or even by chance in the street.

In many cases photographs had been shown to the witnesses prior to their identifying the accused. In the case of Bertram Campbell accused of a series of cheque frauds, eyewitnesses were even shown photographs of Campbell with a wax-tipped moustache inked in to make him resemble the real criminal's description. As a result, Campbell, a respectable businessman of impeccable character, was convicted and served three years in jail. He was later pardoned and successfully sued the State of New York for $115,000.[23] Another form of misleading suggestion used by various American police forces is to dress the accused according to the description of the real culprit and to force him to 'perform antics attributed to the guilty man'.[24] Professor Borchard describes the misidentification of

Floyd Flood, a man with no criminal record, by an eyewitness to an armed bank hold-up in Freeburg, Illinois, as follows: 'At police headquarters Flood was placed in the "show-up cage", a contrivance about ten feet square which enables identifying witnesses to examine suspects under floodlights although the suspects are unable to see the witnesses. The police forced Flood to turn his coat collar up, put on a cap not his own and pull it down over his eyes, stretch his hand forward and say "Stick 'em up". The police had been informed that one of the bandits so attired had thus acted. Under these conditions the two women identified Flood as the bandit who had covered them during the robbery.'[25]

A similar misidentification occurred in the case of Clarence Leroy McKinney (in Wilmington, Ohio) who was accused of shooting two police-officers, one of whom died. McKinney was arrested and dressed up in a khaki coat and cap like a description of one of the real culprits. The surviving police officer was now confronted with McKinney in the dark and flashed a light in his face suddenly and briefly, as at the time of the murder. Perhaps by reproducing the unsatisfactory conditions of the original identification, the police thought they were adopting a reliable procedure rather than reinforcing an error. In this case, as in Flood's, however, they in fact provoked a wrong identification by suggestion.[26]

Even where an identification parade was properly held, mistakes still occur and as in England eyewitnesses who were uncertain at first became more certain over time and were unshakable at the trial. Philip Caruso, suspected of armed robbery of a debt collector in Brooklyn, New York City in 1938, was put on an identity parade and picked out by the debt collector. One of the robbers was described by the victim as having had a mole on his upper lip and Caruso had a fever blister on his lip at the time of the parade—he had been ill at the time of the robbery. A transcript of the proceedings of the parade shows that the victim said after the parade: 'That don't seem to be the right mark I seen on his upper lip.' In court, however, the witness was certain and denied he had made any statement about his assailant having a mole. The court was not told of his doubts at the identification parade and Caruso was convicted despite strong defence evidence and sentenced to from ten to twenty years. Later the mole-lipped robber was arrested for another robbery and confessed, thus exonerating Caruso. The judge now directed that all police records concerning the case be submitted to the court and this revealed what had happened at the identity parade.[27]

One use of identity parades in America that does seem likely to lead to error is the habit of some police forces of putting a person suspected of one crime on a large number of identity parades (the other people on the parade often being other suspects). He is 'paraded' for eyewitnesses to a variety of other crimes even though there is no evidence linking him to these crimes, until they find an eyewitness who is willing to pick him out. This procedure is even more dangerous where the witnesses are simply confronted with the suspect. Vance Hardy, who was arrested on suspicion of helping a prisoner to escape from gaol in 1924, was put on display for a number of witnesses to various murders that had occurred in Detroit. Eventually a witness was found who identified him though he was very uncertain having been 120 feet away at the time of the murder. Hardy was convicted of first degree murder, though he had never met the victim, and sentenced to life imprisonment on this flimsy evidence. He spent twenty-seven years in jail (ten years of this in solitary confinement) from his conviction in 1924 to his acquittal after a new trial in 1951.[28]

As always, the man with a previous criminal record is most at risk of being misidentified. He is more likely to be a suspect, more likely to be put on an identity parade, more likely to have his photo picked out of the photos in the police files. (The bulk of these photos are taken when a man is first convicted. If you have not got a record, the police probably will not have a photo of you to show prospective witnesses.) In America, however, a surprisingly large number of respectable citizens with no criminal record or associates do seem to get convicted as a result of misidentification following some chance meeting with the victim who then denounces them to the police or as a result of some other accidental coincidence. This seems to happen most frequently in connection with cheque frauds with prosperous business and professional people including a large number of women being wrongly convicted of this offence.[29] Presumably the courts take the view that (since this is one of the few offences frequently committed either by women or by the middle classes) evidence of previous good character and current prosperity is irrelevant in such cases. However, such people do also sometimes get misidentified in cases of robbery, murder and sexual assaults. In over one-half of the cases of misidentification (where the facts regarding a man's character are known) the accused had no previous record. Of this group, about one-half had criminal associates or were in some way shady characters but this left over one-quarter of the misidentified as entirely respectable people caught up in a false accusation and conviction by some hideous coincidence.

Confessions by the feeble-minded, by the psychologically disturbed, by immigrants and others with language difficulties are a source of wrongful conviction in America as in England. Moreover these groups have further problems to contend with during their trial. Again these are more common in America than England partly because more Americans seem to come in each of the three categories and partly because American society is more willing and able to use them as scapeboats.

We have earlier quoted Block on the confession of the feeble-minded Harold Israel (p 52). Borchard cites also the cases of John Johnson who was convicted of murdering a child and later pardoned after spending ten years in jail, and of Stielow and Green who were convicted of murdering their landlord but later exonerated. The report of a commission of inquiry into the Johnson case to the Governor of Winconsin noted: '.... It is of course clear that ordinary people do not ordinarily accuse themselves falsely of the commission of crime. If Mr Johnson were a man of ordinary strength of character and of ordinary prudence and sagacity, I should find it difficult to disbelieve him when he stated that he committed this offence. But I find he was and is far below the ordinary individual in mentality. The testimony establishes in fact to my satisfaction at least that he was a man conspicuously weak, weak almost to the degree of irresponsibility.'[30]

On the Stielow and Green case Borchard commented: 'Nelson Green is described as practically half-witted and Stielow himself as of inferior mentality. It did not take much skill to work upon their minds and shortly after their arrest . . . what were called confessions had been extracted from them . . . every material fact in the alleged confession of Stielow in so far as it was not patently obvious, actually could not have occurred.'[31]

It would seem as easy to get confessions out of the feeble-minded by persuasion and suggestion (let alone harsher methods) in America as it is in England. The psychologically unstable too are at risk though for rather different reasons as is illustrated by the case of Ralph W. Lobaugh. A series of sadistic rapes and murders occurred in Fort Wayne, Indiana, during the years 1944-5. Two years later Lobaugh went to the police and confessed to three of them. He later repudiated his confession and engaged a lawyer to defend him who pointed out the striking inconsistencies in his confession, the degree to which it failed to match the known facts of the various cases and the fact that Lobaugh had strong alibis for each occasion. Lobaugh, however, dismissed his lawyer, confessed again and pleaded guilty to the several crimes. He was sentenced to death but now again recanted. Further investigation revealed that Lobaugh had nothing to do with the crimes, and the real culprits were caught. The Governor of Indiana now commuted his sentence to life imprisonment and on the recommendation of the psychiatrists had him transferred to a mental hospital. He was later declared sane but cannot be released, because he is held to be a dangerous criminal who has confessed to a series of violent crimes. No one believes he did them, no one believes he is mad, yet he cannot be released. Whilst the committing of such crimes might be seen as good reason for protecting the public by detaining him, it is difficult to see why his merely confessing to them should constitute such a danger.[32]

Those whose English is deficient are similarly at risk in making statements to the police or the courts. Until the ending of mass immigration into America after the First World War, there were a number of cases of Hungarian, Polish, Irish, Croat, Norwegian and other immigrants speaking little or no English being wrongly imprisoned partly because of misunderstandings or mistranslations during or before the trial.[33] Today the chief problem lies with the Spanish-speaking Mexicans and Puerto Ricans.[34]

If of course you are able to speak little English *and* are thought to be insane then you are doubly at risk. Such was the case of Victor Rosario, a Puerto Rican whose wife called the police and accused him of assault. In court Rosario said in his defence that his wife was having an affair with their lodger, who to demonstrate his virility drank his own blood and wrote in this blood on the wall of their apartment. As a result of claiming that such an unbelievable event took place, Rosario was declared unfit to plead and placed in a maximum security prison for the criminal insane. As the law stands in New York State he could have been kept there indefinitely without trial so long as the doctors declared he was unfit to stand trial. Rosario spent four years in this hospital-prison writing in turn (alphabetically) to all the lawyers in New York asking them to take up his case. When he got to 'H' a Mrs Sara Halbert investigated the case and got a statement from his wife saying that her lover did in fact drink his own blood. She showed this to the head of the prison hospital who declared Rosario fit to face trial. The assault charge was dismissed (1962) and Rosario released. During his four years in the 'hospital' Rosario was interviewed seventeen times by nine different psychiatrists, all of whom thought he must be mad because of the story about the blood. Indeed this was the only evidence that he was at all unbalanced and at one point the doctors even offered to declare him sane, if only he would admit the story was a mere fantasy.[35]

Confessions and guilty pleas involving some degree of plea-bargaining are also fairly common in the United States, though the practice is frowned on in some States. One extreme version of this is where an innocent man facing a capital charge realizes that the prosecution have an apparently strong case and that he will probably be found guilty whatever he pleads and so chooses to plead guilty to avoid being sentenced to death. This is an extremely rational procedure to adopt since if new evidence exonerating him should later crop up he can always be released from jail and compensated—but this is not possible if he has been sent to the electric chair or the gas chamber. Such a case was that of Louis De More, a Chicago man, who for some reason moved to St Louis and changed his name. The same day that he arrived a robber held up a tram and killed a policeman who was pursuing him. De More heard some policemen discussing the case in a cafe an hour later, and overheard one police-officer read out the description of the robber to the others. De More humorously pointed out that he fitted the description, and was promptly arrested when it was found that he had no alibi and was signed in at his hotel under a false name. He was confronted with the tram-driver who identified him and taken to the bedside of the dying policeman who nodded his head when looking at him, which ambiguous gesture was taken as further identification. In gaol, other prisoners told De More that he was certain to be convicted and executed if he pleaded not guilty but that he might get life imprisonment if he confessed. The assistant prosecutor confirmed that this was so in a discussion with De More before the trial. De More pleaded guilty to first degree murder and confessed in detail to the crime explaining away his lack of a gun by saying he had thrown it in the river afterwards. The prosecution stuck to their side of the bargain and within five days of the murder he was sentenced to life imprisonment. Ten days later the police arrested the real murderer on suspicion and found the gun in his possession (it had not been in any water). He was identified by the tram-driver and several of the passengers and De More was exonerated and pardoned.[36]

Perhaps the oddest case of a man confessing to a crime for the benefits the confession might bring was that of Eugene Padgett of Belton, Texas. While serving a twenty-year sentence for burglary he confessed to the murder of a garage-owner. He pleaded guilty at his trial, was sentenced to ninety-nine years, and sent back to jail. He now revealed that his confession was false and that he had only made it in the hope of being put in a small town jail during his trial, from which he hoped to make an easy escape. Instead he was kept in a high security jail. The courts continued to play out this bizarre game by refusing to act on his appeal until he had finished his burglary sentence. The jail insisted that he serve the full twenty years because he had contemplated trying to escape in this way. Only fifteen years later was his appeal allowed and the conviction for murder set aside.[37]

Perjury as a cause of wrongful imprisonment is more widespread and more blatant in America than in England. Some, however, of the categories of perjury and perjurors are similar in the two countries. Women and children,[38] especially in sex cases or where their pride is hurt, and immigrants (notably Italians) enmeshed in a tight network of family and community ties[39] are often responsible for a man or woman being convicted on perjured evidence. Cases involving perjury by children or young girls seem common enough to move Edward D. Radin to comment '. . . [They] for reasons too devious for simple adults to grasp, solemnly swear away an innocent man's freedom. Sometimes they are honestly mistaken; occasionally they let their imagination run away with the few facts but more often they are outrageous liars spinning a web of fantasy that has an aura of reality to it. Any attempt by defence counsel to subject them to a rattling cross-examination will bring instant frowns from the jurors and a warning scowl from the presiding judge.'[40]

This very much confirms our experience in England, but 'hurt pride' does seem to make untruthful witnesses go to greater lengths in America to ensure the conviction of the person who has offended them, than anything we have seen in England. The case of Condy Dabney of Coxton, Kentucky, provides a good example. Several women had disappeared in the area where Dabney lived, including a 14-year-old girl Mary Vickery who had been seen in Dabney's taxi. Dabney was arrested but released for lack of evidence. Later a US marshall looking for a still found a girl's body in some old mine workings expressively called the Bugger Hollow shaft and the body was identified as that of Mary Vickery by her father. A Marie

233

Jackson now came forward and said that she had seen Dabney embrace Mary Vickery and then kill her and hide the body in the mine, threatening to kill Marie Jackson if she were to reveal this. Largely on this evidence Dabney was convicted and sentenced to life imprisonment. A year later a patrolman who knew the case saw the name 'Mary Vickery' in a hotel register in another town—purely by chance—and following this lead tracked her down and found her alive and well. She had simply run away from home without telling anyone. Dabney was now pardoned and Marie Jackson convicted of false swearing. Her motive appears to have been resentment at Dabney's refusal to leave his wife for her, assisted by the promise of a $500 reward.[41]

Another such case was that of Lonnie Jenkins of Detroit whose wife shot herself (leaving a suicide note) and was found by the coroner's inquest to have committed suicide. The police, however, continued to investigate because they were puzzled by Jenkins's description of his wife's position after she shot herself, a very unusual one for a suicide case. At an earlier time Jenkins and his wife had had a 15-year-old girl living with them partly to help the wife and partly because otherwise the girl would have been put in an institution as beyond anyone's control. The girl became infatuated with Jenkins who rebuffed her and eventually asked her to leave. This girl now told the police that she had had an affair with Jenkins who had promised to kill his wife and marry her. She also claimed to have written notes for Jenkins in an imitation of his wife's hand-writing. Jenkins was tried for murder, found guilty, and sentenced to life imprisonment. His defence lawyer continued to work on the case and worked out carefully how a person could shoot herself and fall in the same position as Mrs Jenkins. He then went to the police to demonstrate how this could be done but accidentally used a loaded pistol and shot himself dead in the police station. Jenkins's daughter who knew he had been devoted to her mother and had rejected the girl collected new forensic evidence over a period of years and got the case reopened. The girl now admitted that she had invented the story out of resentment at being scorned by Jenkins. Jenkins's conviction was now set aside (1940), but he had spent nine years in jail.[42]

The notion of 'female' perjury was given a new twist in the case of William Green, convicted of murdering a nightwatchman on the evidence of two eyewitnesses and sentenced to life imprisonment in 1947. Ten years later one of the witnesses voluntarily went to the

District Attorney's office and admitted that he had committed perjury because the other witness had paid him $100. The other witness was a homosexual who had once been beaten by Green, a tough navy veteran, for making an indecent proposal to him. This was his method of getting revenge. Neither witness had in fact been anywhere near the crime. Once again we have a case of a person prevented by physical weakness (relative to Green) and social convention (which allows normal people to attack homosexuals with impunity under certain circumstances but will not allow homosexuals to retaliate) from direct aggressive retaliation. Nor was legitimate legal redress for his beating open to the homosexual. Under these circumstances he sought to use the criminal courts as his weapon in working off his grudge against Green.[43]

The American legal system is very similar in many ways to the English, not surprisingly since it derives directly from it. The common law, jury trials for serious criminal offences, an accusatorial system, characterize the American as well as the English systems of criminal justice. The details of trial procedures do, however, differ from those of England, and within America may differ widely from State to State. Though there are Federal offences and Federal courts, most trials occur under the aegis of the governments of the individual States. The conducting of criminal trials and the determining of trial procedures is left in the hands of the States by the American Constitution,[44] though the constitution does lay down basic safeguards and the Supreme Court has on many occasions given rulings as to what does and does not constitute a fair trial.[45] It is, however, probably broadly true to say that the jury has even less help reaching its decision than is the case in England and that it is even more difficult to appeal[46] against that decision on grounds of fact.[47] On the former issue Professor Morgan has noted that in many States 'the trial judge is prohibited by constitution, statute or controlling decision from commenting upon the weight or credibility of the testimony. . . . In some States he may review the evidence but he must not indicate his opinions about it; and in none [of these States] can he say a word as to the credibility of a particular witness. . . . The prevailing practice is unwise and it should be provided by statute [thus]: The trial judge may express to the jury after the close of the evidence and arguments, his opinion as to the weight and credibility of the evidence or any part thereof.'[48] We have already discussed in an earlier chapter comparisons between English and American procedures for appeal against criminal conviction. It need only be added here that in practice the wrongly convicted do find it difficult to appeal unless there has been some legal or procedural error at their trial. Indeed, in some States there is no criminal appeal court and no legal procedure for reopening a case on the basis of new evidence.[49] The jury seems to be placed on an even higher pedestal than in England and its errors are accordingly probably more frequent and more difficult to rectify.

The other great shibboleth of the English legal system, the protection against self-incrimination, with its corollaries, the right to silence and the caution, is even more strongly entrenched in America since it is inscribed in the Constitution in the Fifth Amendment. It creates the same general problem there as in England,[50] and it is difficult to disagree with Professor Borchard's comment that 'the supposed privilege against self-incrimination is of but little help to an innocent man.'[51] Indeed, because of the way the privilege against self-incrimination interacts with other elements of trial procedure, this right is both hopelessly weakened as a protection for the accused and used as a justification for practices that are actively harmful.[52]

Many States in America lack what are probably two of the most important procedural protections for an accused man. Many States allow the accused's former convictions to be introduced as evidence by the prosecution. Again, in many States there is no proper provision for a preliminary hearing at which the prosecution puts forward the details of its case. As a result the defence may not know of the case it has to answer, until the actual trial itself. Both of these factors load the scales heavily against the defence and undoubtedly contribute to many wrong convictions.

In some States the trial may indeed open with the introduction by the prosecution of details of the accused's prior convictions.[53] In many other States where the prosecution is not allowed to introduce such evidence directly, nevertheless the prosecuting counsel can cross-examine the accused on his past record. For this reason many defendants choose not to give evidence at their trial—they seek refuge from such questions in their constitutional right to remain silent. As a result the jury, which is naturally and rightly suspicious of any failure to testify, may also conclude (rightly or wrongly) from the defendants' silence that he has a criminal record that he wishes to conceal. The fact that cross-examination of the accused on his record is permitted in this way thus effectively robs the right to silence of any value it might have. If the defendant's record is directly or indirectly revealed to the jury, this will go against him very strongly. As Jerome and Barbara Frank put it: 'Because the prosecutor may always reveal that any witness has been previously convicted of a major crime—on the theory that the testimony of an ex-convict is not likely to be trustworthy—most of the courts apply the same theory to the accused if he elects to testify. The judges to be sure will admonish the jurors that such evidence bears solely on the truth of the defendant's testimony and that they must not treat it as proof of the defendant's guilt of the crime for which he is now on trial. However, most judges and trial lawyers agree that a jury will probably seldom heed that cautionary admonition. They believe that the jury will usually conclude that since the defendant was a proved criminal in the past, he is still a bad man with a criminal propensity who probably committed the crime with which he is now charged. (Most lawyers and judges think that the accused will be better off if the judge does not give the jury such a warning. For that sort of warning tends to rub in the very fact that the jury is cautioned to disregard.) As a result, a defendant whether guilty or innocent who was formerly convicted of a major crime is very likely to be again convicted if he testifies.'[54] Both Borchard and the Franks indicate that this is a key source of wrongful imprisonment in the United States.[55]

In many American States the accused is not told in advance of his trial what evidence the prosecution will present against him. America (more precisely the States of which this is true) is unique in this respect—in most other countries and particularly in England, great stress is laid on the preliminary court hearing at which the suspect hears the testimony of the prosecution witnesses, is able to cross-examine them and also to examine any documents or forensic exhibits the prosecution intends to use. This is probably essential if the accused and his lawyers are to be able to prepare a defence that meets the salient points of the prosecution case. Alibis cannot be established unless the timing of events alleged by the prosecution is known, cross-examination of witnesses cannot be prepared unless the outline of their testimony is known. Paradoxically, the lack of disclosure of the prosecution case hinders the innocent man's defence more than that of the truly guilty. The guilty man after all knows the details of the crime anyway because he was there. It is only the innocent man who is left floundering and wondering what it is the prosecution will try to prove. The justification for this odd procedure is according to the Franks curiously bound up with the right not to testify. They comment: 'There is still another argument made against discovery [disclosure of the prosecution case] in criminal cases: as the defendant has a constitutional right not to testify or to disclose his evidence before the trial begins, the State, it is argued, ought to be in the same position: what is sauce for the goose is sauce for the gander. This reciprocating argument has not won favour in England or Canada. If it has any validity then it might be provided that a defendant in order to obtain discovery from the government must disclose the evidence he intends to present in his defence. Something similar is already the practice in the Federal courts and in some States.'[56]

English lawyers when upholding the right of a man to avoid incriminating himself often refer back to the need for such a privilege in the days when men were unfairly tried for essentially political offences before the Star Chamber.[57] It may be retorted that with the abolition of the Star Chamber the need for this right is greatly diminished. America, however, still has the Star Chamber in the form of its congressional committees. This is perhaps not strictly relevant in a discussion of wrongful imprisonment resulting from criminal trials. But in America there are important cultural continuities between the two situations. Ronald Seth discussing the House committee on un-American activities (which can cover anything from the Communist Party to the Ku-Klux-Klan) notes that 'like all congressional committees it had almost Star Chamber powers. Its proceedings were privileged as are those in courts of law the world over but it had *no rules of evidence*. As a consequence, the members of the committee might all ask whatever questions they wished and make any comments that might occur to them whether sensitive to proof or not and no matter how prejudicial such comments might be to the witness. The witness unless he invoked the Fifth Amendment to the Constitution which gave him the right to refuse should his answer tend to incriminate him, had to reply or risk action for contempt of Congress.'[58]

The result of course is that people being interrogated by the committee invoke the Fifth Amendment to a ludicrous extent. Here for example is a typical passage from the interrogation of Henry Collins by R. E. Stripling, the chief investigator of the committee on un-American affairs, in open session of the committee.

Stripling: Do you know an individual known to you as Carl in 1935?

Collins: I refuse to answer that question on the grounds of possible self-incrimination. . . .

Stripling: Mr Collins did you ever live at St Matthew's Court in Washington.

Collins: I did.

Stripling: Did you ever meet John Abt at that apartment?

Collins: I decline to answer that question on the grounds of possible self-incrimination.

Stripling: Did you ever meet Alger Hiss at that apartment?

Collins: I decline to answer that question for the same reason.

Stripling: Did you ever meet in the apartment of Alger Hiss on P Street in Georgetown in 1935?

Collins: I decline to answer that question on the grounds of possible self-incrimination.[59]

The whole process is reduced to farce if the witness is allowed to stonewall in this way. Indeed the only reason for allowing him to do so is that this is the only protection he has against an essentially unfair set of procedures. The answer though is not to enshrine the right against self-incrimination but to curb the powers of congressional committees. Alternatively, the right could be retained in this context but considerably diminished in criminal trials along the lines we have suggested in Chapter 10. There are, after all, other and better safeguards for the accused in a criminal trial. In an American context of course any such whittling away of this right would have to be accompanied by much stronger protection of the accused in other ways—notably by forbidding the prosecution to bring up his past record.

The main problems in America, however, do not lie in the structure of the legal system but in the attitudes the prosecution and defence, judge and jury, accused and witness, police-officer and press reporter and all those connected with the process of criminal justice, bring to the system and to their role in it. These are largely determined by the values of the wider society for the legal system is not detached and insulated from the rest of society to the extent it is in other countries. The dominant values of American society have been described by S. M. Lipset as 'Equality' and 'Achievement'.[60] In America all men are equal and all strive to become more equal than the others. From American egalitarianism is derived the intense influence that crass and unmediated popular prejudice can have on the conduct of trials and law enforcement agencies. The people can and do assert their right to determine the course of these events and the behaviour of these officials. It is their will that prevails, not that of the lawyer, the expert or the intellectual. At times, public opinion can even exert direct pressure on the conduct of particular cases and trials. Press comment on trials is much more unrestrained in America than in England. More generally the sheriffs, judges and others who administer the system are elected by direct vote or hired and fired at will by local politicians to a greater extent than in Europe. Political power is in some ways much more decentralized in America and the operation of the courts and the police in particular are as much more subject to *local* pressure as a result.

Equality in America means that anyone can reasonably aspire to become a police-officer, a lawyer or a judge, however lacking in ability, education, probity or sense of public duty he may be. It is difficult to become a successful lawyer on Wall Street, or a Justice of the Supreme Court or an agent of the FBI for at the top, the standards of ability and integrity are very high. But it is very easy to join a local police force, to become a bad though fully qualified lawyer, or a small-time local judge.[61] You don't need to be clever and you don't need to be honest, for America is in her terms a democratic country. The result is a system of criminal justice that is admirable at its tiny peak and all too frequently corrupt and incompetent at the lower levels.

The problems are compounded by the other all-pervading American value—the zeal to succeed at all costs regardless of whether you stay within the rules.[62] In some ways this aggressive and ruthless competitiveness has been a great asset to America. It is the source of the economic and political vitality that has made her the richest, and most powerful and efficient nation the world has ever known. But it is not an appropriate approach for a criminal trial. What's good for General Motors is not good for the USA versus John Doe. Also although competitiveness is a virtue it must be bounded by clear rules as to what are legitimate and what are forbidden modes of attaining success. These rules are lacking in America, perhaps because the pervasive egalitarianism forbids the making of distinctions between different routes to the top. A lack of restraints on the desire to win is disastrous for the proper functioning of a system of criminal justice and this is particularly true for an accusatorial system. Too much zeal for gaining a conviction leads to corrupt and brutal practices on the part of police and prosecution which often lead to wrongful imprisonment. An unrestrained desire for revenge or reward leads to perjury by witnesses, to deliberate frame-ups or to corruption of officials. A defence lawyer's keenness to get his client off may give rise to pettifogging obstruction and the deliberate thwarting of justice which may provoke equally unfair retaliation from the prosecution. The combination of the drive for success and the love of equality gives rise to the ethic of rugged individualism and self-reliance held by so many Americans which has stifled the growth of certain welfare services there. As a result proper legal aid is lacking in many towns and States since local sentiment rejects it as paternalism, as collectivism and as throughly un-American.

Public interest and passion is easily aroused about criminal trials in America especially in small communities and frequently has an effect on the verdict. Borchard notes that this was an important factor in fourteen of his cases of proven wrongful imprisonment.[63] A classic case of such influence was that of James Foster convicted of murder in Jefferson, Georgia, in 1956 and later exonerated when the real culprit confessed. Public feeling ran so strongly against Foster that he could not be held in the local jail for fear of a lynch-mob. Edward D. Radin described the effect of public opinion on this and similar cases thus: 'People are emotionally aroused by a crime and display above normal interest; there is a restless rumbling by this disturbed public and a sharp increase in letters and telephone calls to police, to newspapers, to officials all insistently demanding action. Newspapers reflect the general temper of their readers and become more shrill and so the heat is on. Police, prosecution and even judge may be goaded into hasty action; judgment becomes blurred under the pressure; suppositions replace facts and since jurors are selected from among this excited public little attention is paid to the actual evidence, the guilty verdict is a foregone conclusion, and the net result is a legal lynching. And a study of cases where innocent persons have been convicted shows this happens more frequently than is realized. . . . After his [James Foster's] arrest children were observed outside the jail carrying home-made nooses; on the opening day of his trial a gospel preacher mounted the court-house steps and delivered what local reporters described as a "hell-fire" oration and eighteen minutes after the jurors had retired to deliberate they were called back to the court-room and asked if they had reached a verdict.'[64]

Public opinion also exerts more indirect pressures—notably via the ballot box—on sheriffs and prosecutors who need to seek re-election. The election manifestos of candidates for these offices frequently stress their zeal in winning cases. As Radin notes: '. . . because a prosecutor's office is frequently a stepping-stone to political advancement and a high "batting-average" [that is proportion of prosecutions won] looks impressive at first glance, some trial assistants are more anxious to win their cases than they are concerned over the innocence or guilt of the person on trial. . . .'[65] Radin also notes: 'The sheriff is an elected official, his staff quite often is largely a non-professional group and there is nothing like a conviction in a good case to win re-election for sheriff and job insurance for political appointees.'[66]

Local influence can extend even beyond the stage of prosecution and trial. In the case of Charles F. Stielow and Nelson Green convicted of murder in the small community of West Shelby in upstate New York, the locals played a big part in preventing the case from being reopened, even though another man had confessed and Stielow had been proven innocent. The Governor of New York State had ordered a special investigation of Stielow's conviction by a leading attorney because of doubts about the case. The attorney reported that Stielow was innocent and named the real culprit. He presented his evidence to a special grand jury but they rejected it and refused to allow the case to be re-examined. E. B. Block comments: '. . . the jury's action reflected the attitude of a country community that had thoroughly satisfied itself on the guilt of two men and did not wish its conclusions to be changed. . . . The townsfolk believed they had heard too much of the case for too long and were angered that more than $75,000 of public funds had been expended, even though the money had been used to correct a miscarriage of justice. And there was still another factor—resentment against the employment by the State of an investigator from another county to undo the work of their own elected officials. Against these circumstances the fate of two of their fellow citizens did not seem to matter.'[67] A similar instance of such obstruction occurred in the case of Leonard Hankins convicted of robbery and murder in Minneapolis, Minnesota, in 1932 and sentenced to life imprisonment by a local court. Three years later the FBI captured one of the real robbers who named his accomplices, stating Hankins was innocent. The FBI notified the Minneapolis authorities but this merely led to a dispute about who was entitled to keep the files on the case. Only after Hankins had spent eighteen years in jail was he pardoned and released in 1951, fifteen years after his innocence was established.[68]

The press plays a notable role in America in influencing trials partly because of the greater intensity of local feelings and influence, and partly because there are far fewer restrictions on press reporting of trials. As Lord Devlin notes in *Trial by Jury*: 'Comment on matters that are *sub-judice* has always been punishable by contempt of court; but the court [in England] is especially vigilant whenever there is a danger of a jury being prejudiced. . . . This may be contrasted with the practice in America. In the Hiss case the supposed evidence of a witness which had been excluded as inadmissible on the first trial was published by a newspaper, apparently without objection notwithstanding that a second trial was pending.'[69]

Press reporting of this sort can in fact be the main cause of a wrongful conviction as was shown by the case of James W. Preston, convicted of burglary, robbery and assault in Los Angeles in 1924. Preston was arrested on suspicion of robbing a widow in her home but it was found that his fingerprints did not match those found in the house. The Los Angeles papers, however, carried a false story claiming that he was the robber and that the prints matched. The victim read this in the press and when confronted with Preston in hospital identified him as her assailant. The jury was not told in court anything about the fingerprint evidence but of course may well have read about it in the press. Preston was convicted and got from eleven years to life. The only man who thought he was innocent was the police fingerprint expert who some eighteen months later caught the real culprit. This man's prints did match those found and Preston was pardoned.[70]

In the past, many Americans have been convicted of serious crimes and given heavy sentences without there being any lawyer for the defence because the defendant could not afford one. In some cities and States the indigent accused was defended by a public defender, a salaried employee of the district; in other places there were publicly- or privately-financed legal aid schemes. But until the Supreme Court ruled in the Gideon case[71] that all defendants were entitled to counsel even if indigent there was no compulsion on the State or city governments to make any provision at all. Now in theory every defendant is adequately defended at the expense of the State, but in practice the lawyer assigned to him may be so incompetent or inexperienced as to be useless. Also these schemes only cover the totally destitute defendant. The accused person who has some small means is at the mercy of the cheap but inept and careless lawyers who make up the bulk of the criminal bar in large cities in America.[72] Even if the State pays for a lawyer, a man may still be imprisoned solely because he is unable to pay to have his alibi checked or to engage a handwriting expert or a pathologist. Poverty still remains a major cause of wrongful imprisonment in America, even in major cases.[73]

The drive to get a conviction at all costs by police or prosecutor is a major factor causing wrongful imprisonment in America. In Borchard's study alone are listed twenty cases where over-zealous action by police or prosecutor or some other party procured a wrongful conviction; in ten cases the police were negligent in over-looking evidence of innocence and in one case they actually suppressed it.[74] This is largely the result of continuous public pressure on the police and prosecutors to get convictions due to the very high rates of crime and especially violent crime in America. The main harmful responses to this pressure are (a) the police are tempted to get a confession out of a suspect by threats or violence; (b) the police sometimes pin a crime on a suspect and fix the evidence to back this up;[75] and (c) the prosecutor may withhold evidence favourable to the defence and hence secure a wrong conviction.

In England we have come across no *proven* cases of wrongful imprisonment which were the result of a false confession extorted by threats or brutality. Cases of wrongful imprisonment following a confession usually involved people of low mentality unable to cope with the rigours of ordinary interrogation in the way a normal person can. In America the methods used are sometimes such that even the normal person cannot stand up to them and may break down and confess to a crime he did not commit. Cases like that of Geither Horn who was taken by the police to an open grave and told he would be buried alive if he didn't confess to a local killing (he served twenty-four years, 1935–59, before he was freed, exonerated and compensated)[76] or like Johnson who was told there was a howling lynch-mob outside the goal and that the police would hand him over to the mob if he didn't confess to the murder of a child,[77] are crude examples of how American police may get such a confession. Normally they are slightly more subtle. The 'subtle' methods may be illustrated by quoting from the forty-five-hour interrogation of Gerald Anderson of Mountain Home, Idaho, who in 1954 was induced by the office of special investigation to confess to the murder of the wife and child of a neighbour. (Anderson had nothing to do with the crime and was later totally exonerated.)

Interrogator: We both know it happened and you and I are the only two that know for certain it happened.

Anderson: No sir, I swear to God I didn't.

Interrogator: Your subconscious mind knows you did it. Your conscious mind had to know you did it. I'm not asking whether you did it or not. We know. I'm only asking one thing—why? That's all I want, Gerald. I explained to you this morning how I could understand that it takes a lot of courage to do it. The problem now is why you did it. Was it something you were provoked into doing, either mentally or psychically? Was it just at a time that you went insane for just a split second? What better excuse could a man have? Something that they cannot disprove and something they cannot hold you responsible for. There is not a board or a court that would. They can't send a man up that has been proven insane and you know that. You must have been insane, drunk perhaps frightened . . . something . . .'

'You've got to level with me so that I can present a reasonable solution. I'm ready to listen to anything. She could have taken after you with a butcher's knife and you got into a fight and you took it from her and it was accidental. You could have gone in and she was beating up this child and you tried to stop her and it happened . . .'

'You're a sick man. You're sick. Did you ever think about that. You're sick. Did you ever think about that. You're sick. You're a twisted up, violent and sick man. That's what you are. Look at yourself, inspect your heart, inspect your mind, look at your brain. . . . Are you proud of what you are, huh?. . . . [If you don't confess your wife will be arrested as an accessory.] And when I do that, I put those three young kids [of yours] in a reformatory or an orphanage.'[78]

After forty-five hours of this, Anderson was totally confused and made an inaccurate confession to the murder, which he later repudiated. He was so completely bemused by the questioning that an attempt by the local police to give him a lie-detector test well after the interrogation had to be abandoned because Anderson was still totally confused.

In theory, the prosecution in America should not withhold evidence favourable to the defence. As the Canon of legal ethics of the American Bar Association puts it: 'The primary duty of a lawyer engaged in a public prosecution is not to convict but to see that justice is done. The suppression of facts or the secretion of witnesses capable of establishing the innocence of the accused is highly reprehensible.'[79] In practice in this as in many areas of American life, greater stress is placed on the importance of winning than on using the correct and legitimate means of doing so.[80] This may be illustrated by reference to the case of Walter A. Pecho, of Lansing, Michigan, who was convicted of killing his wife in 1954 when in fact she had committed suicide with a shotgun. (She left a suicide note and had made a previous attempt.) He was sentenced to from fifteen to twenty years' gaol. After the trial the defence lawyer learnt that the police had found his wife's fingerprint just behind the trigger-guard. This lawyer asked for a new trial on the grounds that evidence had been concealed. The prosecution denied this and said that the police had been willing to give this information and that it was up to the defence to elicit it during cross-examination. The defence lawyer stated that he knew there had been fingerprint tests but that he did not know the result and had not asked about them because he was afraid he might walk into a trap set by the prosecution. The judge refused to grant a new trial and the conviction was upheld on appeal. Only in 1960 after Pecho had been in jail five years was there a full investigation which resulted in the Governor granting Pecho an unconditional pardon on the grounds of his complete innocence.[81] It is remarkable that not merely did the prosecution behave in this way but that the other legal functionaries connived at this and accepted the situation.[82]

It is perhaps understandable if not excusable that the prosecutors in America should cut corners to get convictions in view of the crime situation there. They are at least motivated to some degree by a (misplaced) sense of public duty. What is rather more shocking is that they should use their position to gain the conviction of an innocent man purely for private reasons whether for reward or out of malice. Cases that illustrate two common sources of corruption in American life are those of James Montgomery, and of Louis Gross.

James Montgomery was a negro living in Waukegan, Illinois, in 1923 who had a well-paid skilled job in a factory and who owned two houses, one of which he rented out. He was arrested following a baseless accusation of rape by an elderly and mentally deficient spinster who had fantasies about such things. A medical examination showed that there was no evidence of rape and that she was in fact a virgin. The day after his arrest, when Montgomery was confronted with his 'victim' she failed to identify him and said she had never seen him before. However, the local public prosecutor was a member of the Ku-Klux-Klan who had a grudge against the accused because he had lost a civil law suit to Montgomery following an attack on Montgomery's property by the Klan. Now was his chance for revenge on this 'uppity nigger'. He had Montgomery so badly beaten up by the police that he still had the scars twenty-six years later when he was released. At the trial, the jury was in effect chosen by the prosecution. The negro defence lawyer was threatened by the Klan and failed to call any of Montgomery's twelve alibi witnesses. The entire trial took twenty minutes, Montgomery was found guilty and sentenced to life imprisonment. He served twenty-four years before he was exonerated and released in 1949.[83]

Louis Gross was a Jewish pedlar who traded in a largely Syrian neighbourhood in Detroit. In 1932 a wealthy Syrian was shot dead while asleep at his home. The police had difficulty in getting information partly because of the language problem and partly because of the tangle of lies and counter-lies that are told by members of a tightly knit immigrant community in this kind of situation. One of the suspects conveniently 'remembered' that Gross had told him he did it, in order to forestall a difficult question during his interrogation by the police. Gross had in fact been offered money by one of the suspects to do the murder but he had refused. At the trial many witnesses showed a lack of concern with telling the truth and some were threatened with prosecution for perjury. All the evidence given was contradictory and contradicted. There were accusations and counter-accusations and lies all round. In the confusion Gross was convicted and given life imprisonment. He sought to appeal and requested a transcript of the trial. The court reporter now discovered that his shorthand notes of the trial were missing. He applied to the new prosecutor (the successor of the man who had handled the case) for a transcript but the prosecutor discovered that the police file on the case, the shorthand notes of the preliminary hearing and the locked files of the prosecution department were also missing. The prosecutor began an investigation but he shortly afterwards failed to get re-elected to his office due to a solid block of organized votes by interested persons and their supporters plumping for his opponent. Thus even though the theft was revealed in open court this did not help Gross. Later a new police captain assigned to the neighbourhood learnt from the Syrians that Gross had been framed in this way and began to investigate. The investigation was blocked by a local politician and the police captain was sacked. Gross now remained in jail for sixteen years. He told his story to the prison rabbi who took it to the 'Court of Last Resort' an organisation of lawyers and detectives who investigate such cases in America. By now there was yet another new prosecutor and he initiated a new investigation despite violent and corrupt resistance to it. It was shown that a key witness had lied and that both the witness and the murder victim had been involved in a gambling racket. Gross was now granted a new trial and the charge dismissed.[84]

No one was punished following the revelations of what had happened in these two cases nor was there any proper State investigation of who was responsible. It seems likely that if you are a black man or on the fringe of a well-organized racket there are many places in America where you may well be wrongly imprisoned because of corrupt practices before or during your trial.

It is not necessarily the police or prosecution who are responsible for innocent men being framed or otherwise convicted on perjured evidence. In addition to the types of perjury discussed earlier there is a good deal of deliberate perjury by criminals and others. Borchard discusses nineteen cases in which perjury was a major ingredient and Radin several others.[85] In many of these the key element is perjury by criminals seeking some advantage. Three situations may be distinguished. Firstly, prisoners in gaol accuse an innocent man with a crime possibly with the hope of gaining favour with the authorities. This often happens when a man is held in gaol before trial and shares a cell with men already convicted. They may then later claim that the man on trial admitted to them that he had committed the crime when they occupied the same cell. Secondly, a prisoner under arrest names innocent men as his accomplices in the hope of getting a more lenient sentence. Thirdly, a man sentenced to death or a long sentence seeks to work out a last revenge on someone who has thwarted him. In the case of Dale Bundy an associate of his, Russel McCoy nearly succeeded in killing him in this way. McCoy committed several hold-ups and four murders in Uniontown, Ohio, in 1957 before being caught by the police. Bundy, a friend of McCoy's, helped the police with their investigations and McCoy threatened to kill him for it later. When caught McCoy confessed to the murders in such a way as to implicate Bundy. Bundy was convicted of first degree murder and sentenced to die in the electric chair. A great deal of new evidence was now produced indicating that Bundy was innocent but the judge refused a new trial since Bundy was held to have received 'substantive justice'. His appeal was denied and the Ohio Supreme Court affirmed the conviction. Three days before the execution, a woman read an account of the case in a crime magazine which featured a photo of McCoy. She recognized him as the man who had boasted to her that he had killed four people and was about to arrange a legal murder. As McCoy put it: 'I'm going to have the law do it for me'. Bundy was now granted a new trial and acquitted, but he spent a year in jail altogether.[86]

As in England most wrongly convicted Americans got off because of random factors such as the real culprit confessing. Far more than in England were eventually exonerated though as a result of further police or prosecution investigation. This does not reflect greater assiduousness on their part in seeking to free the wrongly convicted but rather that they are more willing than the British police to take a case to court that they are not sure about and to get a conviction. Having safely notched up a success, they go on investigating because they are still not sure of his guilt. For similar reasons more men are exonerated because it is discovered that no crime was ever committed (for example the 'victim' of a murder turns up alive) or because similar and sometimes distinctive crimes go on happening after the convicted (though innocent) man is in jail.[87]

The morals of the American experience for England are largely negative. We can see that mis-identification, false confessions by the mentally inadequate, and nearly all the other main causes of wrongful imprisonment in England are not peculiar to our legal system or our culture. We can be sure that these are factors we must guard against. We can see the real value of such safeguards as prohibiting the use of a man's record as evidence or the proper disclosure of the prosecution's case in a preliminary hearing—safeguards which America lacks and which there are a potent cause of wrong convictions. We can see that it is vital to keep political influence out of the legal system and to have a judiciary, lawyers and police-officers whose first loyalty is to the rule of the law and not to faction or their electorate. It is curious that the notoriously legalistic Americans with their veneration for 'government by laws not by men' should succumb to this problem. But perhaps they need this principle precisely because they cannot trust their officials to exercise discretionary power in a disinterested way. We can see that the accusatorial system which we share with the Americans works well only if all parties concerned in it stick to the rules of the game. In England it works reasonably well for this reason. In America the eagerness to win leads the prosecution to break these rules and cause wrongful convictions. The defence too by pettifogging obstruction in court, by challenging the jurors until it has packed the jury-box, by dragging in irrelevant political issues, by endless frivolous appeals on technicalities can thwart justice. In the long run, wrongful acquittals achieved in this way lead to wrongful convictions because the prosecution is forced to retaliate with its own brand of sharp practice. As Glanville Williams has well put it: 'The evil of acquitting a guilty person goes much beyond the simple fact that one guilty person has gone unpunished. It frustrates the arduous and costly work of the police who if this tendency goes too far may either become daunted or resort to improper methods of obtaining convictions. If unmerited acquittals become general, they tend to lead to a disregard of the law and this in turn leads to a public demand for more severe punishment of those found guilty. Thus the acquittal of the guilty leads to a ferocious penal law. . . . For all these reasons it is true to say with Viscount Simon that "a miscarriage of justice may arise from the acquittal of the guilty no less than from the conviction of the innocent".'[88]

This piece of theoretical analysis can almost be taken as a description of America's problems. These problems stem as much from the zeal of the crusading liberal lawyer as from the actions of the law-enforcement agencies. On both sides can be seen the operation of the central failing of American society and the American people, viz. an overweening desire to win at all costs and a disregard for rules, procedure and restraints.

Chapter 10

Scales of Injustice

'The object of any satisfactory system of criminal justice should be to ascertain the truth in every case and to secure with even-handed impartiality the conviction of the guilty and the acquittal of the innocent. The sting of any unjust acquittal is, however, spread over the community at large. An unjust conviction bears directly upon the individual, his family and friends. It is for this reason that until now the English system of investigating and prosecuting crime has been heavily weighted in favour of the accused.'[1]

These sentiments are admirable, but they result in a lot of guilty people getting off.[2] It might be thought that some of the reforms we have suggested would make things even more difficult for the police. Some of these, for example the rules with regard to identification, and prosecutions initiated by someone like the Procurator-fiscal rather than the police, are similar to the situation already obtaining in Scotland. Some benefits of the Scottish system can be seen in the fact that the acquittal rate in jury trials is much lower (22 per cent in Scotland as against 39 per cent in England and Wales); and that during the period 1950–70, only two free pardons were granted in Scotland to people who had received prison sentences (both these pardons were on relatively technical grounds). Only six cases since the passing of the Criminal Appeal (Scotland) Act, 1926, have been referred (under Section 16) to the High Court of Justiciary (as Court of Criminal Appeal). Of these, only the first, the celebrated case of Oscar Slater, resulted in the conviction being quashed. Since we have no reason to suppose that it is more difficult to get an appeal or a pardon in Scotland, and even allowing for the smaller population, we feel that these figures do indicate a much lower rate of wrongful imprisonment in Scotland. But the clear-up rate for crime in Scotland is also much lower than that in England. Both these phenomena may well stem from the distinctive characteristics of the Scottish legal system.

Is it in fact ever possible to introduce extra safeguards for the innocent without making the prosecution's job more difficult? Given the present structure of our legal system, we feel that there are many areas where it is. Tom Sargant, the Secretary of 'Justice', had this to say about the present set-up: 'Our system of criminal justice appears to me to have perhaps too many safeguards for the guilty person and too few safeguards for the innocent.'[3] We agree with this. Ironically, the more the system is reformed along the lines suggested below, the closer we get to a position where further reform would involve making a hard choice of this nature.[4] But at present it is still possible to win both ways.

Historically, the two bases of the English system of criminal justice have been that the burden of proof lies on the prosecution; and that the defendant may not be compelled to incriminate himself. In many ways these two principles are closely tied together. If you cannot compel a man to give evidence against himself, then it is up to you to provide other evidence to prove your case. Our quarrel is not with these principles; but we feel that legalistic adherence to them has at times led to the conviction of the innocent and the acquittal of the guilty. Procedural reforms in the application of these principles could lead to an improvement in both directions. It is not that the principles have never yet been breached. Two cases in point are the relatively recent requirement that the defence disclose before the trial details of any alibi they are proposing to use; and the introduction of the breathalyser. These innovations both impinge on the immemorial principle that it is for the prosecution to prove its case, not for the suspect to prove his innocence or to help the prosecution prove its case. In the case of the breathalyser, the tipsy motorist is expected to provide the evidence of his own unfitness to drive, and may be prosecuted if he fails to do so. In the case of the alibi defence, the accused is no longer allowed to remain completely passive *vis-à-vis* the prosecution right up until the moment of the trial. In effect, he has to assist the prosecution by enabling them to investigate his alibi. Both these reforms have helped to convict more of the guilty, but also to exonerate the innocent. With the breathalyser, the guilty motorist is no longer able to pretend that he was not really drunk, and a protection is afforded the genuinely confused, shocked or asthmatic driver. As for the disclosure of the alibi, this makes it much more likely that the innocent man's alibi will be properly investigated and confirmed.

Three main areas of controversy at the moment are the question of the caution, the accused's right to silence, and the disclosure of evidence at the preliminary hearing.

The caution is essentially a guard against inadvertent self-incrimination. It is supposed to be administered at the point where in the mind of the investigating police-officer the period of open-ended inquiry has come to an end, and he feels justified in charging the man he has been questioning, who has now become his chief suspect.[5] It is difficult to see quite how the interests of justice or of the innocent man are served by giving him an explicit warning at this particular point. It is one thing to argue that a suspect should not be compelled to incriminate himself; but we cannot see why he should not be allowed to. The important distinction to make is not that between inadvertent and deliberate statements, but between voluntary and coerced. As Sir Norman Skelhorn put it: 'A voluntary statement means a statement which has not been induced by any force or threat, or by any promise of favour or reward. It does not mean that it is one that the accused was necessarily anxious to make.'[6]

There are many disadvantages to the caution rule. When it is adhered to, there are at least two possible unfortunate results: the man being questioned may decide to say nothing more at all, and consequently get off; and, more important, this must be a great source of frustration to the police. If it is not adhered to, then the suspect may be acquitted because his defence lawyer can prove that the rule was broken; and, again more important, it may lead to a general disregard of rules, including more important rules, on the part of the police. Either way, it is probably very bad for police morale. It is perhaps time that this superfluous symbol was discarded, despite its historical and sentimental attractions. All that is necessary is that, when a person is finally charged, he be told exactly what he is being charged with.

The other great prop of the principle against self-incrimination is the right to silence. At present, the suspect is not required to say anything to the police during the pre-trial period, nor can he be compelled to go into the witness-box during the trial. We do not see how this can be of any help to the innocent man. Indeed, it might lead to his conviction because of the suspicion his silence might arouse in the minds of the jury. (We have come across some cases of this kind, where the accused's silence was a contributing factor in his being found guilty.) In other cases, a guilty man may escape conviction simply because he is never exposed to proper questioning.

Clearly, this is an unsatisfactory situation. The question arises, at what stages can it profitably be changed?

Diverse groups of people advocate the introduction of an examining magistrate at the pre-trial stage (see p. 64). They suggest that if the suspect refuses to answer his questions, this should be regarded as *prima facie* evidence of guilt which he should have to refute at his trial. All interrogations would have to be carried out before the magistrate, and no other statements or confessions would be admissible in court.[7]

We reject this suggestion for a number of reasons. One is, that it seems completely to shift the burden of proof away from the prosecution and on to the defendant, and might well result in more rather than less wrongful imprisonment. Secondly, if we are to judge by the experience of other countries, cases would take much longer to come to court under this system; and there is no proven correlation between slowness and accuracy. However, this correlation does seem to be assumed by the participants in this kind of system, and consequently there is a greater reluctance to reopen cases which have been investigated in this way. Wrongful imprisonment might thus become not only more frequent, but more final. Thirdly, there seems little doubt that this would frustrate the police even more than the present system does, and in ways which they would regard as unreasonable. In France, where the examining magistrate system prevails, and where police interrogation is theoretically not permitted (except in certain specific cases) we have nevertheless come across far more cases of police brutality in extorting confessions than we have found in England. Yet officially the suspect in France is protected by regulations which allow the police far less latitude than their counterparts in England.[8]

In America, the suspect's right to silence and his privilege against self-incrimination, are specifically written into the Constitution. Americans are even more concerned with the right to silence than the British—indeed, it might fairly be said that they are obsessed with it. The effect on the behaviour of their police has not been a salutary one. Professor Edwin Borchard says of this: 'It seems probable that the privilege [against self-incrimination by refusing to testify] is not an essential condition of the impartial administration of justice and that it does not afford to the accused the protection assumed. On the contrary, it is probably responsible for many abuses, not least of all the "3rd degree" which subjects accused persons to far more brutal and intolerable ordeals than any obligation to tell the truth in open court. Refusal to take the stand—under circumstances where an explanation from the accused is naturally expected—even if it cannot be commented upon by judge or prosecutor, inevitably affects the jury unfavourably; but in addition the accused's known privilege of refusing to testify influences the police to exact "confessions" which, whether true or not, stigmatize the system of obtaining them as public disgrace.'[9]

It would seem that, paradoxically, the less the right to silence is written into the rules, the more likely the police are to behave properly.

In an English context, we feel that certain abridgements of the right to silence ought to be introduced. These would be, firstly that the accused should be compelled to be a witness at his own trial, and have to face cross-examination. He could, of course, refuse to answer any specific question. Any inference the jury might draw from this would be no worse than the inference they might draw at present if he refuses to go into the box at all, and might indeed be more accurate. Secondly, when the accused does give evidence at his trial, and if he has previously refused to give any explanation or defence, he should be liable to face cross-examination on this point. This is to some extent an extension of the present practice that he can be cross-examined and commented upon if he previously had produced a different defence or only a part of his final one.[10] These suggestions are far more in keeping with the English tradition than the introduction of an examining magistrate. In England, evidence given during the trial is generally considered to be more important than what has happened at the pre-trial stages. An examining magistrate system reverses this stress, and consequently it would be very difficult to fit it into the English system.

Our third proposal is that there should be more discovery of evidence on both sides before the trial. At present, the prosecution is required to divulge its case in detail at the preliminary hearing, so that when the defence goes into court it knows more or less what each witness has to say and how he will say it. The defence, on the other hand, needs only give details if it intends to run an alibi defence. What we suggest is an extension of the area of discovery on both sides. The prosecution should be required to give details of any evidence it may possess which is favourable to the defence, whether or not it is proposing to use it during the trial. The advantage of this is that it would eliminate the kinds of cases of wrongful imprisonment we have discussed which have been due to the prosecution withholding such evidence. The defence on its side should be required to give some details of the case it intends to present, even where this is not an alibi defence. It is argued that to require the defence to disclose its case in this way is to shift the onus of proof away from the prosecution, because it is forcing the defence to help the prosecution. This is held to imply that the prosecution would no longer have to prove its case. We feel this is a fallacious argument. The fact that the prosecution knows the defence case makes their job easier, but not by altering the burden of proof. The defence has to show its hand, but this does not mean that it plays its cards in co-operation with the other side. In any case, most defences are alibi defences, and so are disclosed already.

What we have been trying to do is to sort out which of the existing safeguards are essential and should be strengthened, and which are superfluous and perhaps indirectly harmful. Apart from the specific suggestions which we have made in each separate chapter of this book, there are two main features of the English legal system which are essential and which should be retained and strengthened. One is the onus of proof—the fact that if there is any reasonable doubt, the jury is to be instructed by the judge to give the accused the benefit of it, and acquit. The other is the two-sided nature of the trial procedure, with a clear separation of prosecution and defence, and an equitable balance of power between them.

Nevertheless, there will always be cases of wrongful imprisonment. What is the moral position of the wrongly imprisoned man? Is it, as William Paley put it in his *Principles of Moral and Political Philosophy*, that: 'He who falls by a mistaken sentence may be considered as falling for his country. He suffers under the operation of those rules by the general effect of which the welfare of the community is maintained.'[11] By implication, the common good should always prevail over the rights of the individual. But our society is based on the opposite principle: that society consists simply of the individuals who compose it, rather than some personification of the general will that must not be opposed. And wrongful imprisonment, far from buttressing our kind of society, undermines it.

Epilogue

Since we wrote the bulk of the book before June 1972, we were unable to take into account the important suggestions made by the Criminal Law Revision Committee in its 11th report. We should therefore like to comment briefly on them.

We find ourselves in agreement with most of their detailed suggestions. Such concrete evidence as we have been able to collect as to how mistakes are made seems to buttress most of these suggestions.

We are also glad that they have explicitly emphasized the view that '. . . the law should be such as will secure as far as possible that the result of the trial is the right one.' As they go on to say: 'The habit has grown up of looking at a criminal trial as a kind of game to be played, according to fixed rules, between the prosecution and the defence.'[1] It is good to see that the Committee seems determined to break this insidious habit.

It seems a pity, then, that they have not been equally willing to attack other institutions and assumptions which are generally regarded as basic to our system of criminal justice, such as the sanctity of trial by jury. We find it, for instance, impossible to agree with their assumption that 'the judge will not (as for example in France) retire with the jury when they consider their verdict.'[2]

We agree with much of what they have to say about the problems involved in the interrogation of suspects. We do not see how such regulations as the right to silence and the caution are specially helpful to an innocent man. Nor indeed were many of the other Judges' Rules.

However, there are some precautions which are needed and which the Committee has not recommended. An important one seems to be the special protection needed by the inadequate and feeble-minded. On the matter of tape-recorders, we would like to see them wisely and generally used, but only a minority of the Committee agree with us.

We are relieved to note that the Committee has not recommended any major changes in the rules regarding the admission of the accused's previous record in court, despite strong pressure from a minority. We are, however, concerned at the suggestion that the accused's record might be admissible where it 'tends to confirm the correctness of an identification of the accused by a witness for the prosecution'.[3] As is well-known, and as we have shown in the text, identification evidence tends to be unreliable. The combination of a disclosed past record with a possibly shaky identification is very likely to lead to conviction, whether or not the accused committed the crime.

We agree that juries ought to be warned of the dangers of identification evidence, but we are not sure what is the safest way to do this. Such warnings can backfire.

We agree in general with the recommendations concerning children and sexual offences, but we feel that the safeguards for the accused should be, if anything, a little stronger. Possibly corroboration should be insisted on, although we recognize that this might present problems.

We are glad to see that the Committee has recommended relaxing some of the more artificial restrictions on the admissibility of hearsay evidence. Possibly more could be done in this direction.

We feel, however, that no matter how many emendations are made to any legal system, mistakes will inevitably be made. Perhaps we should more honestly face this fact. If our aim is to find the truth of the matter rather than to uphold the existing rules of the legal game, then surely this should apply after trials as well as during them. In our opinion the area in which most reform of this kind is needed is that of appeals and Home Office reviews of conviction.

Appendices

Appendix A
Statistical Analysis

Table I. Free Pardons in Cases carrying a Liability to Imprisonment, 1950–1970

Number	Court	Date	Nature of Offence	Sentence	Date of Free Pardon	Time Served[1]
1.	Quarter-sessions	16.6.49	Housebreaking and larceny	Borstal training	Dates not available	
2.	Quarter-sessions	16.6.49	Housebreaking and larceny	Borstal training	Dates not available	
3.	Assizes	22.3.48	Throwing corrosive liquid with intent to do grievous bodily harm	Bound over on condition that she enter a mental home for 1 year	26.2.50	12 months
4.	Assizes	20.5.52	Shopbreaking	18 months	30.6.52	1 month
5.	No details available		Larceny as a bailee	2 years	No details	
6.	Quarter-sessions	28.7.52	Malicious damage	—	7.2.53	
7.	Quarter-sessions	27.4.53	Stealing	2 years	2.6.53	2 months
8.	No details available		Driving whilst disqualified	6 months	No details available	
9.	Assizes	26.1.54	Causing grievous bodily harm to a policeman	10 years	14.1.56	24 months
10.				7 years		24 months
11.				4 years		24 months
12.	No dates available		Storebreaking and larceny	2 × 18 months concurrent	No details available	
13.	Quarter-sessions	16.2.60	Shopbreaking and larceny	Borstal training	26.3.60	1 month
14.	No details available		Larceny	—	No details available	
15.	Magistrates' court	5-5-59	Wilful damage	Entered a mental deficiency institution	8.7.59	2 months
16.	Magistrates' court	28.9.60	Larceny	—	19.4.61	
17.	Juvenile court	6.10.60	Robbery	28 days in a remand home	11.5.61	1 month
18.	Juvenile court	29.12.60	Receiving stolen money	—	13.5.61	
19.	Magistrates' court	16.3.61	Stealing	4 months	13.7.61	1 month
20.	Magistrates' court	16.1.61	Taking and driving away a motor vehicle without authority. Driving without insurance	9 months and 2 months consecutive	24.4.61	3 months

No.	Court	Date	Offence	Sentence	Date	Sentence
23.	Magistrates' court	14.3.61	…wounding and assault	6 months	19.1.62	6 months
24.	Magistrates' court	7.3.62	Road traffic offences	On remand awaiting sentence	19.7.62	2 months
25.	Magistrates' court	1.3.62	Stealing church candlesticks	Subject of hospital order	16.10.62	6 months
26.	Magistrates' court	8.3.62	Stealing	—	14.11.62	
27.	Magistrates' court	2.7.62	Indecent assault. Unlawful possession of firearm	—	14.3.63	
28.	Quarter-sessions	6.6.62	Housebreaking and larceny	Borstal training	7.12.62	6 months
29.	Quarter-sessions	9.4.63	Possessing explosives	2 years	2.9.63	5 months
30.	Quarter-sessions	9.4.63	Possessing explosives	12 months	2.9.63	5 months
31.	Magistrates' court	2.8.63	Driving whilst disqualified	6 months	13.12.63	3 months
32.	Magistrates' court	28.3.64	Loitering with intent	1 month	4.4.64	2 months
33.	Magistrates' court	16.10.64	Driving whilst disqualified	2 months	5.1.65	8 months
34.	Assizes	15.12.64	Robbery with violence	5 years	5.8.65	8 months
35.	Assizes	15.12.64	Robbery with violence	3½ years	5.8.65	8 months
36.	Assizes	15.12.64	Robbery with violence	3 years	5.8.65	8 months
37.	Magistrates' court	12.11.65	Larceny	3 months' detention	29.3.66	2 months
38.	Magistrates' court	28.6.66	Pavilion breaking and larceny	—	15.8.66	
39.	Magistrates' court	20.6.64	Wilful damage	3 months	27.4.67	3 months
40.	Quarter-sessions	14.3.66	Attempted buggery with a chicken. Larceny	3 months' detention	31.7.67	3 months
41.	Magistrates' court	15.8.67	Shopbreaking and larceny	3 months	8.9.67	1 month
42.	Magistrates' court	8.5.67	Unlawful possession of drugs	In remand centre awaiting sentence	12.6.67	1 month
43.	Magistrates' court	14.6.68	Various offences	12 months	9.12.68	5 months
44.	Quarter-sessions	6.11.68	Larceny	2 years	20.8.69	7 months
45.	Magistrates' court	6.6.69	Wilful damage	3 months	1.1.70	3 months
46.	Magistrates' court	13.8.69	Driving without insurance. Driving whilst disqualified	2 × 3 months consecutive	19.11.69	3 months
47.	Quarter-sessions	30.7.68	Larceny	4 months	16.4.69	8 months
48.	Quarter-sessions	8.4.68	Shopbreaking and larceny	9 months	17.3.69	9 months
49.	Magistrates' court	30.9.68	Larceny	6 months	25.1.69	4 months
50.	Magistrates' court	10.10.69	Driving whilst disqualified	3 months	27.7.70	3 months
51.	Assizes	9.7.68	Larceny	4 years	21.5.70	22 months
52.	Assizes	23.1.69	Assault with intent to rob, robbery	4 years	28.11.69	10 months

Table II. Cases Referred to The Court Of Appeal under Section 19(a) of The Criminal Appeal Act, 1967 (Now Section 17(a) of The Criminal Appeal Act 1968) Leading to the Conviction being Quashed, 1950–1970

Number	Court	Date of Conviction	Nature of Offence	Sentence	Date of Reference	Date Conviction Quashed	Time Served
1.	Central criminal court	25.11.49	Bigamy	18 months	28.8.50	23.10.50	11 months
2.	Assizes	6.12.49	Bigamy	6 months	18.9.50	16.10.50	6 months
3.	Sessions	27.2.51	Attempting to take and drive away a motor car without the consent of the owner	3 years' corrective training	29.9.52	13.10.52	20 months
4.	Quarter-sessions	21.9.61	Burglary and larceny	2 years' corrective training	14.3.62	20.3.62	6 months
5.	Assizes	20.12.61	Conspiring to rob some person or persons unknown whilst armed with an automatic pistol	18 months	26.9.62	29.10.62	10 months
6.	Central criminal court	22.7.63	Having an offensive weapon in a public place	12 months	18.12.63	20.12.63	5 months
7.			Offences of demanding money with menaces and possessing an offensive weapon	12 months	18.12.63	20.12.63	5 months
8.				3 years	7.7.64	27.7.64	19 months
9.	Central criminal court	18.12.62		5 years	7.7.64	27.7.64	19 months
10.				15 months	7.7.64	27.7.64	15 months
11.				5 years	7.7.64	27.7.64	19 months
12.				7 years	7.7.64	27.7.64	19 months
13.	Quarter-sessions	18.6.64	Shopbreaking and larceny	2 years	6.5.65	26.7.65	13 months
14.	Crown court	12.10.66	Receiving a stolen cheque-book and obtaining goods by false pretences	2 years	4.10.67	4.12.67	14 months
15.	Assizes	11.7.68	Possessing and uttering forged bank notes	21 months	24.4.69	16.5.69	10 months
16.	Crown court	15.5.69	Robbery	3 years	30.4.70	14.5.70	12 months
17.	Quarter-sessions	3.6.70	Burglary	12 months	19.11.70	14.12.70	6 months
18.	Quarter-sessions	3.6.70	Burglary	12 months suspended for 2 years			

Table III

Length of Sentence	Number of men pardoned	Number of men whose sentences quashed by Appeal Court on Referral	Total Number
Under 6 months	10	0	10
6 months and above but under 1 year	9	1	10
1 year and above but under 2 years	4	7	11
2 years and above but under 3 years	4	3	7
3 years and above but under 5 years	5	3	8
5 years and above	3	3	6
Borstal	4	0	4
Mental institution	3	0	3
Remand home	1	0	1
Time Served[1]			
Under 3 months	12	0	12
3 months and over but under 6 months	11	2	13
6 months and over but under 9 months	9	3	12
9 months and over but under 12 months	2	3	5
12 months and over but under 15 months	1	3	4
15 months and over but under 18 months	0	1	1
18 months and over but under 2 years	4	5	9
2 years and over	0	0	0

The seventy cases provided by the Home Office (together with Ron Avard's case, making seventy-one) can be broken down into four groups. The first group consists of those offences where a pardon was granted or a conviction quashed on rather technical grounds involving the discovery that documents used in obtaining the conviction were in error. Under this heading we have the following offences (see Table IVa).

Table IVa

Offence	No. of cases
Bigamy	2
Driving without insurance and/or while disqualified and other traffic offences	7
Unlawful possession of firearms	1
Unlawful possession explosives	2
Unlawful possession of drugs	1
TOTAL	13

The second group consists of the seven cases associated with Detective-Sergeant Challenor. The third group consists of four cases. It was found difficult to classify then either because the description of the offence was vague (for example 'various offences') or because the description did not match our knowledge of the cases. This left a total of fifty cases (three individuals were convicted of two separate offences and were pardoned for both. Effectively they got two pardons and can be treated as two individuals), which can be broken down by offence as follows.

Table IVb

Offence	Number of persons pardoned or whose conviction was quashed following a sentence of imprisonment 1950–70		Number of persons (male) sent to prison for each of these offences in 1968	
	Number	%	Number	%
Violence against the person	3	6	3,190	8·4
Sexual offences	3	6	1,321	3·4
Breaking and entering	13	26	12,746	33·0
Larceny and stealing	14	28	12,883	34·0
Receiving	2	4	1,536	4·0
Frauds etc.	2	4	1,890	4·9
Robbery	6	12	967	2·6
Assaults	1	2	967	2·6
Taking motor vehicle without owner's consent	2	4	1,818	4·8
Malicious or wilful damage	4	8	896	2·3
TOTAL	50	100	38,214	100·0

Inspection of the two main columns indicates that the relative proportions of offences committed among the pardoned group and among those sent to prison generally are very similar except in the case of three offences or categories of offences, namely robbery, malicious or wilful damage, and sexual offences. On the basis of our case studies this is the kind of distribution of offences we would have predicted. We expected that robbery would be relatively more common among the pardoned group because it is an offence in which the crucial evidence is often the identification of the robber by an eyewitness who has never seen him before. (This is almost certainly more often the case with robbery than almost any other offence.) Malicious and wilful damage and sexual offences (especially the kinds of sexual offences represented here) are often committed by persons of low mentality from whom it is easy to extract a false confession. In the case of sexual offences there is the added problem that witnesses often commit perjury. However, apart from these categories where the nature of the evidence predisposes the courts to convict a man erroneously there is a good match between the two columns. This again we predicted from our findings concerning how men got off who were wrongly convicted. We stressed that men got off largely because of chance factors. If this is the case, then one would expect these chances to occur randomly throughout the innocent members of the prison population. If the innocent members are themselves spread randomly throughout those going to gaol then the distribution by offence of the men who got off should be very similar to that of all the people (innocent and guilty) who go to gaol. This seems to be the case thus confirming our view that the men who were exonerated owe this to the operation of purely random chances. In fairness, it should be noted that in Table IVa we have excluded a number of types of offence where a man is more likely to get off because of the operation of systematic factors such as the routine checking of documents or the checking of such documents by request of the prisoner.

This general picture is on the whole confirmed by a closer look at the statistics. If we apply the chi-square test to the categories of robbery, malicious or wilful damage and sexual offences we find that the number of cases in the first two categories differs significantly from what might be expected on the basis of the distribution of offences in the general prison population. However, the number of cases expected is very small and it is advisable to calculate the exact probability of getting as many as six cases of robbery and as many as four cases of malicious or wilful damage in a sample of fifty cases.

Table Va

	Observed	Expected
Robbery	6	1·3
Other cases	44	48·7
TOTAL	50	50

$p = 0.0018$

Observed = as in Pardons sample. Expected = number in each offence category if distribution was the same as in people sent to prison as a whole.

Table Vb

	Observed	Expected
Malicious or wilful damage	4	1·15
Other cases	46	48·85
TOTAL	50	50

$p = 0.0279$.

In both cases the probabilities are very low, that is the probability of getting as many cases of robbery or malicious damage in our sample by chance alone is very low. It seems likely, therefore, that some such systematic factors of the kind we have suggested are operating.

If we now take the remaining forty cases, their distribution by offence is now remarkably similar to that of the general prison population.

Table VI

Offence	Number of persons pardoned or whose convictions were quashed following a sentence of imprisonment 1950–70		Number of persons (male) sent to prison for each of these offences in 1968	
	Number of cases	%	Number of cases	%
Violence against the person	3	7·5	3,190	8·8
Sexual offences	3	7·5	1,321	3·6
Breaking and entering etc.	13	32·5	12,746	35·0
Larceny and stealing	14	35·0	12,883	36·0
Receiving	2	5·0	1,536	4·2
Frauds etc.	2	5·0	1,890	5·2
Assaults	1	2·5	967	2·6
Taking a motor vehicle without the owner's consent	2	5·0	1,818	5·0
TOTAL	40	100·0	36,351	100·4

If we now re-group these categories into larger ones and calculate the observed and expected numbers of cases in each of these categories we get Table VII.

Table VII

	Observed	Expected
Offences against the person (sex and violence)	7	6·03
Breaking and entering etc.	13	14·03
Larceny and stealing	14	14·18
Other	6	5·77
TOTAL	40	40·01

If we now calculate the value of chi-square for this table we get

$$\text{chi-square} = 0.2448 \quad 97.5 > p > 95$$

This shows a significant goodness of fit (beyond the 5 per cent level), that is there is a very close match between the distribution of the pardoned group by offence and the distribution by offence of men going to gaol.

All these calculations based on the distribution of persons pardoned by offence do seem to support the more intuitively based hypotheses incorporated in the text of the book. However, it must be pointed out that there are a number of arbitrary factors built into our calculations, notably our decision to exclude certain cases (mainly those in Table IVa) and our use of the prison intake figures for the year 1968 only, rather than for the whole period 1950–70. We chose to do this simply because 1968 was the only year during this period in which the prison statistics were broken down in the same way as the data on pardons supplied to us by the Home Office.

There were many other calculations we would have liked to have done on this original data and on data we acquired later but we feel these would have been of even more limited validity than the above. The main problem was that we only had time and money enough to get further details (than those given in this Appendix) on about half of the cases involved. Since we were not at all sure that this half was representative of the whole (owing to differential publicity given to such cases it could be atypical) we chose not to make any further detailed calculations.

Home Office Circular on Identification Parades (January 1969)

1. The object of an identification parade is to make sure that the ability of the witness to recognise the suspect has been fairly and adequately tested.

2. Identification parades should be fair, and should be seen to be fair. Every precaution should be taken to see that they are so, in particular, to exclude any suspicion of unfairness or risk of erroneous identification through the witnesses' attention being directed specially to the suspected person instead of equally to all the persons paraded.

Conduct of identification parades

3. If an officer concerned with the case against the suspect is present, he should take no part in conducting the parade.

4. Wherever possible the officer arranging the parade should be of not less rank than inspector.

5. Once the identification parade has been formed, everything thereafter in respect of it should take place in the presence and hearing of the suspect, including any instructions to the witnesses attending it as to the procedure that they are to adopt.

6. All unauthorized persons should be strictly excluded from the place where the identification parade is held.

7. The witnesses should be prevented from seeing the suspect before he is paraded with other persons, and witnesses who have previously seen a photograph or description of the suspect should not be led into identifiying the suspect by reason of their recollection of the photograph or description, as for instance by being shown the photograph or description shortly before the parade.

8. The suspect should be placed among persons (if practicable eight or more) who are as far as possible of the same age, height, general appearance (including standard of dress and grooming) and position in life. If there are two suspects and they are of roughly similar appearance they may be paraded together with at least twelve other persons. Where, however, the two suspects are not similar in appearance, or where there are more than two suspects, separate parades should be held using different persons on each parade.

9. Occasionally all members of a group are possible suspects. This may happen where police officers are involved (for example an allegation concerning a police officer which can be narrowed down to a number of officers who were on duty at the place and time in question). In such circumstances

an identification parade should not include more than two of the possible suspects. For example, if there were twelve police officers on duty at the time and place in question, there should be at least six parades, each including ten officers who were not implicated and not more than two who might have been: the twelve possible suspects should not be paraded together. Two suspects of obviously dissimilar appearance should not be included on the same parade. Where police officers in uniform form an identification parade, numerals should be concealed.

10. The suspect should be allowed to select his own position in the line and should be expressly asked if he has any objection to the persons present with him or the arrangements made. He should be informed that if he so desires he may have his solicitor or a friend present at the identification parade.

11. The witnesses should be introduced one by one and, on leaving, should not be allowed to communicate with witnesses still waiting to see the persons paraded; and the suspect should be informed that he may change his position after each witness has left.

12. The witness should be asked whether the person he has come to identify is on the parade. He should be told that if he cannot make a positive identification he should say so.

13. It is generally desirable that a witness should be asked to touch any person whom he purports to identify; but when the witness is nervous at the prospect of having to do this (as may occur when, for example, the witness is a woman or child who has been the victim of a sexual or violent assault or other frightening experience) and prefers not to touch the person, identification by pointing out may be permitted.

14. If a witness indicates someone but is unable to identify him positively, this fact should be carefully noted by the officer conducting the parade, as should every other circumstance connected with it, whether the suspect or any other person is identified or not.

15. It may sometimes happen that a witness desires to see the suspect with his hat on or his hat off, and there is no objection to all persons paraded being thereupon asked to wear or remove their hats. Sometimes again there may be something peculiar in the suspect's gait or tone of voice, and if the witness desires to see the person walk or to hear the person speak, there is no objection to the person paraded being asked to walk or to speak. When any such request is made by a witness, the incident should be recorded.

Identification parades in prison

16. If the suspect is in prison and is willing to take part in an identification parade, arrangements should be made with the governor for his production at the nearest convenient police station where the parade may take place. A parade should be held in prison only if special security considerations make it unwise to hold it outside or the suspect refuses to take part in a parade unless it is held in prison.

17. Where a parade has to be held in prison, the governor will be responsible for the assembly of the parade and a prison officer will be present throughout in charge of the discipline of the prisoners taking part. A police officer, unconnected with the case, will otherwise be responsible for the parade (including the introduction of witnesses to the parade and the noting of all that takes place). He must ensure that the parade is conducted in the same way as a parade outside prison.

Use of photographs in identifying criminals

18. Photographs of suspects should never be shown to witnesses for the purpose of identification if circumstances allow of a personal identification. Even where a mistaken identification does not result, the fact that a witness has been shown a photograph of the suspect before his ability to identify him has been properly tested at an identification parade will considerably detract from the value of his evidence.

19. Any photographs used should be available for production in court if called for.

20. If a witness makes a positive identification from photographs, other witnesses should not be shown photographs but should be asked to attend an identification parade.

21. Where there is other evidence identifying the accused with sufficient certainty to prefer a charge, a witness who has made a firm identification by photograph should not normally be taken to an identification parade. There may however be circumstances when it is desirable to ask the witness to identify the suspect from a parade. For example, identification may have been made from a poor or out-of-date photograph; the photographic identification may have been made so long previously that the present ability to identify is uncertain; the suspect's appearance may have materially altered since the photograph was taken; or the witness may think his identification is likely to be assisted by having an opportunity of hearing a suspect speaking or observing his gait. The decision whether a witness should, in such circumstances be taken to an identification parade should, wherever possible, be made by an officer of not less rank than inspector.

22. Where there is no evidence implicating the suspect save identification by photograph, the witnesses as to identification should be taken to an identification parade notwithstanding that they may already have made an identification by photograph.

23. The police should inform the defence of any case where an identification is first made from photographs since it cannot normally be said in court that an identification was made from photographs without revealing the existence of a criminal record.

24. Where it is necessary to show a photograph of the suspect, it should be shown among a number of other (unmarked) photographs having as close a resemblance to it as possible, and the witness should be left to make a selection without help and without opportunity of consulting other witnesses.

Appendix C

Judges' Rules

NOTE

The origin of the Judges' Rules is probably to be found in a letter dated 26 October 1906, which the then Lord Chief Justice, Lord Alverstone, wrote to the Chief Constable of Birmingham in answer to a request for advice in consequence of the fact that on the same Circuit one judge had censured a member of his force for having cautioned a prisoner, whilst another judge had censured a constable for having omitted to do so. The first four of the present Rules were formulated and approved by the judges of the King's Bench Division in 1912; the remaining five in 1918. They have been much criticised, inter alia for alleged lack of clarity and of efficacy for the protection of persons who are questioned by police-officers; on the other hand it has been maintained that their application unduly hampers the detection and punishment of crime. A committee of judges has devoted considerable time and attention to producing, after consideration of representative views, a new set of Rules which has been approved by a meeting of all the Queen's Bench Judges.

The judges control the conduct of trials and the admission of evidence against persons on trial before them: they do not control or in any way initiate or supervise police activities or conduct. As stated in paragraph (e) of the introduction to the new Rules, it is the law that answers and statements made are only admissible in evidence if they have been voluntary in the sense that they have not been obtained by fear of prejudice or hope of advantage, exercised or held out by a person in authority, or by oppression. The new Rules do not purport, any more than the old Rules, to envisage or deal with the many varieties of conduct which might render answers and statements involuntary and therefore inadmissible. The Rules merely deal with particular aspects of the matter. Other matters such as affording reasonably comfortable conditions, adequate breaks for rest and refreshment, special procedures in the case of persons unfamiliar with the English language or of immature age or feeble understanding, are proper subjects for administrative directions to the police.

JUDGES' RULES

These Rules do not affect the principles

- (a) That citizens have a duty to help a police-officer to discover and apprehend offenders;
- (b) That police-officers, otherwise than by arrest, cannot compel any person against his will to come to or remain in any police station;
- (c) That every person at any stage of an investigation should be able to communicate and to consult privately with a solicitor. This is so even if he is in custody provided that in such a case no unreasonable delay or hindrance is caused to the processes of investigation or the administration of justice by his doing so;

(*d*) That when a police-officer who is making inquiries of any person about an offence has enough evidence to prefer a charge against that person for the offence, he should without delay cause that person to be charged or informed that he may be prosecuted for the offence;

(*e*) That it is a fundamental condition of the admissibility in evidence against any person, equally of any oral answer given by that person to a question put by a police-officer and of any statement made by that person, that it shall have been voluntary, in the sense that it has not been obtained from him by fear of prejudice or hope of advantage, exercised or held out by a person in authority, or by oppression.

The principle set out in paragraph (*e*) above is overriding and applicable in all cases. Within that principle the following Rules are put forward as a guide to police-officers conducting investigations. Non-conformity with these Rules may render answers and statements liable to be excluded from evidence in subsequent criminal proceedings.

RULES

I. When a police-officer is trying to discover whether, or by whom, an offence has been committed he is entitled to question any person, whether suspected or not, from whom he thinks that useful information may be obtained. This is so whether or not the person in question has been taken into custody so long as he has not been charged with the offence or informed that he may be prosecuted for it.

II. As soon as a police-officer has evidence which would afford reasonable grounds for suspecting that a person has committed an offence, he shall caution that person or cause him to be cautioned before putting to him any questions, or further questions, relating to that offence.

The caution shall be in the following terms:

'You are not obliged to say anything unless you wish to do so but what you say may be put into writing and given in evidence.'

When after being cautioned a person is being questioned, or elects to make a statement, a record shall be kept of the time and place at which any such questioning or statement began and ended and of the persons present.

III (*a*) Where a person is charged with or informed that he may be prosecuted for an offence he shall be cautioned in the following terms:

'Do you wish to say anything? You are not obliged to say anything unless you wish to do so but whatever you say will be taken down in writing and may be given in evidence.'

(*b*) It is only in exceptional cases that questions relating to the offence should be put to the accused person after he has been charged or informed that he may be prosecuted. Such questions may be put where they are necessary for the purpose of preventing or minimising harm or loss to some other person or to the public or for clearing up an ambiguity in a previous answer or statement.

Before any such questions are put the accused should be cautioned in these terms:

'I wish to put some questions to you about the offence with which you have been charged (*or* about the offence for which you may be prosecuted).

You are not obliged to answer any of these questions, but if you do the questions and answers will be taken down in writing and may be given in evidence.'

Any questions put and answers given relating to the offence must be contemporaneously recorded in full and the record signed by that person or if he refuses by the interrogating officer.

(c) When such a person is being questioned, or elects to make a statement, a record shall be kept of the time and place at which any questioning or statement began and ended and of the persons present.

IV. All written statements made after caution shall be taken in the following manner:

(a) If a person says that he wants to make a statement he shall be told that it is intended to make a written record of what he says. He shall always be asked whether he wishes to write down himself what he wants to say; if he says that he cannot write or that he would like someone to write it for him, a police-officer may offer to write the statement for him. If he accepts the offer, the police-officer shall, before starting, ask the person making the statement to sign, or make his mark to, the following:

'I, ..., wish to make a statement. I want someone to write down what I say. I have been told that I need not say anything unless I wish to do so and that whatever I say may be given in evidence.'

(b) Any person writing his own statement shall be allowed to do so without any prompting as distinct from indicating to him what matters are material.

(c) The person making the statement, if he is going to write it himself, shall be asked to write out and sign before writing what he wants to say, the following:

'I make this statement of my own free will. I have been told that I need not say anything unless I wish to do so and that whatever I say may be given in evidence.'

(d) Whenever a police-officer writes the statement, he shall take down the exact words spoken by the person making the statement, without putting any questions other than such as may be needed to make the statement coherent, intelligible and relevant to the material matters: he shall not prompt him.

(e) When the writing of a statement by a police-officer is finished the person making it shall be asked to read it and to make any corrections, alterations or additions he wishes. When he has finished reading it he shall be asked to write and sign or make his mark on the following Certificate at the end of the statement:

'I have read the above statement and I have been told that I can correct, alter or add anything I wish. This statement is true. I have made it of my own free will.'

(f) If the person who has made a statement refuses to read it or to write the above mentioned Certificate at the end of it or to sign it, the senior police-officer present shall record on the statement itself and in the presence of the person making it, what has happened. If the person making the statement cannot read, or refuses to read it, the officer who has taken it down shall read it over to him and ask him whether he would like to correct, alter or add anything and to put his signature or make his mark at the end. The police-officer shall then certify on the statement itself what he has done.

V. If at any time after a person has been charged with, or has been informed that he may be prosecuted for an offence a police-officer wishes to bring to the notice of that person any written statement made by another person who in respect of the same offence has also been charged or informed that he may be prosecuted, he shall hand to that person a true copy of such written statement, but nothing shall be said or done to invite any reply or comment. If that person says that he would like to make a statement in reply, or starts to say something, he shall at once be cautioned or further cautioned as prescribed by Rule III(a).

VI. Persons other than police-officers charged with the duty of investigating offences or charging offenders shall, so far as may be practicable, comply with these Rules.

ADMINISTRATIVE DIRECTIONS ON INTERROGATION
AND THE TAKING OF STATEMENTS

1. *Procedure generally*

(a) When possible statements of persons under caution should be written on the forms provided for the purpose. Police-officers' notebooks should be used for taking statements only when no forms are available.

(b) When a person is being questioned or elects to make a statement, a record should be kept of the time or times at which during the questioning or making of a statement there were intervals or refreshment was taken. The nature of the refreshment should be noted. In no circumstances should alcoholic drink be given.

(c) In writing down a statement, the words used should not be translated into 'official' vocabulary; this may give a misleading impression of the genuineness of the statement.

(d) Care should be taken to avoid any suggestion that the person's answers can only be used in evidence against him, as this may prevent an innocent person making a statement which might help to clear him of the charge.

2. *Record of interrogation*

Rule II and Rule III(c) demand that a record should be kept of the following matters:

(a) when, after being cautioned in accordance with Rule II, the person is being questioned or elects to make a statement—of the time and place at which any such questioning began and ended and of the persons present;

(b) when, after being cautioned in accordance with Rule III(a) or (b) a person is being questioned or elects to make a statement—of the time and place at which any questioning and statement began and ended and of the persons present.

In addition to the records required by these Rules full records of the following matters should additionally be kept:

(a) of the time or times at which cautions were taken, and

(b) of the time when a charge was made and/or the person was arrested, and

(c) of the matters referred to in paragraph 1(b) above.

If two or more police-officers are present when the questions are being put or the statement made, the records made should be countersigned by the other officers present.

3. *Comfort and refreshment*

Reasonable arrangements should be made for the comfort and refreshment of persons being questioned. Whenever practicable both the person being questioned or making a statement and the officers asking the questions or taking the statement should be seated.

4. *Interrogation of children and young persons*

As far as practicable children (whether suspected of crime or not) should only be interviewed in the presence of a parent or guardian, or, in their absence, some person who is not a police officer and is of the same sex as the child. A child or young person should not be arrested, nor even interviewed, at school if such action can possibly be avoided. Where it is found essential to conduct the interview at school, this should be done only with the consent, and in the presence, of the head teacher, or his nominee.

5. *Interrogation of foreigners*

In the case of a foreigner making a statement in his native language:

(a) The interpreter should take down the statement in the language in which it is made.

(b) An official English translation should be made in due course and be proved as an exhibit with the original statement.

(c) The foreigner should sign the statement at (a).

Apart from the question of apparent unfairness, to obtain the signature of a suspect to an English translation of what he said in a foreign language can have little or no value as evidence if the suspect disputes the accuracy of this record of his statement.

6. *Supply to accused persons of written statement of charges*

(a) The following procedure should be adopted whenever a charge is preferred against a person arrested without warrant for any offence:

As soon as a charge has been accepted by the appropriate police-officer the accused person should be given a written notice containing a copy of the entry in the charge sheet or book giving particulars of the offence with which he is charged. So far as possible the particulars of the charge should be stated in simple language so that the accused person may understand it, but they should also show clearly the precise offence in law with which he is charged. Where the offence charged is a statutory one, it should be sufficient for the latter purpose to quote the section of the statute which created the offence.

The written notice should include some statement on the lines of the caution given orally to the accused person in accordance with the Judges' Rules after a charge has been preferred. It is suggested that the form of notice should begin with the following words:

'You are charged with the offence(s) shown below. You are not obliged to say anything unless you wish to do so, but whatever you say will be taken down in writing and may be given in evidence.'

(*b*) Once the accused person has appeared before the court it is not necessary to serve him with a written notice of any further charges which may be preferred. If, however, the police decide, before he has appeared before a court, to modify the charge or to prefer further charges, it is desirable that the person concerned should be formally charged with the further offence and given a written copy of the charge as soon as it is possible to do so having regard to the particular circumstances of the case. If the accused person has then been released on bail, it may not always be practicable or reasonable to prefer the new charge at once, and in cases where he is due to surrender to his bail within forty-eight hours or in other cases of difficulty it will be sufficient for him to be formally charged with the further offence and served with a written notice of the charge after he has surrendered to his bail and before he appears before the court.

7. *Facilities for defence*

(*a*) A person in custody should be allowed to speak on the telephone to his solicitor or to his friends provided that no hindrance is reasonably likely to be caused to the processes of investigation, or the administration of justice by his doing so.

He should be supplied on request with writing materials and his letters should be sent by post or otherwise with the least possible delay. Additionally, telegrams should be sent at once, at his own expense.

(*b*) Persons in custody should not only be informed orally of the rights and facilities available to them, but in addition notices describing them should be displayed at convenient and conspicuous places at police stations and the attention of persons in custody should be drawn to these notices.

Reference Notes

CHAPTER I   WRONGFUL IMPRISONMENT ?

1. The term 'wrongful imprisonment' or similar terms such as 'false imprisonment' are sometimes used in a different sense, viz. to denote cases where a man has been improperly held in custody without trial, that is where the correct legal procedure has not been followed.

2. For details of how and why the Home Secretary may do this, see D. R. Thompson and H. W. Wollaston, *Court of Appeal, Criminal Division* (Charles Knight, 1969), p. 114.

3. We have deliberately not considered the problems associated with bail because there are already several excellent books on the subject.

4. Tom Sargant, Secretary of 'Justice', in his memorandum on the individual cases sent to the Donovan Committee on Criminal Appeals commented: 'whereas the judicial consideration of the results of an investigation could lead the court to the view that no jury would have convicted with all the facts before it, this is not the case once an appeal has been dismissed. Thereafter, absolute proof of innocence is required.' (p. 6)

5. Our figures differ from those listed under 'Prerogative of Mercy' in the Home Office criminal statistics. In these tables even the category of pardon listed as 'on grounds of affecting the original conviction' contains a large number of cases where a pardon has been granted on essentially technical grounds (procedural errors at the trial, the famous speeding convictions where the lamp-posts turned out to be too far apart, etc.). Also many of these convictions did not result in a custodial sentence and a sentence of imprisonment could not have been imposed in some of these cases. We prefer to regard cases where the conviction was quashed on appeal or a re-trial has resulted in acquittal as part of the normal working of the legal system and not calling for special comment.

6. 'Justice', *10th Annual Report*, pp. 17–18.

7. Some people have commented that in that case it did not matter. We disagree.

8. Compare F. H. McClintock and E. Gibson, *Robbery in London* (Macmillan, 1961), p. 38: 'Where a problem of detention arose it was found that the reason for the offender remaining undetected was the vagueness of the description obtained from the victim or eyewitness.' The circumstances which created this problem of detection also lead to frequent misidentification.

CHAPTER 2   IDENTIFICATION EVIDENCE

1. See T. B. Smith, *British Justice: The Scottish Contribution* (Stevens & Sons, 1961), p. 126. There is a general requirement of corroboration in Scots law, In Ireland corroboration is now specifically required in cases involving eye-witness identification.

2. Justice, *2nd Memorandum on Identification*, submitted to the Criminal Law Review Committee, p. 1, para. 3.

3. Jerome and Barbara Frank, *Not Guilty* (Victor Gollancz, 1957), p. 61. Professor Edwin M. Borchard, *Convicting the Innocent* (Plenum Publishing Co., 1970), p. xiii.

4. Trial transcript, p. 14.

5. Trial transcript, p. 4.

6. There are special provisions for identity parades involving police officers—see Appendix B, rule 9.

7. *Sun* (11 May 1968).

8. This is in accordance with Home Office Rule 15—see Appendix B.

9. Appeal allowed, 4 December 1967.
10. Justice, *2nd Memorandum on Identification*, submitted to Criminal Law Review Committee, pp. 14–15.
11. *Police Review* (21 February 1969).
12. *Police Review* (May 1970).
13. NCCL, *Memorandum on Identification Parades and Procedures* (18 April 1968), p. 1.
14. These are groups of people who regularly appear in cases of wrongful imprisonment, whatever the cause, as victims, perpetrators and witnesses, and as victims of the crimes.
15. Appeal allowed, 9 April 1970.
16. Frank, op. cit., p. 61.
17. Compare Borchard, op. cit., p. xiii.
18. Trial transcript, pp. 96–7.
19. Justice, *2nd Memorandum on Identification*.
20. The use of photographs is discussed in some detail in the Home Office circular on identification parades—see Appendix B.
21. The defence may be unable to challenge the identification evidence on these grounds because to do so would reveal that the defendant had a police record. For a discussion of this dilemma for the defence, see Glanville Williams, *The Proof of Guilt: A Study of the English Criminal Trial* (Stevens & Sons, 1963), p. 123.
22. Speaking of the importation of detail in the same experiment, Bartlett says: 'The subject easily at the head of the list of importations in each of the groups was the most definite visualizer of the whole group. He remarked that he had cultivated a habit of visualizing, and practised himself in it constantly. . . . Even when material is arranged in a short series, is small in bulk and simple in objective structure and when it is so given to the observer that he will be asked to define it later . . . accurate recall is the exception and not the rule' (F. C. Bartlett, *Remembering* (CUP, 1932), pp. 58 and 61). These problems are also discussed in M. L. Johnson Abercrombie, *The Anatomy of Judgemnt* (Hutchinson, 1960); in Patrick M. Wall, *Eyewitness Identification in Criminal Cases* (C. C. Thomas, 1965) and in Williams, op. cit., pp. 86 and 97.
23. The description of the witness as having given evidence on several separate occasions is probably in error but this is how the defendant remembers it. It must have seemed repetitive and reinforcing to him.
24. The Criminal Justice Act, 1967, may have had some effect in this direction but it is still largely a question of practice.
25. Bartlett, op. cit., p. 55.
26. Rupert Furneaux, *Michael John Davies* (Stevens Crime Documentary No. 4, 1962), pp. 33 ff.
27. It is part of the duties of the police-officer supervising the parade to note this kind of thing—see Appendix A, rule 14.
28. Julian Symons, *A Reasonable Doubt* (Cresset Press, 1960), pp. 129–30.
29. Ibid., p. 132.
30. Trial transcript.
31. Cmnd 2315 (November 1904), p. 5.
32. E. Lustgarten, *Verdict in Dispute* (Alan Wingate, 1949), p. 59.
33. Williams, op. cit., p. 112.
34. Du Cann, op. cit., p. 269. This is not strictly true. In his book, *Under My Wig* (Arthur Barker, 1961), John Parris says: 'Even fingerprints can be faked by the police, though one would have a hard time persuading a jury that this is so. Once in possession of a man's prints, it is not a difficult task to reconstruct a plausible facsimile of them in plasticine and to impress this on glass or

some other object. In a photograph they are indistinguishable from the real thing. A number of times I have been told by men who have admitted their guilt: "It's a lie about my fingerprints being found. I wore gloves, of course" (p. 153).' See also C. H. Rolph, *Personal Identity* (Michael Joseph, 1957), pp. 56 ff.

35. Criminal Appeal Act, 1907, section 9, paras d and e; *Law Reports* (1907), p. 104.

36. In fairness it should be noted that the special commission is asked for advice on the specific facts and issues of a particular case, not on the broad, general problems involved in considering evidence of a given kind. The problems arising from identification evidence or confessions or statements tend to be similar for many cases of this type rather than special technical problems particular to a given case.

37. The way in which we 'organize' beliefs of this kind is described in Milton Rokeach, *The Open and Closed Mind* (Basic Books, 1960), especially pp. 39 ff.

38. Frank, op. cit., p. 61.

39. Compare ibid., pp. 111 ff.

40. Justice, *2nd Memorandum on Identification*, p. 2, para. 5a.

41. See, for comparison, the Home Office Rules in Appendix B.

42. See Williams, op. cit., pp. 97-9 for a discussion of the issues involved.

CHAPTER 3   CONFESSIONS AND STATEMENTS

1. For a full discussion of the legal position see R. Cross, *Evidence*, 3rd edn (Butterworth, 1967), pp. 55 ff. The statement of the law quoted above is by Lord Sumner in Ibrahim *v* Rex [1914 A.C. 599] given in Cross.

2. See Appendix C for a list of the Judges' Rules.

3. *Police Review* (31 January 1964).

4. Brabin Report.

5. *Observer* (6 June 1971).

6. *Southern Echo* (May 1969).

7. Details from the *Daily Mail* (24 June 1964) and the *Guardian* (24 June 1964).

8. See also William Sargant, *Battle for the Mind* (Pan Books, 1959), pp. 170-1 and 180-6, in Chapter 9, 'The Eliciting of Confessions'.

9. E. B. Block, *The Vindicators* (Alvin Redman, 1963), p. 87.

10. H. J. Eysenck, *Crime and Personality* (Routledge, 1964), p. 91.

11. Eysenck, op. cit., p. 56.

12. Jan Svartvik, *The Evans Statements: A Case for Forensic Linguistics* (Acta Universitatis Gothoburgensis in the Gothenburg Studies in English Series, Göteborg, 1968). See also Richard Arens and Arnold Meadow, 'Psycholinguistics and the Confession Dilemma', *Columbia Law Review* (January 1956).

13. Personal communication.

14. The Royal Commission on Capital Punishment, 1949-53 (Cmnd 8932, p. 78), notes that: 'We are told that, as is not unnatural, persons who have been found insane on arraignment and ordered to be detained during Her Majesty's pleasure sometimes exhibit a strong sense of grievance on the grounds that they have not been proved to have committed any crime and ought not therefore to be detained in an institution for criminal lunatics.'

15. Under the Mental Health Act, 1969, the authorities anyway have very wide powers to detain a mentally disordered person in hospital against his will quite regardless of what he has done. See *Public General Acts, 1959*, p. 1283 and Mental Health Act, 1959, part IV.

16. See Appendix A.

17. Other studies, for instance Susanne Dell, *Silent in Court* (G. Bell & Sons, 1971), seem to us to bear out our point of view.

18. P. Laurie, *Scotland Yard* (Bodley Head, 1971).
19. C. G. L. Du Cann, *Miscarriages of Justice* (Muller, 1960), p. 229; see also Clive Davies's article in the *Law Guardian* (March 1970).
20. John Parris, *Under My Wig* (Arthur Barker, 1961), pp. 51–2.
21. *New Society* (28 May 1970).
22. Tom Sargant, *Memorandum to the Donovan Committee on Criminal Appeals*, p. 3.
23. 5th Scientific Congress of the British Academy of Forensic Sciences.
24. *The Times* (2 May 1963).
25. Du Cann, op. cit., p. 229.

CHAPTER 4   TRIAL PROCEEDINGS

1. This seems to be true not just of the British system but of other very different systems, for example the French—see p. 209 ff.
2. Compare W. Cornish, *The Jury* (Pelican, 1971), p. 165: 'In Scotland it is the Crown's practice to prosecute only in cases where there appears to be a substantial chance of conviction. In England some police forces are not so strict, and they have only to demonstrate to the magistrate at committal proceedings that there is a *prima facie* case for the accused to answer.
3. *Police Review* (28 June 1968).
4. Jerome and Barbara Frank, *Not Guilty* (Gollancz, 1957), p. 156.
5. Commonwealth *v.* Wentzel, 360 Penn. State Reports 137 (1948).
6. W. F. Wyndham-Brown (ed.), *The Trial of William Herbert Wallace* (Gollancz, 1933), p. 293.
7. Wyndham-Brown, op. cit., pp. 270–1.
8. Commonwealth *v.* Webster, 5 Cush. (59) Mass, 295, 312 (1850).
9. Report of the Home Office forensic science laboratory on material submitted for examination by the Chief Constable, Liverpool City Police, in accordance with receipt dated 26 May 1966.
10. 4 October 1967.
11. David Lewis and Peter Hughman, *Most Unnatural: An Inquiry into the Stafford Case* (Penguin, 1971), pp. 169–70.
12. Glanville Williams, *The Proof of Guilt* (Stevens & Sons, 1963), p. 97.
13. Ibid., p. 99.
14. Julian Symons, *A Reasonable Doubt* (Cresset Press, 1960), p. 53.
15. E. Lustgarten, *Verdict in Dispute* (Allan Wingate, 1949), pp. 150–1.
16. Archbold, *Criminal Pleading, Evidence and Practice*, 37th edn (Sweet & Maxwell, 1969), p. 532. The cases referred to are: R. *v.* Hall, 43 Cr. App. R. 29 (CCC) and R. *v.* Xinaris (1955) 43 Cr. App. R. 30n.
17. Bryant and Dickson, 31 Cr. App. R. 151.
18. Report of the 'Justice' Committee on the Laws of Evidence, p. 3.
19. Ibid., p. 6.
20. Compare Frank, op. cit., pp. 242–4.
21. This has been the case since the Criminal Justice Act, 1967. See *Public General Acts and Measures of 1967*, para. 1,633.
22. J. H. A. McDonald, *Criminal Law of Scotland*, 5th edn (W. Green & Sons, 1948), pp. 265 ff., for a complete list.
23. Sybille Bedford, *The Faces of Justice* (Collins, 1961), p. 12.
24. Cmnd. 2964 (HMSO, May 1966), p. 4. See also Williams, op. cit., p. 196, for another analysis of the problems involved.
25. The Law Reform Committee Report, however, is critical of the usefulness of this in the context of civil proceedings (p. 5).
26. *Sunday Mirror* (4 January 1970).
27. Cornish, op. cit., p. 93.

28. Ibid., p. 186.
29. Civil Evidence Act, 1968, in *Public General Acts and Measures of 1968*, Book II, Chap. 64, Part 1, p. 1,543 ff.
30. Du Cann, *Miscarriages of Justice* (Muller, 1960), p. 76.
31. For a full discussion of the position, see R. Cross, *Evidence*, 3rd edn (Butterworth, 1967), pp. 338 ff.; or Harris, *Criminal Law*, 21st edn (Sweet & Maxwell, 1968), pp. 743 ff.
32. H. Fletcher Moulton (ed.), *The Trial of Steinie Morrison* (William Hodge, Notable British Trials Series, 1922), p. 277.
33. E. M. Borchard, *Convicting the Innocent* (Plenum Publishing Co., 1970), p. xv.
34. Cornish, op. cit., pp. 99–101.
35. Moulton, op. cit., pp. 36–7.
36. Symons, op. cit., p. 32.
37. Trial transcript, pp. 77–8.
38. There is a good analysis of the pros and cons of joint trials in Michael Ogden *et al.*, *Scales of Justice* (Conservative Political Centre, 1962), pp. 26–7.
39. Cornish, op. cit., p. 195.
40. John Parris, *Under My Wig* (Arthur Barker, 1961), p. 101. See also Williams, op. cit., p. 277.
41. These hazards are well summarized in Ogden, op. cit., pp. 27–8, and in Williams, op. cit., pp. 249 ff.
42. Compare 'Justice' report, *Complaints against Lawyers* (Charles Knight, 1970), p. 5.
43. Figures from H. Kalven and H. Zeisel, *The American Jury* (Little, Brown & Co., 1966).
44. And of course for very many cases in the magistrates' courts no legal aid is provided at all.
45. *The Times* (30 January 1969).
46. *Morning Telegraph* (Sheffield) (16 March 1966).
47. For lucid statements of these distinctions, see E. Durkheim, *The Division of Labour* (Free Press, 1965), p. 69; and H. H. Gerth and C. W. Mills, *From Max Weber* (Routledge, 1970), p. 9.
48. R. *v.* Rivett (1950) 34 Cr. App. R. 87.
49. Commonwealth *v.* Webster, 5 Cush. (59) Mass. 295, 312 (1850).
50. *Daily Mail* (22 July 1971).
51. Cornish, op. cit., p. 66, and Williams, op. cit., p. 302.
52. *The Times* (25 June 1966).
53. Du Cann, op. cit., p. 97.
54. Compare Geoffrey de Parmiter, *Reasonable Doubt* (Arthur Barker, 1938), pp. 1–3. More recently, Mr Justice Lawton has suggested that Parliament may soon have to consider whether cases involving commercial or financial matters would not be better tried by a judge and a team of assessors of established reputation with expert knowledge of the branch of finance or commerce concerned. See *Daily Mail* (22 July 1971).
55. See Cornish, op. cit., pp. 123–5.
56. Williams, op. cit., p. 326.
57. Frank, op. cit., p. 111.
58. Ibid., p. 122.
59. Compare R. K. Merton, *Social Theory and Social Structure* (Free Press, 1958), p. 19 on the concept of manifest and latent function. For a discussion of the phenomenon from a different standpoint see Williams, op. cit., p. 327.
60. R. *v.* Lester (1938) 27 Cr. App. R. 8.
61. Lord Devlin, *Trial by Jury* (Stevens & Sons, 1966), p. 83.

62. Belton Cobb, *Trials and Errors* (W. H. Allen, 1962), p. 36.
63. See, for example, the case of Murtagh and Kennedy (1955) 39 Cr. App. R. 72. Glanville Williams comments on this case: 'Owing to the restrictions imposed upon an appeal from a verdict of a jury it was not considered possible to challenge the conviction on the facts and instead an appeal was argued on the question of law and whether the direction of the judge was adequate (Williams, op. cit., p. 191).
64. Court of Criminal Appeal (20 December 1963).
65. *Home Office Criminal Statistics*, 1969, Cmnd. 4398, p. 194.
66. Compare 'Justice' report on *Home Office Reviews of Criminal Convictions* (Stevens & Sons, 1968), pp. 9–10, para. 17.
67. Ibid., pp. 8–9, para. 15.
68. Justice, *10th Annual Report*, p. 15.
69. *Criminal Law Review* (July 1969), pp. 368 ff.
70. Court of Criminal Appeal (20 October 1964).
71. By an 'ideal typical' jury, we mean a hypothetical jury in which the typical qualities of the jury are maximized, in which 'juryness' is pushed to its logical conclusion. In this context it is not just the supposed virtues of the jury that are evoked but in some sense all the qualities of the jury, though naturally the virtues are stressed. For a discussion of the ways in which the concept of an 'ideal type' can be used see Gerth and Mills, op. cit., p. 59.
72. These points are discussed at length by Lord Devlin who comes to different conclusions. See Devlin, op. cit., pp. 61–7.
73. D. Karlen, *Appellate Courts in the United States and England* (New York University Press, 1963), p. 147.
74. E. M. Borchard, op. cit., p. xxi.
75. D. R. Thompson and H. W. Wollaston, *Court of Appeal, Criminal Division* (Charles Knight, 1969), p. 106.
76. Ibid., p. 119.
77. *Donovan Committee Report*, Cmnd. 2755, p. 32, paras 140–1. The Court expressed the same attitude in the course of an application concerning the reference of the case of Alfred Hinds by the Home Secretary to the Court of Appeal. The 'Justice' report, *Home Office Reviews of Criminal Convictions*, quotes the Lord Chief Justice as saying in this case: 'We are not a court of inquiry investigating this matter; we still are a Court of Appeal treating this as an appeal.' The report adds: 'The following exchange also took place between the Lord Chief Justice and the counsel for the Crown, when the latter observed: "I approach it deliberately in a rather tentative way because it seems to me to open up something very much in the nature of an inquest rather than a hearing by the Court of Appeal." To which the Lord Chief Justice replied: "That is my difficulty when you get a reference of this sort, that it does not seem to be that this Court is the proper body to deal with it, we have not got the inquisitorial powers that a commissioner or tribunal set up to hear it would have. . . . I think it would be wrong for this Court to turn itself into a body of that sort. We shall just have to see where we get to" (p. 20, para. 42).'
78. Thompson and Wollaston, op. cit., pp. 119–20. Indeed, the Committee cites examples of cases where 'the Court has acted as a jury and come to the conclusion that, on the totality of the evidence, some of which was one way and some the other, it would be unsafe to allow a verdict of guilty to stan'd (*Donovan Committee Report*, p. 34, para. 148).
79. Thompson and Wollaston, op. cit., p. 111.
80. Ibid., pp. 113, 121, 123.

81. Ibid., p. 114.
82. Justice, *10th Annual Report*, p. 15.

CHAPTER 5   WITNESSES CREDIBLE AND INCREDIBLE

1. This appears to be a fairly common situation in such cases. C. H. Rolph describes the predicament in his book, *Personal Identity* (Michael Joseph, 1957), p. 121: 'His own solicitors probably won't believe him and will advise him to drop it; and therefore to produce the alibi too soon is to put a needless strain on solicitor-and-client relationships.'
2. Ibid., p. 118.
3. Ibid., p. 131.
4. Ibid., p. 120.
5. Compare the case of Steinie Morrison discussed on p. 74. See also Julian Symons, *A Reasonable Doubt* (Cresset Press, 1960), p. 53.
6. Mr Justice Maude in the case of Augustine John Fletcher (see p. 107).
7. C. G. L. Du Cann, *Miscarriages of Justice* (Muller, 1960, p. 218.
8. Donovan Committee Report (HMSO, 1970), pp. 34–5, para. 150.
9. Compare Harris, *Criminal Law*, 21st edn (Sweet & Maxwell, 1968), pp. 723–4.
10. This case is discussed in minute detail by L. Kennedy in the *Sunday Times* (April 1971).
11. Compare J. Piaget, *The Moral Judgment of the Child* (Routledge, 1932), pp. 159–64.
12. Ibid.
13. Compare Kinsey, Pomeroy, Martin and Gebhard, *Sexual Behaviour in the Human Female* (Saunders, 1953), p. 121.
14. See Harris, op. cit., pp. 723–4.
15. *Daily Telegraph* (29 October 1959).
16. H. Kalven and H. Zeisel, *The American Jury* (Little, Brown & Co., 1966), Appendix C, pp. 514–16.
17. Du Cann, op. cit. Another similar case, the Johnson-Woodman case, is also cited here. See also Glanville Williams, *The Proof of Guilt* (Stevens & Sons, 1963), pp. 176–8.
18. *South Wales Evening Post* (27 July 1971) and *Western Mail* (27 July 1971).
19. Compare Du Cann, op. cit., where another such case, that of George Edalji, is also discussed.
20. Compare Lionel Tiger, *Men in Groups* (Nelson, 1970), especially pp. 80 ff. for an analysis of why this is so.
21. *Sunday Mirror* (28 June 1964).
22. *Daily Telegraph* (20 March 1970).
23. Belton Cobb, *Trials and Errors* (W. H. Allen, 1962), pp. 163 ff.
24. Symons, op cit., p. 10.
25. Ibid., pp. 19–20.
26. H. Fletcher Moulton (ed.), *The Trial of Steinie Morrison* (William Hodge, 1922), pp. 275–6.
27. Compare Piaget, op. cit., pp. 104–7.
28. J. Enoch Powell, who holds an interpreter's certificate in several Asian languages, would be especially well qualified to fill this kind of role. See A. Roth, *Enoch Powell: Tory Tribune* (Macdonald, 1970), p. 44.

CHAPTER 6   HOW THEY GOT OFF

1. 'Justice' report, *Home Office Reviews of Criminal Proceedings*, pp. 7–8, para. 13.
2. Ibid., p. 30, Appendix B.

3. Mars-Jones Report, Cmnd. 2526, p. 7.
4. Ibid., p. 6.
5. Memorandum on individual cases sent to the Donovan Committee, p. 7.
6. *People* (10 May 1964).
7. *Sunday Mirror* (31 May 1970).
8. *Observer* (5 June 1971).
9. Details in David Lewis and Peter Hughman, *Most Unnatural: An Inquiry into the Stafford Case* (Penguin, 1970).
10. *Daily Telegraph* (3 February 1971).
11. Mars-Jones Report, p. 112. We have deliberately quoted the whole of this rather ambiguous passage.
12. Idem.
13. A. Hinds, *Contempt of Court* (Bodley Head, 1966), p. 256.
14. Compare W. Cornish, *The Jury* (Pelican, 1971), pp. 97–8.
15. Compare the case of Percy Denyer in C. G. L. Du Cann, *Miscarriages of Justice* (Muller, 1960).
16. *Daily Express* (25 September 1962).
17. *Willesden and Brent Chronicle* (16 June 1967).
18. Compare the case of Charles Peace, who confessed as he was about to be hanged exonerating a man previously convicted and imprisoned for another murder which Peace had committed some years before the crime for which he was convicted and hanged.
19. Details from E. R. Watson (ed.), *The Trial of Adolf Beck* (Hodge & Co., 1921)
20. *Evening News* (July 1971).
21. *Western Daily Press* (18 March 1964). The appeal was rejected.
22. This is what appears to have happened in the cases of Thompson (see p. 36) and Hall (see p. 27).

CHAPTER 7   CONSEQUENCES

1. See Appendix A, Table III.
2. Jerome and Barbara Frank, *Not Guilty* (Gollancz, 1957), p. 133.
3. *Colchester Express* (17 March 1966 and 3 August 1967); and *Essex County Standard* (4 August 1967).
4. W. F. Wyndham-Brown (ed.), *The Trial of William Herbert Wallace* (Gollancz, 1933), p. 304.
5. Compare J. P. Martin and D. Webster, *Social Consequences of Conviction* (Heinemann, 1971), p. 102.
6. *Daily Telegraph* (2 December 1963).
7. Total institutions, that is institutions cut off from the rest of society in which the inmates spend all aspects of their lives, including sleep, work and recreation. For a discussion of the nature of these institutions (prisons, asylums, public schools, armies, monasteries, kibbutzim, etc.), see Erving Goffman, *Asylums* (Penguin, 1968), pp. 15–22.
8. There is an interesting discussion of some of the issues involved here in H. Garfinkel, 'Conditions of Successful Degradation Ceremonies', *American Journal of Sociology* (1955–6).
9. For a more general finding to this effect, see Martin and Webster, op. cit., p. 214.
10. Ibid., pp. 134–5.
11. Wyndham-Brown (ed.), op. cit., pp. 307 ff.
12. These extracts are from Wallace's diary for: 15 June 1931, 16 June 1931, 28 June 1931, 6 October 1931, and 20 March 1932.
13. *People* (30 July 1967), and *Colchester Express* (3 August 1967).

14. *Daily Telegraph* (26 July 1968).
15. In the case of persons executed in error, compensation is usually in kind. For instance, Timothy Evans after his pardon was reburied in consecrated ground.
16. Perhaps the best way to calculate the value of these earlier sums now would be to multiply them by the ratio of the money income *per capita* today to the money income *per capita* then. This would take care of both the rise in our real standard of living and the fall in the value of money. This could then be directly compared with the present-day awards.
17. *Daily Express* (21 December 1963).

CHAPTER 8   THE FRENCH SYSTEM

1. *Guardian* (9 March 1964 and 13 March 1964).
2. R. Floriot, *Les Erreurs Judiciaires* (Flammarion, 1968), p. 7.
3. M. Besnard, *The Trial of Marie Besnard* (Heinemann, 1963).
4. Hamson, 1955 CLR 276.
5. Floriot, op. cit., p. 93.
6. Ibid., p. 92.
7. Ibid., p. 109.
8. The motivations and attitudes towards the concept of abstract truth in this case recall several of the cases we discussed in the chapter on 'Witnesses Credible and Incredible'—that of Steinie Morrison and those involving Italian and Asian immigrants. In all these cases, clan loyalties conflict with the demands of the law. Are these types of cases more commonly encountered in France, where this type of family set-up is more usual, than in England?
9. *Sunday Mirror* (16 October 1966).
10. Mannheim, 53 LQR 112.
11. Hamson, 1955 CLR 272.
12. Floriot, op. cit., p. 149.
13. Ibid., p. 8.
14. Ibid., p. 90. While we are on the subject of the abuse of technical powers, it might be worth mentioning another type of judicial error which is more usual in France than in England. The French penal code is far more definite than the English about what constitutes a crime. Under the rule of *pas de peine sans texte*, anything is permitted in France which is not specifically forbidden. Thus we get the possibility of judges being faced with someone who has undoubtedly committed an offence, but not a listed one, and stretching the law so that he may be punished. Strictly speaking, this may result in wrongful imprisonment. (But it can be argued that this doctrine affords greater protection to the defendant than the looser common law doctrine of precedent, which relies on the reluctance of judges to extend the boundaries of crime. See John Parris, *Under My Wig*, pp. 106–7.)
15. One might have thought that, if this happened, it would conclusively prove the innocence of the murderer, and he would be released. But in a celebrated case in Italy, where the legal system is in many ways similar to the French, this did not happen. Salvatore Gallo, a Sicilian peasant, was convicted of the murder of his own brother. Seven years later, the brother was found alive and well, living an isolated life; he said he had not appeared at his brother's trial, for fear that he might go to prison himself. He was charged with calumny on the ground that his conduct had brought about the condemnation of an innocent person, but acquitted after telling the court that he had been knocked unconscious with a stone and had fled once he regained consciousness, being convinced that his brother was one of his assailants. Salvatore meanwhile had been provisionally released and was awaiting judicial rehabilitation,

without which he had no civil rights (such as the right to vote, or hold public office). At this stage the public prosecutor declared that there was no alternative but to send him back to prison. In order to allow a hearing for appeal, he would have to be able to show that the events in which he was said to have been involved did not take place or that he had not been responsible for them. The prosecutor alleged that the events certainly did take place, and that even if the brother did not die, there was a quarrel in which Gallo was involved. As he could not show that he had nothing to do with the incident, he had no right to ask for the reversal of a verdict already upheld on appeal. Taking this argument to its logical conclusion, the prosecutor called not only for the rejection of the plea, made on Gallo's behalf, for a hearing in the *cour de cassation*, but also asked for his re-arrest so that he could complete the life-sentence passed on him. In the event, he was gaoled for four years for assaulting his brother, and immediately freed (*Daily Telegraph*, 9 October 1961); *The Times* (10 July 1965 and 7 April 1966).

16. Floriot, op. cit., p. 11.
17. *The Times* (6 March 1969).
18. Brutality may be more endemic in the structure of the French police force than in the English—for a full discussion of this, see Christie Davies (Pitman, 1973).

CHAPTER 9   THE AMERICAN EXPERIENCE

1. The abhorrence of sex and the acceptance of violence in America is well illustrated by the case of an American woman who confessed to a murder she had not committed in order to avoid revealing the details of her sex life to the court (see Edward D. Radin, *The Innocents* (William Morrow, 1964).

2. Edwin M. Borchard, *Convicting the Innocent* (Plenum Publishing Co., 1970), p. xiii.

3. To some extent the larger number of the American cases of wrongful imprisonment is due to the larger population of that country and to the fact that the studies we have cited cover a longer time-span than our British study. The American cases are spread fairly evenly over this century and a few occurred in the nineteenth century. We have only looked in detail at the last twenty years of the British experience. On the other hand our list is a complete one, whilst the American cases are a small non-random selection of the proven cases of wrongful imprisonment that occur in America.

4. It has been suggested that there are more proven cases of wrongful imprisonment in America because it is easier to get a pardon there than it is in England, that is the number of wrongfully imprisoned people is the same but in America you stand a better chance of ultimately being exonerated and released. In fact it is extremely difficult to get a pardon in most of the American States. Good examples of just how difficult it is are the Shephard and Lester case cited in the Franks book, *Not Guilty* (Gollancz, 1957) and the Gunter case discussed in Borchard's book *Convicting the Innocent*.

5. Of the 139 listed American cases where the previous record and the associates of the defendant are known—in 59 cases the man wrongly convicted had a criminal record, in 21 cases he had no record but was known to have criminal associates, and in 59 cases he was entirely respectable.

6. Also, America has about four times as many inhabitants as England and Wales, so the absolute number of such offences will be even greater there.

7. In 1963-7 the United States had on average 12 rapes per 100,000 population. England and Wales had only 2. The Americans had 77 robberies per 100,000 population. England and Wales had only 9. Also America has about four times as many inhabitants as England and Wales, so the absolute number of such

offences will be even greater there. See D. J. Midinhill, M. M. Tumin, L. A. Curtis, *Crimes of Violence*, a staff report submitted to the National Commission on the Causes and Prevention of Violence (December 1969), p. 124.

8. See *Crimes of Violence*, p. 119, or *FBI Law Enforcement Bulletin* (May 1971), p. 30 for details.

9. Borchard notes that 'in several of the cases the convicted prisoner later proved innocent was saved from hanging or electrocution by a hairbreadth (Brown; Dabney; Hess and Craig; Purvis; Steilow and Green; the Sydney Men—Berdue; Wilson). Only by rare good fortune were some of the sentences of hanging and electrocution commuted to life imprisonment or indictments for first degree murder modified by verdicts of second degree murder so that the error could still be corrected (Brown; Hess and Craig; Lyons; McKinney; Purvis; Steilow and Green; Toth; Woods and Miller).' Presumably there are also cases of wrongly convicted men who were not lucky in this way and who were in fact executed.

10. A total of 101 cases of this type are cited in the various American studies.

11. Six cases cited in the American studies.

12. Five such cases cited.

13. Five such cases cited.

14. Four cases cited.

15. Eleven cases cited.

16. Seven cases cited.

17. For example, the case of Craig and Hess of St Louis, Missouri, 1929, in Borchard, op. cit.

18. For example, the cases of Thomas Oliver, New York City, 1945 (Radin), and James Long, Chicago, Illinois, 1934 (Frank). Some States acknowledge the problems involved in joint trials. Thus the State of Ohio requires separate trials of each accused in cases of first degree murder. See Borchard, op. cit., p. 160.

19. Five cases cited in the various American studies.

20. In Britain in contrast to America it is the person who receives a bad cheque who has reason to feel aggrieved with the legal system.

21. If a graph is plotted of the number of eyewitnesses against the number of mistakes made (y) it fits reasonably well to the rectangular hyperbole

$$y = \frac{60}{x} - 10$$

over the range $x=1$ to $x=6$. It might be objected that this inverse relationship simply reflects the greater probability of there being only a small number of witnesses present at the crime. If this is so then the equation would hold for correctly observing witnesses as well as mistaken ones. It is difficult to see though why the number of witnesses correct and mistaken taken together should follow such a pattern. In particular the predominance of the single witness is difficult to explain, especially since most people work and travel in groups as often as they do alone.

22. Borchard, op. cit., p. xiii ff.

23. Frank, op. cit.

24. Borchard, op. cit., p. xx.

25. Borchard, op. cit., p. 64. He also cites the similar cases of J. Anthony Barbera and Joseph Nedza.

26. Borchard, op. cit., p. 163.

27. Frank, op. cit.

28. Source of information: Radin, op. cit., and from E. S. Gardner's *The Court of Last Resort* (Morrow, 1952). For a different but similar procedure see the case of Lesher, Garvey and Rohan of Los Angeles discussed in Borchard, op. cit.

29. For example, the case of Bertram Campbell, an ex-Wall Street broker mentioned earlier in this chapter; the case of Clifford Shephard, a partner in a fund-raising organization, and Betty Lester, a borading-house owner (Frank); the case of Jere Snodgrass, a pharmicist (Frank); the case of Mary Berner, a private secretary to a Congressman (Borchard); and the cases of Dorothy Moerer, Lois Palmer and Minnie Pence—all respectable housewives (Radin).
30. Borchard, op. cit., p. 119.
31. Ibid., p. 245, and also the case of George Harland Bilger, cited in Frank, op. cit., and in Radin, op. cit.
32. Radin, op. cit.
33. For example, the cases of Andrew Toth, Michael Sabol and George Rusnok (Hungarians), Louis Thorvik (Norwegian), and Ameer Ben Ali (Algerian Arab) in Borchard, op. cit.
34. A good example is the case of Santos Rodriguez (Puerto Rican) convicted in Springfield, Massachusetts, 1954 (Radin).
35. Radin, op. cit.
36. Ibid. Other cases of this type are those of John Fry of San Francisco (Radin) and Rudolph Sheeler of Philadelphia (Frank).
37. Radin, op. cit.
38. For an interesting case involving perjury by children, see the case of Louise Butler and George Yelder of Montgomery, Alabama, in Borchard, op. cit. American studies tend to be shy of giving details of sex cases but examples are the cases of Arthur O'Connell of Boston, Massachusetts, 1935 (Frank), and Edward Oscar of Kansas City, Missouri, 1958 (Frank and also Radin)— both of whom were convicted of sexual assault on young girls as a result of totally false accusations by the 'victims'.
39. An example is the case of Luigi Zambino convicted on the perjured evidence of Frank Manfra, his supposed accomplice. Manfra implicated Zambino in order to protect his own brother who was his real accomplice. Details in Borchard, op. cit.
40. Radin, op. cit., p. 158.
41. Borchard, op. cit.
42. Radin, op. cit.
43. Ibid.
44. Compare Anthony Lewis, *Gideon's Trumpet* (Bodley Head, 1966), pp. 12–16, and 87 ff. Also Edward S. Corwin, *The Constitution and What It Means Today* (Princeton University Press, 1958), pp. 226 ff.
45. Compare Lewis, op. cit., Chaps. 8, 12 and 13.
46. See p. 123 in the chapter on Trial Proceedings. Also there is a good discussion of the difficulties facing the appellant in Frank, op. cit., p. 117.
47. Borchard goes so far as to comment: 'A jury's verdict is often a difficult if not insurmountable obstacle to overcome on the road to justice' (Borchard, op. cit., p. 327).
48. Quoted in Borchard, op. cit., p. xxviii.
49. See, for example, the problems faced by Theodore Marcinkiewicz and J. Majozek (Frank) and Robert J. Enzensperger, Jr (Radin), in getting their cases reopened.
50. See also p. 62.
51. Borchard, op. cit., p. 209. For a similar view see Frank, op. cit., p. 111.
52. See p. 254 on the relationship between the right to silence and the use of the third degree.
53. Compare Borchard, op. cit., p. xv and 136.
54. Frank, op. cit., pp. 111 ff.

55. Borchard cites eighteen cases like that of Broughton. Frank discusses a number of such cases and so does Radin.
56. Frank, op. cit., pp. 242–4.
57. See, for example, Rt Hon. Sir John Hobson, QC, MP, Sir John Foster, QC, MP, Ian Percival, QC, MP and Rt Hon. Sir David Renton, QC, MP, *The Silence of The Accused* (Conservative Political Centre, 1966), p. 7: 'It is contrary to our history, to our sense of fair-play and to our notions of individual liberty (pace the Liberals) that a man should be put in a position where he must either commit perjury or convict himself out of his own mouth. . . . The principal objection in the seventeenth century to the proceedings of the Court of Star Chamber—otherwise a most efficient court—was its power to insist on any man answering on oath any question put to him and to punish him for his failure to do so.'
58. Ronald Seth, *The Sleeping Truth* (Leslie Frewin, 1968), p. 13. The extraordinary powers of the committee are justified by its supporters on the ground that witnesses subpoenaed to give evidence are not formally on trial.
59. Seth, op. cit., p. 106.
60. Notably in his perceptive, if chauvinistic, book, *The First New Nation* (Heinemann, 1964).
61. Compare Glanville Williams, *The Proof of Guilt* (Stevens & Sons, 1963), pp. 4 and 22.
62. For an illuminating discussion of this feature of American life, see R. K. Merton's essay 'Social Structure and Anomie' in his book *Social Theory and Social Structure* (Free Press, 1957).
63. Borchard, op. cit., p. xviii. The cases of Boorn; Boyd; Brown; Butler and Yelder; Dabney; Galindo, Hernandez and Mendival; Johnson; MacGregor; Purvis; Stain and Cromwell; Steilow; Berdue, Toth; Wilson. The cases of Hankin and Sell in Radin, op. cit., provide further examples.
64. Radin, op. cit., p. 55.
65. Ibid., p. 36.
66. Ibid., p. 135. See also similar cases in Radin's book and the case of Will Purvis in Borchard's.
67. E. B. Block, *The Vindicators* (Alvin Redman, 1963), p. 219.
68. Radin, op. cit.
69. Lord Delvin, *Trial by Jury* (Stevens & Sons, 1966), pp. 44–5.
70. Details from Frank, op. cit. Similar factors operated in the case of James Foster (p. 241) where the local press and other media gave very biased and inaccurate reports of the case prior to his trial.
71. Compare Lewis, op. cit.
72. See Frank, op. cit., pp. 85–7 for a discussion of this point.
73. Good examples of this are the cases of Nancy Bott; Shephard and Lester (Frank); Oscar Krenger (Borchard); Walter A. Pecho; Samuel Curlow (Radin).
74. See Borchard, op. cit., p. xv.
75. Borchard gives cases showing that at least six women were framed by the police in this way in America in one town alone.
76. Radin, op. cit.
77. Borchard, op. cit., pp. 117–20 and p. xvii. There is also the similar case of John Valletuti discussed in Radin, op. cit.
78. These extracts are taken from Radin, op. cit., p. 187.
79. Quoted in Frank, op. cit., p. 154.
80. See also Merton 'Social Structure and Anomie' in op. cit., pp. 131 ff.
81. Radin, op. cit.
82. A similar case is that of Raymond Riley cited in Frank, op. cit.

K

83. Frank, op. cit., and Block, op. cit.
84. Gardner, op. cit., and Block, op. cit.
85. Borchard discusses the cases of Brown; Butler and Yelder; Dabney; Evans and Ledbitter; Lesher, Garvey and Rohan; Murchison; Prevost; Stain and Cromwell; Sweeney; Walker; Wilson; Chesterman; Gunter; Micks; McManus; Sans; Zambino. Radin cites the cases of Meredith; Kendal and Vickers; Foster.
86. Radin, op. cit.
87. In the case Sutherland and Mathis who were wrongly convicted of an armed bank robbery, the real robbers assisted them to prove their innocence by deliberately re-enacting the crime two years later using the same bank and the same technique.
88. Williams, op. cit., p. 189.

CHAPTER 10 SCALES OF INJUSTICE

1. Sir John Hobson *et al.*, *The Silence of the Accused* (Conservative Political Centre, 1966).
2. This point is made by Lord Devlin, *The Criminal Prosecution in England* (Oxford University Press, 1966).
3. *Memorandum to the Donovan Committee on Criminal Appeal*, p. 7.
4. The jury, of course, is frequently faced with a choice of a very similar nature in doubtful cases: does it acquit, and risk letting a guilty man go free, or convict, and risk wrongfully imprisoning an innocent man?
5. See the Judges' Rules in Appendix C.
6. Norman Skelhorn, *Crime and the Punishment of Crime*, Address to the 3rd Commonwealth and Empire Law Conference, 1965.
7. We have earlier (p. 64) quoted a 'Justice' report on the subject. Another advocate of this kind of reform is the Conservative lawyer and politician Leon Brittan who at the Conservative party conference in Brighton in 1969 declared: 'Persons reasonably suspected by the police of serious crimes should be brought as soon as possible before an examining magistrate and required to answer searching questions about their conduct. If they refuse to answer, this should be regarded as *prima facie* evidence of guilt which they should have to disprove at their trial. . . . If the effect of the change is not to make it any worse for the innocent but to make it more difficult for the guilty to get off, surely it is a change which should be supported by this conference however radical it may be.' *Brentford and Chiswick Post* (17 October 1969).
8. Compare Glanville Williams, *The Proof of Guilt* (Stevens & Sons, 1963), p. 50.
9. E. M. Borchard, *Convicting the Innocent* (Plenum Publishing Co., 1970), p. xvii.
10. For a full discussion of this point, see Williams, op. cit., pp. 63–4.
11. Quoted in the Franks, *Not Guilty* (Gollancz, 1957), p. 68.

EPILOGUE

1. *11th Report*, Evidence (General) of the Criminal Law Revision Committee, June 1972, Cmnd. 4991, p. 15, para. 27.
2. Ibid., p. 8, para. 13.
3. Ibid., p. 174, Part 1, Section 3, Subsection 2c.

APPENDIX A

1. The times spent in prison were calculated by us. This information was not supplied by the Home Office. Where the figures given for time spent in prison in the Appendix do not agree with those given in the text, this is because the figures in the text include time spent awaiting trial.

Index

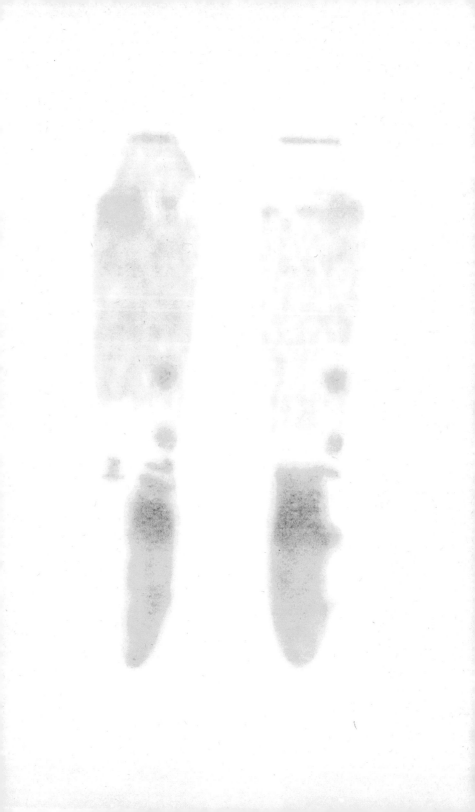